INDIGENOUS STATISTICS

This second edition of the groundbreaking *Indigenous Statistics* opens up a major new approach to research across the disciplines and applied fields. While qualitative methods have been rigorously critiqued and reformulated, the population statistics relied on by virtually all research on Indigenous Peoples continue to be taken for granted as straightforward, transparent numbers. Drawing on a diverse new author team, this book dismantles that persistent positivism with a forceful critique, then fills the void with a new paradigm for Indigenous quantitative methods using concrete examples of research projects from first world Indigenous Peoples in the United States, Australia, Aotearoa New Zealand and Canada. Concise and accessible, it is an ideal supplementary text as well as a core component of the methodological toolkit for anyone conducting Indigenous research or using Indigenous population statistics. This is an essential text for students studying quantitative methods, statistics and research methods.

Chris Andersen is Michif (Métis), from the parkland region of Saskatchewan. He is the dean of the Faculty of Native Studies at the University of Alberta, Canada.

Maggie Walter (PhD; FASSA) is Palawa and Distinguished Professor of Sociology (Emerita) at the University of Tasmania, Australia.

Tahu Kukutai (Ngāti Tiipa, Ngāti Māhanga, Ngāti Kinohaku, Te Aupōuri) is Professor of Demography at Te Ngira Institute for Population Research, The University of Waikato, Aotearoa New Zealand.

Chelsea Gabel is Métis from Rivers, Manitoba, and a citizen of the Manitoba Métis Federation. She is an associate professor in the Indigenous Studies Department and the Department of Health, Aging and Society at McMaster University, Canada.

INDIGENOUS STATISTICS

From Data Deficits to Data Sovereignty

Second Edition

*Chris Andersen, Maggie Walter,
Tahu Kukutai and Chelsea Gabel*

Routledge
Taylor & Francis Group
NEW YORK AND LONDON

Designed cover image: Getty Images

Second edition published 2025
by Routledge
605 Third Avenue, New York, NY 10158

and by Routledge
4 Park Square, Milton Park, Abingdon, Oxon, OX14 4RN

Routledge is an imprint of the Taylor & Francis Group, an informa business

© 2025 Chris Andersen, Maggie Walter, Tahu Kukutai, and Chelsea Gabel

The right of Chris Andersen, Maggie Walter, Tahu Kukutai, and Chelsea Gabel to be identified as authors of this work has been asserted in accordance with sections 77 and 78 of the Copyright, Designs and Patents Act 1988.

The Open Access version of this book, available at www.taylorfrancis.com, has been made available under a Creative Commons Attribution-Non-Commercial-No Derivative Licence (CC-BY-NC-ND) 4.0 license.

Any third party material in this book is not included in the OA Creative Commons license, unless indicated otherwise in a credit line to the material. Please direct any permissions enquiries to the original rightsholder.

Trademark notice: Product or corporate names may be trademarks or registered trademarks and are used only for identification and explanation without intent to infringe.

First edition published by Left Coast Press, Inc. 2013

Library of Congress Cataloging-in-Publication Data
Names: Andersen, Chris, 1973– author. | Walter, Maggie, author. | Kukutai, Tahu, 1971– author. | Gabel, Chelsea, author.
Title: Indigenous statistics : a quantitative research methodology / Chris Andersen, Maggie Walter, Tahu Kukutai and Chelsea Gabel.
Description: Second edition. | New York, NY : Routledge, 2025. | Includes bibliographical references and index.
Identifiers: LCCN 2024045213 (print) | LCCN 2024045214 (ebook) | ISBN 9781032002477 (hardback) | ISBN 9781032002507 (paperback) | ISBN 9781003173342 (ebook)
Subjects: LCSH: Indigenous peoples—Statistics. | Indigenous peoples—Research—Methodology.
Classification: LCC GN380 .W35 2025 (print) | LCC GN380 (ebook) | DDC 305.80072/1—dc23/eng/20250107
LC record available at https://lccn.loc.gov/2024045213
LC ebook record available at https://lccn.loc.gov/2024045214

ISBN: 978-1-032-00247-7 (hbk)
ISBN: 978-1-032-00250-7 (pbk)
ISBN: 978-1-003-17334-2 (ebk)

DOI: 10.4324/9781003173342

Typeset in Sabon
by Apex CoVantage, LLC

CONTENTS

Acknowledgements   *vii*

1 Introduction   1
   Maggie Walter, Chris Andersen, Tahu Kukutai and Chelsea Gabel

2 A Decade of Data Revolutions: Big Data and Indigenous Data Sovereignty   10
   Maggie Walter, Chris Andersen and Tahu Kukutai

3 The Statistical Field, Writ Indigenous   30
   Chris Andersen

4 Statistics and the Neo-Colonial Alliance: "Seeing" the Indigene   48
   Maggie Walter

5 Beyond Colonial Constructs: The Promise of Indigenous Statistics   69
   Tahu Kukutai

6   Statistics, Stigmatization and Stereotyping: The Importance of Authentic Partnering and Community Engagement to Validate Indigenous Statistical Research   89
    Chelsea Gabel

7   Métis Population Data in Canada: A Conceptual Case Study   106
    Chris Andersen and Chelsea Gabel

8   "Fixing" the Figures: Tribal Data in the Aotearoa New Zealand 2018 Census   123
    Tahu Kukutai

9   Doing Indigenous Statistics in Australia: The Racial Burden of Disregard   139
    Maggie Walter

Index   *160*

ACKNOWLEDGEMENTS

The authors would like to thank Ngā Pae o te Māramatanga Centre of Research Excellence for awarding a Publishing Support Grant which enabled us to publish this book open access. We would also like to thank the Canadian Institute for Advanced Research and the Canada Research Chairs Program for their financial support regarding research assistance, copy editing and book cover design.

1
INTRODUCTION

Maggie Walter, Chris Andersen, Tahu Kukutai and Chelsea Gabel

Introduction

In 2013, two authors of this book, Maggie Walter and Chris Andersen, published the original *Indigenous Statistics: From Data Deficits to Data Sovereignty*. These two scholars, one palawa, from Tasmania, Australia, the other Métis, from Saskatchewan and living in Alberta, Canada, met as board members of the then nascent Native American and Indigenous Studies Association (NAISA). Their shared interest in quantitative analysis led first to a recognition of their common experiences as Indigenous academics pursuing scholarship using primarily quantitative methodologies. Discussions around these similar experiences led to collaboration around their scholarship built around a shared understanding of the similarity of their experiences. The book they wrote from these was built around three central premises:

1. **Statistics are culturally embedded phenomena rather than neutral data**

    All statistics are, in one way or another, culturally embedded rather than acontextual or neutral numbers. As such, Indigenous statistics reflect the purposes, assumptions and interests of those who have the power to commission, collect, analyse, interpret and disseminate the data, rather than necessarily reflecting the more robust complexity of Indigenous lived realities. For Indigenous Peoples in Anglo-colonized nations (Australia, Canada, Aotearoa New Zealand and the United

States), the common trope of these data is one of *deficit*. The narratives that accompany these data have defined and continue to define, pejoratively, the relationship between Indigenous Peoples and their respective nation-states.

2. **The methodology, rather than the statistics themselves, are what create culturally "loaded" data**

Methods and methodologies are not interchangeable terms. Methods are the mechanisms through which data (in this case, statistics) are collected and analysed. Methodologies are the overall approach that shapes the research: what is considered worth doing; the underpinning assumptions; the key question/s asked; of whom; and why; and the framework through which the data are interpreted. Methodology, unlike method, therefore has almost nothing to do with data and everything to do with the sociocultural positioning, value systems, knowledge systems and lifeworld of the researcher/data commissioning entity. Almost without exception (until recently, at least), for Indigenous statistics, that researcher/data commissioning entity has been non-Indigenous.

3. **Indigenous-led research shares similarity of methodology and legitimacy barriers**

This premise posits that all Indigenous researchers need to be more cognizant of the translative processes through which knowledge is translated into and out of the academy. This point was aimed, in part, at redressing the pointless, but often vigorously pursued, argument that quantitative research is culturally antithetical to Indigenous Peoples. Automatically positioning all quantitative research as positivist in approach, this claim asserts that such research is unable to reflect the culturally complex social relations—the lives and lived experiences, in other words—of Indigeneity. From our methodology-not-method premise, however, we know that it is methodological approach rather than the means of data collection that underpins the social meaning of research. Thus, Indigenous research that is framed by Indigenous perspectives and lifeworlds have more methodological similarities than differences, regardless of method.

*****

The 2013 book was the first to meaningfully address the topics of Indigenous quantitative methodologies and in the Indigenous-specific context of official statistical data. It was positively reviewed multiple times and has been cited nearly 900 times at last count, and the authors are gratified to know that the book has been particularly useful to Indigenous masters and doctoral candidates across the Anglo-colonial world. Anecdotally, the book has provided a tool to help challenge the ubiquity of Western quantitative frameworks and to resist the expectation that their own work will reflect the presumptions inherent in these. Such tools remain a continuing necessity for all Indigenous scholars negotiating research frameworks that allow them to combine scholarly rigour with Indigenous knowledge, cultural integrity and values.

However, in the decade since the first book, a data revolution has taken place in the global data landscape. It is within this new terrain that all Indigenous data sits and within which Indigenous data users find ourselves operating. This book's layout in particular was designed to acknowledge the power of the "big data" revolution. Properly accounting for this new world means that this version is not a straightforward "second edition" in the ways that it might normally be imagined. While our basic argument is largely congruent with the original volume, this edition has been greatly expanded: *theoretically*, to include a broader discussion about data cycles, ecosystems, assemblages, and statistical fields and their relationships with the burgeoning scholarship on Indigenous Data Sovereignty and governance; *methodologically*, to emphasize the broadening expanse of data "inputs and outputs" that Indigenous data users engage with and in (the Indigenous data world now reaches far beyond official statistics, though for reasons we will make clear, official statistics still constitute critical data to engage with); and *empirically*, to offer case studies at the interface of Indigenous Data Sovereignty and statistical practice, in three national contexts: Aotearoa New Zealand (Aotearoa), Australia and Canada.

Though we hope that readers will find this edition's changes enlightening, the rest of this introduction speaks directly to two key forces that are powerfully directing the Indigenous data world: the explosive growth, capaciousness and fungibility of information in the era of *big data* (and big data-driven technologies including artificial intelligence); and the rise of *Indigenous Data Sovereignty and governance* as central tools of Indigenous nation building. The latter is a crucial technology in the resurgence of Indigenous nations, acting as a key resource of policy-relevant information and as a powerful discourse that bolsters Indigenous rights to self-determination and transforms the kinds of Indigenous stories that we can tell.

*****

Notwithstanding differences in historical and socio-political contexts, broad similarities and resonance exist across the various Indigenous Data

Sovereignty movements that have arisen over the last decade or so. As an academic field, Indigenous Data Sovereignty both makes visible and addresses the long-expressed discontent of Indigenous Peoples with how data about us are collected, analysed and used (Davis 2016). The phrase itself emerged from an international workshop held in 2016 in Australia. Since that time Indigenous Data Sovereignty networks have been established in all four CANZUS countries (Canada, Australia, Aotearoa New Zealand and the United States), Scandinavia and the Pacific. Indigenous scholars from Mexico, Spain and South America are also working in this space. These networks have been increasingly influential within their own nation-states and came together in 2018 to form the Global Indigenous Data Alliance (www.gida-global.org). GIDA operates as a network of networks, bringing collective energies and interests together and facilitating the sharing of knowledge, experience and platforms across national contexts. As well as challenging and breaking down the old ways of doing Indigenous statistics, these networks, and the scholars and Indigenous leaders associated with them, are addressing the new challenges associated with the data revolution. For example, the global movement for data sharing, especially the sharing of administrative data collections by governments, can and does expose Indigenous populations to elevated risks of data-related harms. Indigenous Data Sovereignty networks are insisting that the "FAIR Guiding Principles for scientific data management and stewardship" (findable, accessible, interoperable, reusable) (Wilkinson et al. 2016) do not—and indeed, cannot—sufficiently protect Indigenous data or Indigenous Peoples. In response, the collective benefit, authority to control, responsibility and ethics (CARE) principles have been developed to be used as an essential addition to FAIR when researchers and agencies deal with Indigenous data (Carroll et al. 2019). GIDA also published Indigenous Peoples' rights in data describing the specific rights that support Indigenous Peoples' aspirations for control of data and self-determined priorities and activities (GIDA 2023). More recently GIDA has taken universities to task, calling on them to (among other things) implement data management plans that have Indigenous Data Governance principles and mechanisms embedded and to allocate adequate resources for Indigenous Peoples to govern their data on their own terms (Prehn et al. 2023).

*****

In summary, over the past decade, Indigenous Peoples—especially within the CANZUS countries—have increasingly demanded recognition of their rights in relation to data that are generated by them, or about them, their lands, waters and territories. These rights pertain, regardless of where the data are held or by whom. Demands have included:

- decision-making authority on how and why data about them or their lands and waters are collected and used;
- statistical capacity-building within First Nations organizations and communities; and
- production of, and access to, data that meet Indigenous defined needs and priorities.

Indigenous Data Governance is also increasingly advocated by Indigenous leaders who recognize the importance of data for driving change and disrupting the status quo with respect to the policy environments that affect them. An Australian example demonstrates how data has become a core element of Indigenous-state relationships. In 2008, the Australian federal government announced a new Indigenous policy framework, labelled *Closing the Gap*. This framework, which operated between 2008 and 2018, was a dismal failure. Only three of the seven health and socio-economic targets were even "on track" after ten years of operation (McNicol n.d.). Its replacement, a refreshed *Closing the Gap* framework, took the unprecedented move of actively involving Aboriginal and Torres Strait Islander organizations and leaders in its design, targets and priorities via a formal agreement between all Australian governments and the Coalition of Peaks (a group of peak Aboriginal-controlled community organizations). The agreement was built on four priority reform pillars. Priority Reform Four is "Shared access to data and information at a regional level" (Commonwealth of Australia 2020a). The stated outcome was for "Aboriginal and Torres Strait Islander people [to] have access to, and the capability to use, locally-relevant data and information to set and monitor the implementation of efforts to close the gap, their priorities and drive their own development." To achieve this outcome Australian governments committed to including Aboriginal and Torres Strait Islander Peoples in data about us/them by sharing available, disaggregated regional data and information; establishing partnerships to improve collection, access, management and use of data; making data more transparent by reporting what data they have and how it can be accessed; and building capacity to collect and use data (Commonwealth of Australia 2020b). This relatively modest set of data-related agreements represent the first ever Indigenous data rights commitments made by the Australian state. Collaborative work is now underway between government executive members and Indigenous leaders in the field on how these commitments can be operationalized. The

Indigenous Data Sovereignty movement, its principles and its enactment mechanism, Indigenous Data Governance, are discussed in more depth in the later chapters (see, in particular, Chapters 3 and 6).

Indigenous Peoples in This Book Have Similar Indigenous Lifeworlds

Given the diversity of Indigenous Peoples, the United Nations Permanent Forum on Indigenous Issues (UNPFII) declines to adopt an official definition of Indigenous. Instead, the body proposes a

> modern understanding of this term based on the following: self-identification as indigenous peoples at the individual level and accepted by the community as their member; historical continuity with pre-colonial and/or pre-settler societies; strong link to territories and surrounding natural resources; distinct social, economic or political systems; distinct language, culture and beliefs; form non-dominant groups of society; resolve to maintain and reproduce their ancestral environments and systems as distinctive peoples and communities.
>
> *(UNPFII n.d.)*

Those wishing to define Indigenous Peoples (see, for example, Axelsson and Sköld 2011) often use the 1987 working definition formulated by Jose R. Martínez Cobo who, at the time, was a UN special rapporteur:

> Indigenous communities, peoples and nations are those which, having a historical continuity with pre-invasion and pre-colonial societies that developed on their territories, consider themselves distinct from other sectors of the societies now prevailing on those territories, or parts of them. They form at present non-dominant sectors of society and are determined to preserve, develop and transmit to future generations their ancestral territories, and their ethnic identity, as the basis of their continued existence as peoples, in accordance with their own cultural patterns, social institutions and legal system.
>
> *(1986: Add 4, paras 379 and 381)*

We accept the central premises of the UNPFII's criteria and Martinez Cobo's definition. But the definition is a pan-categorization, derived to put some parameters around the meaning of the term "Indigenous." Under such pan-categorization, any attempt to discuss "an Indigenous perspective" is largely meaningless. Yet, we are also aware, from assessment comments for our 2013 book and others' work published over the last decade, that we can rely on non-Indigenous reviewers to ask why we have not included Indigenous examples from Africa or Asia. We regard this regular critique as an artefact of colonization. We point out to our publisher that the term Indigenous is just a category. Demanding that all Indigenous scholarship encompass "the Indigenous world" is as ridiculous as demanding that any Western theory include reference to all White populations (Walter et al. 2021).

We are clear that this book is written primarily in reference to the subgroup of Indigenous Peoples whose own nations have been subsumed through Anglo colonization into Western first world nation-states. These nations form what is known as the CANZUS countries: Canada, Australia, Aotearoa New Zealand and the United States. This grouping elides with Dyck's (1985) definition of the fourth world as those who are Indigenous but have had their sovereignty appropriated; are minorities within their traditional lands; are culturally stigmatized as well as economically and politically marginalized; and are struggling for social justice. Thus, Indigenous Peoples from CANZUS countries have shared histories of dispossession, stigmatization and marginalization. Our Indigenous embedded lived realities, and the social and cultural positioning in which they occur, are not the same as those of our pre-colonization ancestors. Colonization has changed that forever.

Yet we are far more than the sum of Dyck's categories. Colonization does not define us, then or now. As Indigenous Peoples we all retain thousands of years of deep history of our lands, culture, traditions and ways of knowing, and these distinguish and continue to shape our lived realities. It is from these dual Indigenous subjectivities of Peoplehood and colonization that the broader concept of the Indigenous lifeworld is developed (Walter and Suina 2019; Walter et al. 2021). The Indigenous lifeworld encompasses the relational positioning inherent in Indigenous lives framed through

- intersubjectivity within Peoplehood and the ways of being and doing of those peoples, inclusive of traditional and ongoing culture, belief systems, practices, identity, and ways of understanding the world and our place within it; and
- intersubjectivity as colonized, dispossessed marginalized peoples whose everyday life is framed through and directly impacted by our historical and ongoing relationship and interactions with the colonizing nation-state.

The nexus of these two intersubjectivities define the lifeworld similarities and differences between dispossessed Indigenous Peoples. For Indigenous

Peoples such as Aboriginal and Torres Strait Islanders, Māori, Native Americans, Native Hawaiians, Alaskan Natives, First Nations and Métis our identity, traditions, belief systems and everyday practices are geographically and culturally unique. We are distinct peoples. But, critically, the embodied lived experience of that Indigenous intersubjectivity is entangled within our shared positioning as dispossessed, politically marginalized peoples, experiencing systemic, intergenerational disparities and our ongoing conflicted relationships with settler colonial states (Walter and Suina 2019). Anglo colonization also leads to similarities in our nation-states' embrace of the governing rhetorics of liberalism (Rose 1999) that shape how they see and understand us as Indigenous Peoples. The substance of these two intersubjectivities produces a particular relationship with population statistics that is not as evident in other global contexts.

Of course, we believe that our analysis and methodologies can be useful to other Indigenous Peoples. But because methodologies cannot be conceptualized in isolation from an understanding of their historical, cultural, and racial antecedents, we are careful not to assume our analysis applies wholesale to Indigenous Peoples outside of our own personal and research experience. We encourage Indigenous Peoples beyond the CANZUS countries to take what they find useful from our writing.

The Purpose of This Book

This book builds on the original work, *Indigenous Statistics*, but with a broader remit. In designing this new version, one collective aim of the four authors is to further equip Indigenous scholars, leaders and researchers to take the emerging lead roles in the production of Indigenous statistics. To contribute to this aim, this book reiterates the central and still relevant arguments of the previous book while adding discussion and analysis of new statistical developments and their impacts on Indigenous Peoples. In so doing it presents a more "ecological" approach to understanding the conception, creation, collection, analysis and communication of Indigenous statistics from "nose to tail." The book highlights the growing scholarship of Indigenous scholars and also addresses the practical aspects of "doing" Indigenous statistics, providing a discussion on *how* to do Indigenous statistics, from conception to completion.

Toward these ends, the authors made a collective decision to organize and write it in such a way as to emphasize the Indigenous (and colonial) nations that frame any given statistics ecosystem, while bearing in mind the broader comparative elements that hold across geo-political contexts. In practice, this means that we chose to individually write our chapters in ways that speak to that "local" complexity. In effect, each of the chapters offers a distinct lens—theoretical, methodological and/or empirical—through which these structures and dynamics can be examined. And as such, each chapter contains the name of the author (or co-authors) who wrote it.

References

Axelsson, Per, and Peter Sköld, eds. *Indigenous Peoples and Demography: The Complex Relation Between Identity and Statistics*. New York: Berghahn Books, 2011.

Carroll, Stephanie Russo, Desi Rodriguez-Lonebear and Andrew Martinez. "Indigenous Data Governance: Strategies from United States Native Nations." *Data Science Journal* 18 (2019). https://doi.org/10.5334/dsj-2019-031.

Commonwealth of Australia. *National Agreement on Closing the Gap*. Canberra: Parliament of Australia, 2020a.

Commonwealth of Australia. *Priority Reforms, Parliament of Australia*. Canberra: Parliament of Australia, 2020b.

Davis, Megan. "Data and the United Nations Declaration on the Rights of Indigenous Peoples." In *Indigenous Data Sovereignty*, edited by Tahu Kukutai and John Taylor, 25–38. Canberra: ANU Press, 2016.

Dyck, Noel, ed. *Indigenous Peoples and the Nation-State: 'Fourth World' Politics in Canada, Australia, and Norway*. Institute of Social and Economic Research, Memorial University of Newfoundland, 1985.

GIDA. "Indigenous Peoples' Rights in Data." *The Global Indigenous Data Alliance*, GIDA-global.org, 2023. https://doi.org/10.6084/m9.figshare.22138160.

Martínez Cobo, José R. *Study of the Problem of Discrimination Against Indigenous Populations*. United Nations, Sub-Commission on Prevention of Discrimination and Protection of Minorities, 1986. UN Doc. E/CN.4/Sub.2/1986/7/Add.4.

McNicol, Sally. "Closing the Gap." In *Social Policy*. Canberra: Parliament of Australia, n.d. aph.gov.au.

Prehn, Jacob, Riley Taitingfong, Robyn Rowe, Ibrahim Garba, Cassandra Price, Maui Hudson, Tahu Kukutai, and Stephanie Russo Carroll. *Indigenous Data Governance and Universities Communiqué*. Global Indigenous Data Alliance, 2023. https://doi.org/10.6084/m9.figshare.24201585.

Rose, N. *Governing the Soul: The Shaping of the Private Self*. 2nd ed. Free Association Books, 1999.

Walter, Maggie, Tahu Kukutai, Stephanie Russo Carroll, and Desi Rodriguez-Lonebear, eds. *Indigenous Data Sovereignty and Social Policy*. London: Routledge, 2021.

Walter, M., and M. Suina. "Indigenous data, Indigenous methodologies and Indigenous data sovereignty". *International Journal of Social Research Methodology* 22, no. 3 (2019): 233–243.

Wilkinson, M. D., Dumontier, M., Aalbersberg, I. J., Appleton, G., Axton, M., Baak, A., Blomberg, N., Boiten, J. W., da Silva Santos, L. B., Bourne, P. E., Bouwman, J., Brookes, A. J., Clark, T., Crosas, M., Dillo, I., Dumon, O., Edmunds, S., Evelo, C. T., Finkers, R., . . . Mons, B. "The FAIR Guiding Principles for scientific data management and stewardship". *Scientific Data* 3 (2016): 160018. https://doi.org/10.1038/sdata.2016.18.

2

A DECADE OF DATA REVOLUTIONS

Big Data and Indigenous Data Sovereignty

Maggie Walter, Chris Andersen and Tahu Kukutai

CHAPTER LEARNING OBJECTIVES

Objective 1: Be able to map the key technological components of the data revolution.

Objective 2: Understand how the data revolution can, and is, changing the landscape for Indigenous data and population statistics, frequently adding additional dangers and risks.

Objective 3: Conceptualize Indigenous Data Sovereignty and understand how this global advocacy movement is operationalized through Indigenous Data Governance.

Introduction

Indigenous Peoples' lives and futures are intricately entwined with data. Data are powerful and political. As argued in Chapter 1, Indigenous Peoples have long campaigned against the inadequacy and harmful nature of existing Indigenous data. Simultaneously, Indigenous demands for Indigenous-driven and -framed data are an increasing feature of Indigenous interactions with our respective nation-states. These dual data needs were central arguments of our original *Indigenous Statistics* book (Walter and

Andersen 2013) and they remain relevant as we write this book more than a decade later. However, the data ecosystem in which they occur is not the same as it was in 2013. Rather, two strong and potentially conflictual data revolutions have emerged.

The first is the rise of Indigenous Data Sovereignty as a social movement and field of scholarship. Indigenous Data Sovereignty is the coalescence of earlier Indigenous demands for data rights into a coherent concept and related advocacy. Under Indigenous Data Sovereignty, Indigenous Peoples have the right to own and control how their data are collected, managed and used (Kukutai and Taylor 2016). Since its inception in 2015, data sovereignty principles have been developed across the CANZUS countries (Walter et al. 2020). In turn these principles have been increasingly adopted by Indigenous nations, leadership, peak organizations and communities. Relatedly, significant progress has been made in embedding Indigenous data rights into state data processes and in Indigenous Peoples developing their own data processes and data capabilities (Rainie et al. 2019).

The second data revolution relates to new data technologies. Since the turn of this century, the value, breadth and scope of data has increased exponentially. The growth in data sources and the computational power to analyse them has presaged the emergence of big data, inclusive of very large databases (VLDB) and artificial intelligence (AI). Alongside these technologies has been an impetus for increasing accessibility to publicly held data (open data). Big data technologies have transformed the data ecosystem in all CANZUS countries, creating new data functions and possibilities. Proponents of these data technologies promise significant societal benefits from their capacity to harness data power at a scale that was hard to conceive of in 2013. They also create new sites of Indigenous data tensions. While there are potential benefits for Indigenous Peoples, there are also significant risks arising from the uncritical deployment of these data technologies, the monopolistic power wielded by large multinational technology companies (Zuboff 2019) and data infrastructures that do not recognize, let alone support, Indigenous worldviews and Indigenous data rights.

This chapter explores these two data revolutions. The first section covers the field of big data, critically examining and explaining many of the terms as well as the implications of these for Indigenous Peoples. The second section examines the rise of the Indigenous Data Sovereignty movement, globally, but with a focus on the CANZUS countries, again explaining key terms and key developments. The tensions between Indigenous Data Sovereignty and big data technologies are also mapped.

Explaining the Data Revolution

What is the "data revolution" and what is meant by "big data"? The data revolution refers to the veritable explosion of data in the last two decades—an explosion that has accelerated the rise of "big data." Diebold (2019), the economist with whom the phrase big data is often associated, intended it to encapsulate the "explosive growth." McCarthy (2016, 1131) notes, however, that differentiating between "small data" and "big data" is not as easy as the terminology might make it appear. Big data is distinct "in the number of data points, the speed at which data are produced and analysed, variation in the different types and sources of data, and the unpredictable and emergent nature of results." These aspects are summarized in Gartner's (n.d.) definition of big data as "high-volume, high-velocity and/or high-variety information assets that demand cost-effective, innovative forms of information processing that enable enhanced insight, decision making, and process automation."

The ideas that "more data is better" and that "the numbers speak for themselves" anchor much of the current global data revolution and have been described in terms of a number of "Vs." Critical data studies scholars Kitchin and Lauriault (2018, 3), for example, note accelerated changes in the sheer *volume* of data (from terabytes to petabytes to exabytes to zettabytes to now yottabytes, each orders of magnitude larger than the previous data volume term); the *velocity* with which new data are being created; the diversity of the *varieties* of data; their *scope* (in pursuit of an exhaustive accounting of social phenomena); the increasingly fine-grained *resolution* of data; their flexibility, extensionality and scalability; and the growth of personal data collections (e.g., social media accounts such as Facebook, WhatsApp and TikTok). Data not only track but also in many ways shape and even define "private" consumer culture behaviours. "[E]very click, every move has the potential to count for something, for someone somewhere somehow" (Gitelman and Jackson 2013, 2). Others have pointed to the importance of a growth in data's *veracity* and *value* (see Andrejevic 2014; McCarthy 2016; Mittelstadt and Floridi 2016).

Proponents of big data encourage the principle that "more data is better" and offer a number of reasons for why such increased predictive capacity holds tremendous potential as a social "good." Everything from competitive commercial advantage (Bartosik-Purgat and Ratajczak-Mrożek 2018) to increased national security (McCue 2007) to the democratization of health, personal, family and community security outcomes for society globally (Pentland 2009) has been touted as possible positive effects of big data (see Andrejevic 2014, 2007; Mosco 2004 for a detailed discussion of rhetoric pertaining to big data). For Indigenous Peoples, however, more data does not necessarily lead to different or better outcomes (Walter and Carroll 2020). If the data used are the usual measures of Indigenous deficit, it doesn't matter how much data are included, the analysis can still only produce results that centre Indigenous Peoples as a problem.

Critical Data Studies and Big Data

For Indigenous Peoples the global data revolution and the associated belief of the positive potential of big data poses significant and particular risks. Some of these are generic human risks and have been articulated within the growing field of critical data studies (CDS). CDS has traced the last half century of data growth and changing use by public and private institutions, arguing that big data should be understood less in terms of size, speed and/or fungibility and more in terms of a "capacity to search, aggregate, and cross-reference large data sets" (boyd and Crawford 2012, 663), beyond the capability of human consciousness (see Andrejevic 2013). This definition of big data dismisses both the naive assumption that more data are necessarily better and the incorrect assumption that data speak (or could ever speak) for itself. It also exposes the data fallacy challenged by Walter and Andersen (2013) that data are neutral. Boyd and Crawford's (2012, 663) definition of big data instead incorporates its irreducibly messy, sticky and dense *sociality* to include:

> *networks of technology* (i.e., "maximizing computation power and algorithmic accuracy to gather, analyze, link, and compare large data sets");
> *analysis* (i.e., "drawing on large data sets to identify patterns in order to make economic, social, technical, and legal claims") and perhaps most importantly in terms of staking its claims to universality or naturalness;
> *mythology* (i.e., "the widespread belief that large data sets offer a higher form of intelligence and knowledge that can generate insights that were previously impossible, with the aura of truth, objectivity, and accuracy").
> *(boyd and Crawford 2012, 663)*

As such, any nuanced attempt to account for the variegated power of data in contemporary society must consider both the intense internal complexities within which they sit as well as their broader reach into (nearly) all parts of social life.

Data Ecosystems

Accounting for the movement of data into and out of multiple data ecosystems is also important. The increased growth and mobility of data do not exist except in relation to the *im*mobile structures that organize, store, manage and control access to them. As such, data need to be situated in time and space, with attention to the barriers and enablers, and the "data divide" that is produced and reproduced. A concept often used to situate these dimensions is that of a data *ecosystem*.

In their review of the data ecosystems literature, Shah et al. (2020) note that while there is no clear definition of the term, the different discussions include common elements that emphasize their networked character and the various combinations of data, people, organizations, organizational procedures and technology. Their own definition focuses on the networks that connect people, processes, technologies and infrastructures (data and organizational) in the quest for optimal data functionality as a means of producing "good" data that "benefit citizens, businesses, and government bodies itself" (Shah et al. 2020, 254–5).

Kitchin and Lauriault (2018) analytically divide data ecosystems into technical and conceptual "stacks." The former are the "instrumental means by which data are generated, processed, stored, shared, analysed and experienced" (Kitchin 2022, 23). They consist of hardware, infrastructure, software, databases and interfaces. The conceptual stacks are the "discursive and material components related to philosophy and knowledge, financial and politics, law and governance, practices, stakeholders and actors, geography and markets."

The notion of a data ecosystem injects the social and political character of data into discussions that tend to focus on ensuring technical accuracy (see Rainie et al. 2017b, 6). For data collected on Indigenous People, this means acknowledging that history, as well as the tendency of population data to reflect mainstream norms and the presumption of Indigenous *deficit*. As discussed in Chapter 4, the deficit lens, supported by national statistics, continues to pervade public and policy narratives of Indigenous capacities and experiences. Researchers who employ data collected on Indigenous People need to recognize that the reliability of this data can be, and has been, negatively impacted by the purpose of data collection, who it is collected by, and how it is collected. This is why data must be interrogated for how it is obtained, deployed and interpreted, and for whom it serves (Walter et al. 2021). Indeed, as Kitchin (2022, 5) argues, "data are inherently partial, selective and representative, and the distinguishing criteria used in their capture has consequence." As such, data are never "raw": instead, they are always/already "cooked" (Gitelman et al. 2013—also see Bowker 2005) by the contexts of social power within which they are produced and deployed and which they produce and make use.

In the Global North, regular information collection constituted a key historical plank of liberal nation-state building, in ideology and in practice (see Hacking 1986; Foucault 2001; Miller and Rose 1990; Scott 1998; Scott et al. 2002). And although they possess a much longer history dating back to the Babylonian era, in a modern state-building context *censuses* became a key lens through which this knowledge was collected, regularized, analysed and disseminated for public policy purposes (see Curtis 2001; Desrosières 1998; Loveman 2009; Porter 1986). This book emphasizes the power of censuses because of their central power in mediating key policy relationships between Indigenous Peoples and the state. Loveman (2009, 438–9) notes that in both historical and contemporary contexts censuses represents a powerful intersection of what she terms the "three driving projects of modernization":

> the political project of developing the administrative infrastructure and authority of a modern state, the cultural project of constructing the communal bonds (the imagined community) of a modern nation, and the scientific project of producing useful knowledge about the population in whose name the nation state claimed its legitimacy to govern.

The constitutionally mandated removal of census data on the Aboriginal population in Australia that held until 1967, for example (see Chapter 4), denotes the state's recognition of the power of population data and their link to reinforcing the state's authority to govern.

A *population* is a commonly understood and even taken for granted concept that presupposes a set of instruments authorized and able to collect and provide "facts" about it. In many nation-states, a formal *census* fulfils this powerful role, shaping the specific fields of public policy interventions (health, wellbeing, housing, employment, etc.) into national citizenry (see generally Curtis 2001; Dean 1999; Rose 1999; also see Scott et al. 2002). And it is precisely within this context of govern*ing* that the rationalities, programs and technologies of govern*ance* require a vast and detailed knowledge of its citizens' collective characteristics. Over time, census data have come to assume a key role in the formation of policy decisions affecting numerous facets of the lives of a nation-state's citizens, including—and perhaps especially—those of Indigenous communities. The data revolution has vastly expanded the sources of data through which powerful entities (public and the private) attempt to shape everyday lives, including those of Indigenous Peoples.

Data Dependency

That data only exists within the structures and circuits that contain and facilitate them means that gaps exist between the data "haves and have nots" and indeed, data "knows and knows not." These gaps are often defined in terms of a "data divide." McCarthy (2016) argues that while big data can offer powerful insights into and information about our daily lives, neither the insights, information nor their potential benefits are evenly shared (2016, 1131). Instead, he argues that big data have produced inequalities that mirror (and are mirrored in) broader social relations, a point which we elaborate on further with respect to the relationship of Indigenous data dependency to colonialism. Andrejevic (2013) argues that the digital divide is at once infrastructural, "shaped by ownership and control of the material resources for data storage and mining"; epistemological, regarding "a difference in the forms of practical knowledge available to those with access to the database, in the way they think about and use information" (2013, 18); and geographical, to the extent that large parts of the world lack both the capacity and the expertise to engage in advantageous use(s) of big data.

In an Indigenous context, the data divide has produced and maintained a powerful *data dependency* that is a continuation of historical forms of data colonialism. The Latin etymology of the term data positions data as something that is "given." Yet, as argued by Indigenous Data Sovereignty scholar Desi Rodriguez-Lonebear (2016, 255), given the extractive colonial contexts within which much data about Indigenous People have been produced, data might just as easily be understood to refer instead to something "taken." Rodriguez-Lonebear (2016) and others (Cormack and Kukutai 2022; Tsosie et al. 2021) have carefully documented how existing *data dependencies* are rooted in intertwining factors. These include growing colonial requirements for data "on" Indigenous communities and individuals; the dismissal and, over multiple generations, the attempted erasure of pre-existing Indigenous information ecosystems; and the ongoing extraction of data about and from Indigenous Peoples according to the colonially produced categories deemed relevant to the growing nation-states. The violence of colonial data collection was a key strategy through which colonial authorities attempted to wrest control of Indigenous lands, lives, governing systems and collective identities. Statistical logics, classifications and taxonomies were key elements of the epistemology of colonization. Colonial officials, in all CANZUS countries, were endlessly fascinated with the apparent power of quantitative data to "order" and "explain" us (see Appadurai 1993; Cohn 1987, 1996; Cormack and Kukutai 2022; Kalpagam 2000, 2016; Pels 1997; Scott 1995; Briscoe 2003 for discussions about the central role of quantitative knowledge in colonialism). Palawa scholar Maggie Walter (2016, 80–2) describes the modes of data analysis used in all CANZUS countries to "explain" Indigenous populations as the "five Ds" (5D) of Indigenous data: difference, disparity, disadvantage, dysfunction and deprivation. Together, they paint a (seemingly) compelling depiction of Indigenous lives as fundamentally ones of *deficit*, a point as powerfully normative as it is empirical.

It is important to be clear here that quantitative population analysis is not a Western invention. As Chapter 4 notes, population statistics have been used by successive societies since ancient times as part of state good. Indigenous nations have also long used the scientific method, engaging in careful systematic and documented observation of pertinent aspects of the social and physical world. The classification schemes of colonial states, therefore, merely attempted to usurp Indigenous epistemologies with their own (see Smith 2016; Carroll et al. 2019; Cormack and Kukutai 2022; Rodriguez-Lonebear 2016). Indigenous relationships with informational abstraction, therefore, long predate the colonial logics, programmes and interventions that attempted to demean, belittle and, ultimately, overwrite them.

Contemporary forms of data dependency in the era of AI and big data move Indigenous interests even further from the channels of power (Walter and Russo-Carroll 2021). While the potential benefits of big data and data-driven technologies are proclaimed by both the nation-state and private interests, the marginalized social, cultural and political location of Indigenous Peoples suggest we will not share equally in these. The growing pervasiveness of AI within data ecosystems also increasingly affects Indigenous Peoples across unforeseen aspects of our daily lives. Well-documented risks such as racial bias, stigma and hyper-surveillance disproportionately affect marginalized minorities (Buolamwini 2023; Eubanks 2018; O'Neil 2017), and in colonial settler states this invariably includes Indigenous Peoples. Similarly, the growing global tendency for data sharing, especially the sharing of administrative data collections by governments, exposes Indigenous Peoples to elevated risks of data-related harms (Kukutai and Walter 2019).

Readers can draw three general conclusions from the foregoing discussion. First, Indigenous data are more usefully positioned as information "taken" than "given" (Tsosie et al. 2021). Walter and Russo-Carroll ably capture this alternative ontology: "[d]ata do not make themselves. [They] are created and shaped by the assumptive determinations of their makers to collect some data and not others, to interrogate some objects over others and to investigate some variable relationships over others" (2021, 2). As such, the relations of power that control data extraction are not only crucial to the very meanings they possess, but also to the range of meanings they *can* possess.

Second, the inequitable data relationships that produce data about Indigenous Peoples has little to do with Indigenous Peoples' inability to understand or engage with data in robust and nuanced ways in alignment with our collectively economic, political, economic and health objectives. Instead, it has everything to do with long-standing colonial attitudes that refuse(d) to value and respect Indigenous epistemologies, particularly our understanding about the deep sense of responsibility that accompanies information and its ethical collection and use (Carroll et al. 2019).

Finally, despite big data proponents' emphasis on their liberatory potential, the potential benefits of big data are not, nor have they ever been, distributed equally. A growing "data divide" is emerging, in several important contexts: first, between those who possess the capacity to collect, analyse and disseminate data and those from whom such data are collected, analysed and disseminated; second, between those from whom such data are collected but who otherwise lack the infrastructure and expertise to build and/or maintain a relationship to crucial data(bases) and those who can; and third—and relatedly—between entities that can engage with data in ways that are in alignment with their collective principles, values and political/policy objectives and those who cannot.

Each of the three conclusions resonate for Indigenous relationships to data and data ecosystems. We turn now to a discussion of *Indigenous Data Sovereignty and Governance* as lenses for thinking about the origins and present contours of Indigenous data dependency; as a critique to the social relations that, so far at least, have animated this dependency; and as a wellspring of hopeful resurgence for our communities and our nations' broader quest for self-determination.

Indigenous Data Sovereignty

The term Indigenous Data Sovereignty broadly encapsulates "the inherent and inalienable rights and interests of Indigenous Peoples relating to the collection, ownership and application of data about their people, lifeways and territories" (Kukutai and Taylor 2016, 2). This central column of Indigenous rights—and particularly the right of self-determination—is reflected in scholarly descriptions of the concept. In the United States context, for example, Tsosie (2019, 229) defines Indigenous Data Sovereignty in terms of the idea that "Native nations and other Indigenous Peoples ought to control the collection and use of data by and about them"; Carroll et al. (2019) define the term as "the right of Indigenous Peoples and tribes to govern the collection, ownership, and application of their own data" (Rainie et al. 2017, 1); and Rodriguez-Lonebear (2016, 259) defines Indigenous Data Sovereignty as "the right and ability of tribes to develop their own systems for gathering and using data and to influence the collection of data by external actors." In Aotearoa, Kukutai and Cormack (2020) have described the intrinsic linkages between Māori data sovereignty, collective self-determination, *tino rangatiratanga* (absolute chiefly authority) and *mana motuhake* (distinct power and authority, see Mutu 2021). Thus, Indigenous Data Sovereignty can be seen as both an expression and an enabler of Indigenous sovereignty in its wider meaning. It is also supported by Indigenous Peoples' collective rights of self-determination and rights to govern data about our peoples, lands, resources and knowledges as recognized in the United Nations Declaration on the Rights of Indigenous Peoples (UNDRIP) (Taylor and Kukutai 2015).

The Rise of the Indigenous Data Sovereignty Movement

The Indigenous Data Sovereignty movement has its genesis in community, nation-state and international action, advocacy and activism. For several decades the United Nations Permanent Forum on Indigenous Issues has called for statistical frameworks that prioritize Indigenous participation, leadership and data needs (Davis 2016). While data and data justice agendas vary, there is a consistent demand across First Nations for data that are disaggregated; are relevant to Indigenous lifeworlds and nation rebuilding; and disrupt the deficit narrative pervasive across policy spheres (Walter and Russo-Carroll 2021; Carroll et al. 2019; Rainie et al. 2017; Walter 2018).

The ownership, control, access and possession (OCAP®) principles were an early Indigenous response to the ongoing inadequacies of Indigenous data. Developed in the 1990s by Canadian First Nations to provide a new framework for data governance, OCAP® asserts Indigenous Peoples and communities control of their data to their benefit (FNIGC 2016). OCAP® principles have since been applied to Canadian national bodies and educational institutions to empower First Nations' control of their data (Walker et al. 2017).

The Indigenous Data Sovereignty movement extended these data demands to other CANZUS countries and, at its core, seeks to transform the data landscape to the benefit of Indigenous Peoples (Lovett et al. 2019). The movement formally began in 2015 when Indigenous scholars from Australia, the United States, Canada and Aotearoa New Zealand met to consider the implications of UNDRIP for the collection, ownership and application of statistics pertaining to Indigenous Peoples. The workshop was the first such international gathering, and the subsequent edited collection of presented papers, *Indigenous Data Sovereignty: Towards an Agenda* (Kukutai and Taylor 2016), has had wide international reach.

This initial Indigenous Data Sovereignty workshop stimulated the formation of national networks. The Māori Data Sovereignty Network Te Mana Raraunga (temanararaunga.maori.nz) formed in 2015 to advocate for Māori rights and interests in data (TMR 2019). The United States Indigenous Data Sovereignty Network (USIDSN; usingdigenousdatanetwork.org) was constituted in 2016 to ensure that data for and about Indigenous Peoples and nations were used to the benefit of those peoples. In 2017, the Maiam nayri Wingara Aboriginal and Torres Strait Islander Data Sovereignty Collective in Australia (maiamnayriwingara.org) was created to seek to change data practices for Australia's First Peoples. In Canada, the already existing First Nations Information Governance Centre (FNIGC https://fnigc.ca/) continues its advocacy for Indigenous data leadership and governance.

Each of these networks developed sets of aligned, but nationally relevant, Indigenous Data Sovereignty principles. Te Mana Raraunga, for example, advanced principles that assert Māori rights and interests in relation to data and the ethical use of data to enhance the wellbeing of Māori people, language and culture. The principles cover six areas of Māori data sovereignty: *rangatiratanga* (authority) in terms of control, jurisdiction and self-determination; *whakapapa* (relationships) with respect to data context, data disaggregation and future use; *whanaungatanga* (obligations) in terms of balancing rights and accountabilities; *kotahitanga* (collective benefit) to derive benefit, build capacity, and connect; *manaakitanga* (reciprocity) promoting respect and consent; and, *kaitiakitanga* (guardianship) requiring data guardianship, ethics and restrictions (TMR 2019). In Australia, the Maiam nayri Wingara Indigenous Data Sovereignty Collective drew its principals from a summit of Aboriginal and Torres Strait Islander leaders in 2018. Summit attendees asserted that Indigenous Peoples in Australia have the right to exercise control of the Indigenous data ecosystem inclusive of data creation, development, stewardship, analysis, dissemination and infrastructure to ensure that such data are contextual and disaggregated; relevant and empowering of sustainable self-determination and effective self-governance; accountable to Indigenous Peoples; and protective of Indigenous individual and collective interests (*Maiam naryi Wingara* 2018).

These Indigenous Data Sovereignty networks continue to collaborate. For example, in 2018, the newly formed International Indigenous Data Sovereignty Interest Group at the Research Data Alliance (RDA Group; rd-alliance.org) developed the CARE Principles for Indigenous Data Governance (see Chapter 1) (RDA IG 2022). The CARE Principles provide direction to non-Indigenous data actors on the stewardship of Indigenous data (Walter and Russo Carroll 2021). Originally developed as an Indigenous pair to the mainstream findable, accessible, interoperable, reusable (FAIR) principles, CARE is now incorporated more widely. For example, the Australian Institute of Aboriginal and Torres Strait Islander Studies (AIATSIS) have incorporated CARE Principles into the AIATSIS Code of Ethics (2020, 19). This code is applicable to all publicly funded research relating to Aboriginal and Torres Strait Islander Peoples or populations.

In 2019, representatives from national networks and scholars from other nations met at a workshop in the Basque Country in Spain. This workshop concluded that while national networks are best placed to respond to and progress data sovereignty for their peoples and communities, a global alliance was needed to advocate for, and advance, a shared vision of Indigenous Data Sovereignty. The result was the formation of the Global Indigenous Data Alliance (see www.gida-global.org/) (Oñati Indigenous Data Sovereignty Communique GIDA 2019).

Indigenous Data Sovereignty Through Indigenous Data Governance

Indigenous Data Governance is the mechanism by which Indigenous Data Sovereignty is made manifest. *Indigenous Data Governance* asserts Indigenous interests in relation to data by informing the when, how and why Indigenous data are gathered, analysed, accessed and used and ensuring Indigenous data reflect Indigenous priorities, values, culture, lifeworlds and diversity (Maiam nayri Wingara 2018). At its simplest, Indigenous Data Governance means Indigenous decision-making and Indigenous control. Critically, this decision-making and control remains central regardless of who produced the data or who holds the data (see Rodriguez-Lonebear 2016; Smith 2016; Carroll et al. 2019; Rainie et al. 2017; Walker et al. 2017). Indigenous data scholars and practitioners divide data governance into two broad and interconnected areas: *governance of data* and *data for governance* (see Smith 2016; Carrol et al. 2019). Both are necessary to achieve Indigenous Data Sovereignty and require Indigenous leadership (Walter and Russo-Carroll 2021).

Governance of Indigenous Data

The governance of data imperative demands that Indigenous Peoples have decision-making power in relation to Indigenous data holdings. This governance imperative is heightened by the current data revolution. More, and more different kinds of data, both public and private, are being utilized in creating narratives about Indigenous communities, little of which is owned or had meaningful Indigenous leadership involved in its production. Rodriguez-Lonebear (2016) suggests, for example, that only 2 per cent of American Indian data are produced by American Indian nations. In a Canadian context, while First Nations have laboured diligently to create their own comprehensive and culturally appropriate health surveys (through the Regional Health Survey), Métis and Inuit organizations lack similar control over data about them (though the Inuit recently completed their Qanuippitaa? National Inuit Health Survey to provide an overall picture of the health and wellbeing of Inuit, and the Métis Nation of Ontario collaborated with Léger to create the first ever Métis housing survey). In Australia, Aboriginal and Torres Strait Islander population data are primarily collected and controlled by the Australian Bureau of Statistics. Very little are made available to Indigenous scholars or communities. The *Mayi Kuwayi National Study of Aboriginal and Torres Strait Islander Wellbeing* is one of the very few Indigenous-led large-scale surveys to date (Lovett et al. 2020).

Indigenous Data Governance seeks to provide Indigenous Peoples with the right to control data that is about or from them, or their lands, waters and territories. Recent initiatives in this arena have been driven by the various national Indigenous Data Sovereignty networks. Examples include the 2023 release of the Māori Data Governance Model by the national tribal leaders forum in Aotearoa. Designed by Māori data experts, the model provides guidance for the system-wide governance of Māori data across the public service, consistent with the government's responsibilities under *te Tiriti o Waitangi* (Treaty of Waitangi). Māori authority over Māori data is developed across eight data *pou* (pillars): data capacities and workforce development; data infrastructure; data collection; data protection; data access, sharing and repatriation; data use and reuse; data quality and system integrity; and data classification (Kukutai et al. 2023).

In 2023, the Maiam nayri Wingara Indigenous Data Sovereignty collective in Australia convened an Indigenous Data Governance Summit. The more than 130 Aboriginal and Torres Strait Islander Summit delegates asserted that in Australia, the realization of Indigenous Data Governance needs to adhere to six basic principles. These included the foundational elements that all governance activity adhere to the internationally agreed definitions of Indigenous Data Sovereignty and Indigenous Data Governance, with Indigenous leadership and control over all governance processes. The summit attendees agreed that Indigenous Data Governance must be integrated at all data lifecycle stages, investing in digital infrastructure and systems aligned with Indigenous priorities. Further, enactment would require resourcing to build Indigenous data literacy and capability by allocating resources for Indigenous workforce expansion and be based on ensuring accountability of entities that hold Indigenous data, ensuring that data are available to and accessible by the Indigenous Peoples and lands to which they relate. To achieve the aforementioned, summit delegates asserted that the creation of new data should incorporate Indigenous Data Governance mechanisms, guaranteeing that data production is ethical, representative and beneficial (Maiam nayri Wingara 2023).

Governance of data within institutional settings has also been a specific focus of the Indigenous Data Sovereignty movement in recent times. In mid-2023, the Global Indigenous Data Alliance (GIDA) Summit convened in Naarm (Melbourne) met to progress how Indigenous Data Governance is positioned within university settings. Indigenous scholars from Australia, Aotearoa, the United States, Canada, Norway, Sweden, Finland, and Tonga and Samoa (diaspora Aotearoa) called on universities and funders to recognize that any data concerning Indigenous Peoples is Indigenous data, to uphold Indigenous Data Sovereignty and operationalize Indigenous Data Governance through working with the affected Indigenous Peoples. Failure to do so would leave "academic institutions open to claims of complicity in the ongoing structure of colonisation" (Prehn et al. 2023).

Data for Indigenous Governance

Data for governance is also built around the foundations of Indigenous leadership and decision-making. However, rather than focusing on data held by nation-state governments and non-Indigenous entities, the priority is on the data that *Indigenous nations* themselves need to govern effectively, including data collected and held by tribal and First Peoples organizations and entities (Carroll et al. 2019). As Rainie et al. (2017, 1) persuasively argue, the right data are foundational for Indigenous nation-building processes:

> Indigenous nations, like all communities, require data to identify problems, to develop and prioritize solutions, to make strategic decisions and defensible policies, to influence external entities, and, most importantly, to bring the community's vision of a healthy and vibrant society to life.

Beyond data collection and generation, there is also growing recognition of the need for data infrastructure, practices and capabilities that enable communities to protect, utilize and benefit from their own data (FNIGC 2020; Kukutai et al. 2023). In all of these matters, Indigenous nations should be the ones making the decisions. The governance for data imperative is exemplified by Walter et al. (2020) in their discussion of how tribal nations are increasingly challenging existing settler colonial data systems by collecting their own data for tribal governance. As the authors note, the enumeration of American Indians and Alaska Natives (AIANs) in the US official statistics system is directly tied to federal funding. In response, tribal nations are increasingly conducting their own tribal census, collecting data that describe the size, characteristics, conditions and realities of their citizenry. Examples of tribal data of governance activities included the Ho-Chunk Nation Census in 2015, the "K'awaika YOU Count!" Laguna Pueblo Census in 2016 and the Sault Ste. Marie Tribe of Chippewa Indians' Census collected in 2014 and 2019.

In enacting our own data systems, Indigenous nations can and do reject the normative precursors that underlie whitestream data systems. Instead, creating, analysing and deploying data for Indigenous governance objectives include ethical considerations around sustainability, reciprocity, responsibility to kin (human and non-human) and any other forms of culturally relevant objectives deemed important by the Indigenous Peoples designing data collection (see Carroll et al. 2019; Smith 2016 for more extended discussions of such cultural objectives). For example, in planning a survey of the health of the Native toddler population in their area, the Albuquerque Area Indian Health Board replaced the mainstream survey instrument with its own survey. This Indigenous-designed survey posed the overarching research question: "What is a healthy Native toddler?" The survey sought to answer that question through the design and data collection on measures that reflected the cultural, identity, relational, spiritual and lifeworld of Native Peoples in New Mexico, inclusive of the physical and development perspective measures that were the focus of the mainstream survey (Walter pers comm Oct 18 2023).

Conclusion

Data represent powerful tools in the broader context of Native nation building. They do so for two reasons. First, because properly created, collected, stored, analysed, interpreted and communicated Indigenous data provide robust, policy-relevant indicators of the state of our nations and, within that, our communities and our families. Second, Indigenous data crucially shape the kinds of *stories* we can tell and the categories we can use, not only to represent our nations, but also to constitute them. The fact of the matter is that it is incredibly difficult to "good data" our way to good relationships: we can only hope to "good relationships" our way to good data. Hence, this book's emphasis is less about how to altogether avoid deficit-based depictions of our Indigenous communities and more on how to generate and engage with data in ways that make visible our own diverse lifeworlds (see Chapter 1 for further discussion on this). This, in turn, requires a greater measure of Indigenous control over the statistical cycle and, indeed, the data ecosystem.

Finally, for Indigenous Peoples there is also the recognition that research has become increasingly quantitative. As a result, there is an increased demand for Indigenous researchers, communities and organizations to understand quantitative methodologies. Understanding allows us to confidently criticize research and data produced by universities, government and consultants that reflect the traditional 5D trope of Indigenous data. By doing so we also enhance our data capacity during an increasingly demanding period of rebuilding our nations.

References

AIATSIS. *AIATSIS Code of Ethics, Australian Institute of Aboriginal and Torres Strait Islander Studies.* Canberra: AIATSIS, 2020.

Andrejevic, Mark. "The Big Data Divide." *International Journal of Communication* 8 (2014): 1673–1689.

Andrejevic, Mark. *Infoglut: How Too Much Information Is Changing the Way We Think and Know.* New York: Routledge, 2013.

Andrejevic, Mark. *iSpy: Surveillance and Power in the Interactive Era.* Lawrence: University Press of Kansas, 2007.

Appadurai, Arjun. "Number in the Colonial Imagination." In *Orientalism and the Postcolonial Predicament: Perspectives on South Asia*, edited by Carol A. Breckenridge and Peter van der Veer, 314–339. Philadelphia: University of Pennsylvania Press, 1993.

Bartosik-Purgat, Małgorzata, and Milena Ratajczak-Mrożek. "Big Data Analysis as a Source of Companies' Competitive Advantage: A Review." *Entrepreneurial Business and Economics Review* 6, no. 4 (2018): 197–215. https://doi.org/10.15678/EBER.2018.060411.

Bowker, Geoffrey C. *Memory Practices in the Sciences.* Cambridge, MA: MIT Press, 2005.

boyd, danah, and Kate Crawford. "Critical Questions for Big Data: Provocations for a Cultural, Technological, and Scholarly Phenomenon." *Information, Communication & Society* 15, no. 5 (2012): 662–679. https://doi.org/10.1080/1369118X.2012.678878.

Briscoe, Gordon. *Counting, Health and Identity: A History of Aboriginal Health and Demography in Western Australia and Queensland, 1900–1940.* Canberra: Aboriginal Studies Press, 2003.

Buolamwini, Joy. *Unmasking AI: My Mission to Protect What Is Human in a World of Machines.* New York: Penguin, 2023.

Carroll, Stephanie Russo, Desi Rodriguez-Lonebear, and Andrew Martinez. "Indigenous Data Governance: Strategies from United States Native Nations." *Data Science Journal* 18 (2019). https://doi.org/10.5334/dsj-2019-031.

Cohn, Bernard S. "The Census, Social Structure and Objectification in South Asia." In *An Anthropologist Among the Historians and Other Essays*, 224–254. New Delhi: Oxford University Press, 1987.

Cohn, Bernard S. *Colonialism and Its Forms of Knowledge: The British in India.* Princeton: Princeton University Press, 1996.

Cormack, Donna, and Tahu Kukutai. "Indigenous Peoples, Data and the Coloniality of Surveillance." In *The Ambivalences of Data Power: New Perspectives in Critical Data Studies*, edited by Andreas Hepp, Juliane Jarke and Leif Kramp, 121–141. London: Palgrave Macmillan, 2022.

Curtis, Bruce. *The Politics of Population: State Formation, Statistics, and the Census of Canada, 1840–1875.* Toronto: University of Toronto Press, 2001.

Davis, Megan. "Data and the United Nations Declaration on the Rights of Indigenous Peoples." In *Indigenous Data Sovereignty*, edited by Tahu Kukutai and John Taylor, 25–38. Canberra: ANU Press, 2016.

Dean, Mitchell. *Governmentality: Power and Rule in Modern Society*. London: SAGE Publications, 1999.

Desrosières, Alain. *The Politics of Large Numbers: A History of Statistical Reasoning*. Translated by Camille Naish. Cambridge, MA: Harvard University Press, 1998.

Diebold, Francis X. "On the Origin(s) and Development of 'Big Data': The Phenomenon, the Term, and the Discipline." University of Pennsylvania. First draft August 2012, last modified February 13, 2019.

Eubanks, Virginia. *Automating Inequality: How High-Tech Tools Profile, Police, and Punish the Poor*. New York: St. Martin's Press, 2018.

First Nations Information Governance Centre. *A First Nations Data Governance Strategy*. Ottawa: First Nations Information Governance Centre, 2020. https://fnigc.ca/news/introducing-a-first-nations-data-governance-strategy/.

First Nations Information Governance Centre. *Ownership, Control, Access and Possession (OCAP): The Path to First Nations Information Governance*. Ottawa: First Nations Information Governance Centre, 2016.

Foucault, Michel. "Governmentality." In *Essential Works of Foucault, 1954–1984, Volume 3: Power*, edited by James D. Faubion, translated by Robert Hurley and others, 201–222. New York: The New Press, 2001.

"Gartner Glossary: Big Data." *Gartner*, n.d. Accessed July 7, 2024. www.gartner.com/en/information-technology/glossary/big-data.

Gitelman, Lisa, and Virginia Jackson. "Introduction: Raw Data Is an Oxymoron." In *"Raw Data" Is an Oxymoron*, edited by Lisa Gitelman, 1–14. Cambridge, MA: MIT Press, 2013.

Hacking, Ian. "Making Up People." In *Reconstructing Individualism: Autonomy, Individuality, and the Self in Western Thought*, edited by Thomas C. Heller, Morton Sosna, and David E. Wellbery, 222–236. Stanford, CA: Stanford University Press, 1986.

Kalpagam, U. "Colonial Governmentality and the Public Sphere in India." *Journal of Historical Sociology* 13, no. 3 (2000): 418–440. https://doi.org/10.1111/1467-6443.00154.

Kalpagam, U. *Rule by Numbers: Governmentality in Colonial India*. Lanham, MD: Lexington Books, 2016.

Kitchin, Rob. *The Data Revolution: A Critical Analysis of Big Data, Open Data, and Data Infrastructures*. 2nd ed. London: SAGE Publications, 2022.

Kitchin, Rob, and Tracey P. Lauriault. "Towards Critical Data Studies: Charting and Unpacking Data Assemblages and Their Work." In *Thinking Big Data in Geography: New Regimes, New Research*, edited by Jim Thatcher, Josef Eckert, and Andrew Shears, 3–20. Lincoln: University of Nebraska Press, 2018.

Kukutai, Tahu, Kyla Campbell-Kamariera, Aroha Mead, Kirikowhai Mikaere, Caleb Moses, Jesse Whitehead, and Donna Cormack. *Māori Data Governance Model*. Rotorua: Te Kāhui Raraunga, 2023.

Kukutai, Tahu, and Donna Cormack. "Pushing the Space." In *Indigenous Data Sovereignty and Social Policy*, edited by Maggie Walter, Tahu Kukutai, Stephanie Russo Carroll, and Desi Rodriguez-Lonebear, 21–35. London: Routledge, 2020.

Kukutai, Tahu, and John Taylor. *Indigenous Data Sovereignty: Toward an Agenda*. Canberra: ANU Press, 2016.

Kukutai, Tahu, and Maggie Walter. "Indigenous Statistics." In *Handbook of Research Methods in Health Social Sciences*, edited by Pranee Liamputtong, 1691–1706. Singapore: Springer, 2019.

Loveman, Mara. "The Race to Progress: Census Taking and Nation Making in Brazil (1870–1920)." *Hispanic American Historical Review* 89, no. 3 (2009): 435–470. https://doi.org/10.1215/00182168-2009-002.

Lovett, Ray, Makayla-May Brinckley, B. Phillips, J. Chapman, K. Thurber, R. Jones, E. Banks, T. Dunbar, A. Olsen, and M. Wenitong. "Marrathalpu Mayingku Ngiya Kiyi. Minyawaa Ngiyani Yata Punmalaka; Wangaaypu Kirrampili Kara. In the Beginning It Was Our People's Law. What Makes Us Well; to Never Be Sick. Cohort Profile of Mayi Kuwayu: The National Study of Aboriginal and Torres Strait Islander Wellbeing." Canberra: Australian National University, 2020. https://mkstudy.com.au/wp-content/uploads/2021/03/Lovett-et-al_Mayi-Kuwayu_AAS-2020_2.pdf.

Lovett, Ray, Vanessa Lee, Tahu Kukutai, Donna Cormack, Stephanie Carroll Rainie, and Jennifer Walker. "Good Data Practices for Indigenous Data Sovereignty and Governance." In *Good Data*, edited by Angela Daly, S. Kate Devitt, and Monique Mann, 26–36. Amsterdam: Institute of Network Cultures, 2019.

Maiam nayri Wingara (MnW). *Indigenous Data Sovereignty Communique: Indigenous Data Sovereignty Summit 20/06/2018*. Maiam nayri Wingara, 2018. https://static1.squarespace.com/static/5b3043afb40b9d20411f3512/t/5b6c0f9a0e2e725e9cabf4a6/1533808545167/Communique%2B-%2BIndigenous%2BData%2BSovereignty%2BSummit.pdf.

Maiam nayri Wingara Indigenous Data Sovereignty Collective, the Australian Indigenous Governance Institute & the Lowitja Institute. *Indigenous Data Governance Communique*. Maiam nayri Wingara, 2023. https://static1.squarespace.com/static/5b3043afb40b9d20411f3512/t/64f7b64b19d9dd4616bf2c75/1693955660219/Indigenous+Data+Governance+Communique+2023.pdf.

McCarthy, Matthew T. "The Big Data Divide and Its Consequences." *Journal of Information Technology* 32, no. 3 (2016): 1131–1148.

McCue, Clifford J. *Data Mining and Predictive Analysis: Intelligence Gathering and Crime Analysis*. Burlington, MA: Butterworth-Heinemann, 2007.

Miller, Peter, and Nikolas Rose. "Governing Economic Life." *Economy and Society* 19, no. 1 (1990): 1–31.

Mittelstadt, Brent Daniel, and Luciano Floridi. "The Ethics of Big Data: Current and Foreseeable Issues in Biomedical Contexts." *Science and Engineering Ethics* 22, no. 2 (2016): 303–341. https://doi.org/10.1007/s11948-015-9652-2.

Mosco, Vincent. *The Digital Sublime: Myth, Power, and Cyberspace*. Cambridge, MA: MIT Press, 2004.

Mutu, Margaret. "Mana Māori Motuhake: Māori Concepts and Practices of Sovereignty." In *Routledge Handbook of Critical Indigenous Studies*, edited by Brendan Hokowhitu, Aileen Moreton-Robinson, Linda Tuhiwai Smith, Chris Andersen, and Steven Larkin. New York: Routledge, 2021.

Oñati Indigenous Data Sovereignty (ID-SOV) Communique, 2019. www.gida-global.org/whoweare.

O'Neil, Cathy. *Weapons of Math Destruction: How Big Data Increases Inequality and Threatens Democracy*. New York: Crown, 2017.

Pels, Peter. "The Anthropology of Colonialism: Culture, History, and the Emergence of Western Governmentality." *Annual Review of Anthropology* 26 (1997): 163–183. https://doi.org/10.1146/annurev.anthro.26.1.163.

Pentland, Alex. "Reality Mining of Mobile Communications: Toward a New Deal on Data." In *The Global Information Technology Report 2008–2009: Mobility in a Networked World*, edited by Soumitra Dutta and Irene Mia, 75–80. Basingstoke, UK: Palgrave Macmillan, 2009.

Porter, Theodore M. *The Rise of Statistical Thinking, 1820–1900*. Princeton: Princeton University Press, 1986.

Prehn, Jacob, Riley Taitingfong, Robyn Rowe, Ibrahim Garba, Cassandra Price, Maui Hudson, Tahu Kukutai, and Stephanie Russo Carroll. *Indigenous Data Governance and Universities Communiqué*. Global Indigenous Data Alliance, 2023. https://doi.org/10.6084/m9.figshare.24201585.

Rainie, Stephanie Carroll, Desi Rodriguez-Lonebear, and Andrew Martinez. "Policy Brief: Data Governance for Native Nation Rebuilding (Version 2)." 2017a. http://nni.arizona.edu/application/files/8415/0007/5708/Policy_Brief_Data_Governance_for_Native_Nation_Rebuilding_Version_2.pdf.

Rainie, Stephanie Carroll, Jennifer Lee Schultz, Elaine Briggs, Patricia Riggs, and Nancy Lynn Palmanteer-Holder. "Data as a Strategic Resource: Self-determination, Governance, and the Data Challenge for Indigenous Nations in the United States." *International Indigenous Policy Journal* 8, no. 2 (2017b). https://doi.org/10.18584/iipj.2017.8.2.1.

Research Data Alliance International Indigenous Data Sovereignty Interest Group (RDA IG). *CARE Principles for Indigenous Data Governance*. RDA IIDSIG, 2022. www.gida-global.org/care.

Rodriguez-Lonebear, Desi. "Building a Data Revolution in Indian Country." In *Indigenous Data Sovereignty*, edited by Tahu Kukutai and John Taylor, 253–272. Canberra: ANU Press, 2016.

Rose, Nikolas. *Powers of Freedom: Reframing Political Thought*. Cambridge: Cambridge University Press, 1999.

Scott, David. "Colonial Governmentality." *Social Text* 43 (1995): 191–220. https://doi.org/10.2307/466631.

Scott, James C. *Seeing Like a State: How Certain Schemes to Improve the Human Condition Have Failed*. New Haven, CT: Yale University Press, 1998.

Scott, James C., John Tehranian, and Jeremy Mathias. "The Production of Legal Identities Proper to States: The Case of the Permanent Family Surname." *Comparative Studies in Society and History* 44, no. 1 (2002): 4–44.

Shah, S., V. Peristeras, I. Magnisalis. "Government (Big) Data Ecosystem: Definition, Classification of Actors, and Their Roles." *World Academy of Science, Engineering and Technology, International Journal of Computer and Information Engineering* 14, no. 4 (2020): 102–114.

Smith, Diane E. "Governing Data and Data for Governance: The Everyday Practice of Indigenous Sovereignty." In *Indigenous Data Sovereignty*, edited by Tahu Kukutai and John Taylor, 117–138. Canberra: ANU Press, 2016.

Taylor, John, and Tahu Kukutai. *Indigenous Data Sovereignty and Indicators. Reflections from Australia and Aotearoa New Zealand*. Paper presented at the UNPFII Expert Group Meeting on "The Way Forward: Indigenous Peoples and the 2030 Agenda for Sustainable Development". New York: United Nations, 2015.

Te Mana Raraunga (TMR). *Maori Data Sovereignty Network*, 2019. www.temanararaunga.maori.nz.

Tsosie, Krystal S., Joseph M. Yracheta, Jessica A. Kolopenuk, and Janis Geary. "We Have 'Gifted' Enough: Indigenous Genomic Data Sovereignty in Precision Medicine." *The American Journal of Bioethics* 21, no. 4 (2021): 72–75. https://doi.org/10.1080/15265161.2021.1891347.

Tsosie, Rebecca. "Tribal Data Governance and Informational Privacy: Constructing Indigenous Data Sovereignty." *Montana Law Review* 80 (2019): 229.

Walker, Jennifer, Ray Lovett, Tahu Kukutai, Carmen Jones, and David Henry. "Indigenous Health Data and the Path to Healing." *The Lancet* 390, no. 10107 (2017): 2022–2023.

Walter, Maggie. "Data Politics and Indigenous Representation in Australian Statistics." In *Indigenous Data Sovereignty*, edited by Tahu Kukutai and John Taylor, 79–97. Canberra: ANU Press, 2016.

Walter, Maggie. Pers Comm, October 18, 2023.

Walter, Maggie. "The Voice of Indigenous Data: Beyond the Markers of Disadvantage." *Griffith Review* 60 (2018): 256–263.

Walter, Maggie, and Chris Andersen. *Indigenous Statistics: A Quantitative Research Methodology*. London: Routledge, 2013.

Walter, Maggie, Tahu Kukutai, Stephanie Russo Carroll, and Desi Rodriguez-Lonebear, eds. *Indigenous Data Sovereignty and Social Policy*. London: Routledge, 2021.

Walter, Maggie, and Stephanie Russo Carroll. "Indigenous Data Sovereignty, Governance and the Link to Indigenous Policy." In *Indigenous Data Sovereignty and Social Policy*, edited by Maggie Walter, Tahu Kukutai, Stephanie Russo Carroll, and Desi Rodriguez-Lonebear, 1–20. London: Routledge, 2021.

Zuboff, Shoshana. *The Age of Surveillance Capitalism: The Fight for a Human Future at the New Frontier of Power*. London: Profile Books, 2019.

3
THE STATISTICAL FIELD, WRIT INDIGENOUS

Chris Andersen

CHAPTER LEARNING OBJECTIVES

Objective 1: In this chapter readers will learn what a social field is, particularly as it relates to internal agents' struggles, hierarchies and investments.

Objective 2: Readers will learn what makes the statistical field distinctive from a data cycle or ecosystem.

Objective 3: Readers will learn examples of what these distinctive struggles, hierarchies and investments look like in practice.

"If you are not at the table, you are probably on the menu."—activist adage

Autumn, 2003: I have flown to Ottawa, Canada's capital, to attend a national gathering of Indigenous scholars and allies to discuss architectural changes to one of the national granting agencies about how to better include "Indigenous knowledge." Over one of the lunches, I happen to be sitting at a table with a number of education professors who had kindly offered me the table's last seat. As we chat collegially about our research interests, I discuss my focus on statistics. One of the education professors, seemingly genuinely curious, asks, "Chris, can you say a little bit about what you doing at this conference?" Slightly puzzled by her question, I replied, "What do you mean?" She replied,

DOI: 10.4324/9781003173342-3
This chapter has been made available under a CC-BY-NC-ND license.

gently, "Well, you just said you do statistics, not Indigenous knowledge." I replied, cheerfully, "Why are statistics automatically not Indigenous knowledge?" We go back and forth for a bit and, after explaining her work in terms of the storytelling methodology she used, she kindly but firmly ends our conversation by stating, "Listen, I'm not saying that what you do isn't important—I just don't understand how it qualifies as Indigenous knowledge."

The idea that statistics and Indigenous knowledge are incommensurable is still a surprisingly durable one in large swaths of the Indigenous research world. This opposition has certainly made its presence felt in academic scholarship and the training of students. For example, statistics are rarely included in Indigenous research methods courses, though these courses tend to form the curricular backbone of undergraduate and graduate "Indigenous methodologies" training (e.g., Chilisa 2019, 2012; Denzin et al. 2008; Kovach 2010, 2021; Smith 2021, 2012, 1999; Wilson 2008; Windchief and San Pedro 2019). And when statistics are discussed in dominant Indigenous methodologies scholarship they are criticized for their positivist pretensions to rationality (Chilisa 2019; Kovach 2021) or their potential for symbolic violence (Tomaselli et al. 2008, 363). Outside the academy, Indigenous leaders and policy actors in the public policy world are rarely in control of the input or the output of statistical information relating to their citizens. These factors—among many—have helped to cement the argument that statistics do not (and perhaps *cannot*) constitute a valid form of Indigenous knowledge. As such, they have long been disregarded as useful tools for decolonization.

As we learned in the first edition of this book, talking about statistics as a valid form of Indigenous knowledge and as an important tool for Indigenous decolonization efforts raises strong feelings for many. We continue to take the position that Indigenous knowledge must include *any* form of knowledge that benefits Indigenous Peoples. We are not suggesting that *no* differences exist between Indigenous and "Western" forms of knowledge (to give one example of many, ceremonial knowledge can and does form the backbone of Indigenous governing systems, though it would rarely be confused with that of Western governing systems). Our point instead is simply that Indigenous Peoples are powerfully embedded in the last five centuries of colonial projects. As such, any tools that help us push back against such projects, and that assist us in "constituting ourselves anew," are worth discussing. And we will argue further that statistics—literally the "language of state"—*must* be included as one of those tools. It is too important a vector in the fight for Indigenous control of our collective lives and territories not to.

We foregrounded in some detail in Chapter 2 (and in the first edition of this book) that a robust literature has explored the way statistics—particularly "official" statistics—have played a powerful and even ubiquitous role in shaping our understandings of the social world (see Alonso and Starr 1987; Curtis 2002; Hacking 1986; Woolf 1989). Philosopher Ian Hacking (1986) argues that statistics literally "make up people." Or perhaps more precisely, the kinds of categories and the enthusiasm to classify, encouraged by statistics, create "new ways for people to be" (Hacking 1986, 161). Alonso and Starr (1987, 1) paint a compelling portrait of the power and ubiquity of official statistics in the introduction to their important *Politics of Numbers* collection, declaring

> [e]very day, from the morning paper to the evening news, Americans are served a steady diet of statistics. We are given the latest figures for consumer prices and the unemployment rate, lagging and leading economic indicators, reading scores, and life expectancies, not to mention data on crime, divorce, and money supply.

In these senses, statistics operate as extremely powerful lenses that bring into focus selected aspects of the everyday lives of citizens. They offer a nearly unparalleled example of what French sociologist Pierre Bourdieu would refer to as "symbolic power" (more on that concept later). In an Indigenous context, much of the past five hundred years has in fact consisted of non-Indigenous colonial officials and administrators using statistics to produce a very narrow aperture[1] of who we are as Indigenous People (acting as a form of what Foucault [1980, 125] might term a "technology of power"). This chapter is premised on asking (and, indirectly, answering) three questions. First, why do statistics possess such a powerful ability to tell narrow or limited stories about Indigenous communities and our members? Second, why is it so important for us to conceive of statistics not as neutral, taken-for-granted "facts" but as complex, power-laden *political processes* that have produced colonial-racist depictions of Indigenous Peoples and our communities? Third and finally, why is it crucial for Indigenous leaders, policy actors and academics to continue to build the "statistical literacy"[2] required to understand and treat statistics as such?

One possible reason why most people think about statistics—particularly "official" statistics like those produced by governments—as "facts" is because their *inputs* and *outputs* are either largely taken for granted or are not thought about at all (see Latour 1987, 2). In turn, because so many typically spend little time thinking about the *fields* through which data inputs and outputs must pass, we miss the complex politics through which information gets taken from the locality of our communities and turned into data. The legitimacy of statistics in modern society is a powerful example of what Bruno Latour has elsewhere referred to as a "black box." He describes this metaphor in the following terms: "[w]hen a machine runs efficiently, when a matter of fact is settled, one need focus only on its inputs and outputs and not on its internal complexity. Thus, paradoxically, the more science and technology succeed, the more opaque and obscure they become" (Latour 1987, 2–3). If statistics operate as a powerful and objective source of truth, unsettling that taken-for-grantedness requires us to open the black box and look inside.

Certainly, a number of conceptual models are available for thinking about data/statistics as political processes rather than a neutral and objective accounting of an underlying reality. The book's first two chapters engaged in a brief discussion about these, including the idea of a data ecosystem, a data assemblage and a statistical field. My preference is for a *field* approach because I believe it offers us superior tools for thinking about the messiness of this political process. First, it allows us to understand the process as complex. This may seem obvious, but it has important implications, which I explain in further detail later. Second, a social field approach is attentive to internal *hierarchical struggle*. In other words, it understands that different groups hold different amounts of power. Therefore, they can disproportionately affect what the statistics eventually come to look like. And finally, this approach is mindful of the intense *investment* required by Indigenous agents to learn the "rules of engagement" for producing and using data. Perhaps equally important, it asks us to think carefully about the tensions between our professional investment as statistical "agents"[3] and the potential for the misalignment of statistics with the Indigenous values and priorities we adhere to.

Finally, I wish to note two specific aspects of a *social field approach* that make it especially attractive to the contexts within which I use it in this chapter's "thought experiment." First, it emphasizes the power of *borders and boundaries* in and out of any given field. This methodology thus asks readers to reflect on the translative or "refractive" efforts required to produce and use data and their narratives in various social contexts. These include those of our own Indigenous nations and communities. So, how do we make data relevant to the kinds of stories we want to give to our communities and nations, and what are the limits of the current statistical field in (my case) Canada for doing so? Second, social field methodology encourages us to consider different scales of abstraction and granularity. In the words of Loïc Wacquant (one of Bourdieu's more well-known students, now a leading sociologist in his own right), part of the analytical attractiveness of a social field approach lies in its ability to

> range along levels of abstraction and to travel smoothly across analytic scales to link large structures of power . . . and the meso level of institutions . . . to the minutiae of everyday interaction and the phenomenological texture of subjectivity encapsulated by the term of practice.
> (Wacquant 2018, 92)

This no doubt seems complicated in the abstract, but the value of attending to different levels of abstraction will become more apparent as we get into the case study later.

In light of this contextual introduction, this is a chapter of two major halves. The chapter's first half—necessarily fairly dense and abstract—will lay out its major elements[4] to explain how different forms and dynamics of statistical production "fit" within this framework. Following this, the chapter's second half will then lay out some of the major dimensions of the statistical *cycle* (which represents the statistical field "in action"). I do so with an eye for demonstrating how the broader power of colonialism—its governing projects, its forms of authority and the expertise of its personnel—can and have thwarted Indigenous attempts to gain sovereignty over it. From a conceptual standpoint, positioning statistics within a field methodology thus holds important implications for

a. how we understand the role of statistics in society;
b. their potential for reproducing colonial structures and practices, both in and outside of the statistical field;
c. the ability of Indigenous policy agents to "push back" against the historically negative impacts and implications of this field; and
d. the different points along the cycle that Indigenous Data Sovereignty can be asserted and inserted, in instances where Indigenous experts are not yet controlling the entire process.

Thinking about statistics through a social field approach encourages us to think more complexly about the broader "statistical cycle" through which the statistics are conceived of, collected, analysed, communicated and evaluated; the various "agents" and their agendas involved in the cycle's various domains; the forms of expertise necessary to participate in the statistical field and how these requirements effectively repel other forms of knowledge; and the fundamental unfairness built into the system that ensure certain forms of statistics are legitimated while others are marginalized and even dismissed.[5] Since these dynamics comprise important elements of the contemporary global statistical field, we will spend the time to undertake an explanation of now.

Part I: Statistics as a Social Field

> In highly differentiated societies, the social cosmos is made up of a number of . . . relatively autonomous microcosms, i.e., spaces of objective relations that are the site of a logic and a necessity that are *specific and irreducible* to those that regulate other fields.
> (Bourdieu and Wacquant 1992, 97—emphasis in original)

Bourdieu's research into *social fields* is undeniably dense. Yet it offers a powerful tool to help us explore the complexity of our everyday lives and to understand the inequalities of the modern world. This includes the lives most Indigenous People who live in colonial contexts experience. As the prior quote alludes to, Bourdieu understood the social world as being divided into a number of distinct and hierarchically structured spheres of professional practice. Think here of areas like law, medicine, religion, art, literature and the criminal justice system. Or—of the most specific relevance here—statistics. These *fields* have specific rules, forms of knowledge, interrelations and forms of socialization (i.e., habituses) through which internal members compete. Together, these competitions govern the field's relations and its boundaries.

This methodology is widely employed but in the interests of presenting it more precisely here, we focus on several key structural properties to fields to offer a sense of their isomorphic properties (i.e., what structural elements they hold in common across specific fields). In a sense, to position statistics as a social field is to "crack open" Latour's (1987) black box and peer into its inner workings. Social fields ask us to explore conceptually the complex relationships *between* agents *within* it, rather than debating the technical accuracy of the end product (i.e., "are these statistics accurate? If so, why? If not, why not?"). In his useful discussion of Bourdieu's social field methodology, David Swartz (1997, 122) unpacks social fields into four major components. I will explain their conceptual meanings here and then touch on them further in this chapter's second part.

First, fields are foundationally locales of struggle "for control over valued resources," what Bourdieu referred to as *capital*: "[f]ields may be thought of as structured spaces that are organized around specific types of capital or combinations of capital" (Swartz 1997, 117). Using an analogy of a game, Bourdieu argues that the activities that occur within a field relate to the forms of struggle in pursuit of the capital of that field. In fact, part of the struggle is over what counts as capital.[6] Those in dominant positions in each field will attempt to impose broad agreement for their understanding of capital. In doing so, if they "win" they gain "symbolic capital" (i.e., what gets taken for granted as "true"). Hilgers and Mangez (2015, 6) assert, in fact, that "[t]he struggle in a field is . . . a struggle to impose a definition of legitimate recognition, in which victory leads to more or less monopolistic control of the definition of the forms of legitimation prevailing in the field."

The preceding discussion may seem eye-wateringly abstract. But, in fact, it holds powerful real-world consequences for the relationship between Indigenous Peoples and statistics. Let's think about what this might this look like for Indigenous People in a place like Canada: in the *medical field*, medical agents (nurses, doctors, administrators, even ambulance drivers, etc.) might struggle over what counts as legitimate medical knowledge and intervention (think here of the acknowledgment of Indigenous healing traditions and knowledges); in the *juridical field*, agents (lawyers, judges, police officers, etc.) might struggle over what comes to count as the actual substance of law (imagine here the recognition of Indigenous laws and legal orders); in the *artistic field*, agents might struggle over the meaning and boundaries of what can legitimately be called art (think about the increased valuation of certain kinds of Indigenous art in the last three decades); in the *education field*, agents might struggle over what counts as legitimate pedagogy or curriculum, to be taught in schools (in what ways have Indigenous pedagogies and curriculums been fitted—or not—into dominant whitestream education systems?). Each of the agents in these fields struggle to impose their vision of reality within any given field. And more often than not, Indigenous agents in these fields struggle to do so from marginalized positions.

If fields are arenas of struggle, the struggle rarely takes place on an even playing field. It is important to note that a second structural property of fields is that they are, as just noted, fundamentally *hierarchical*. As such, they include "spaces of dominant and subordinate positions based on the types and amount of capital" that those within the field possess (Swartz 1997, 123). For Bourdieu, the strategies that field agents undertake are based on their position in the field (whether dominant or subordinate) and as such, they "struggle" as efficiently as they can, given the resources (capital, but also networks and even access to infrastructure) available to them (Bourdieu and Wacquant 1992, 101) to impose their vision upon the field. We can think here of the differences in power between, for example, the chief statistician of a national government statistical agency and an Indigenous policy analyst, to impose a vision of "correct" data and statistics. Both are socialized into the field (more on this later), but both will ordinarily operate according to different strategies based on the pathways and opportunities for manoeuvring open to them.

Importantly, those in advantageous positions of power tend to want to maintain the field's status quo and what counts as capital (which they will possess higher amounts of). On the other hand, those in subordinate positions often struggle to change the field's relations, their position in them and even what counts as capital. For example, in recent years Indigenous knowledge keepers have challenged the dominant legal interpretations contained in nation-states' constitutional interpretations about Indigenous legal traditions. Similarly, Indigenous experts and organizations in formerly dominated positions within the statistical field have attempted, with differing levels of success, to wrest control of key elements of the statistical cycle from non-Indigenous institutions and personnel and to fundamentally shape what comes to count as legitimate capital within the statistical field—what data summaries will be produced, for example, and what stories about Indigenous communities will be told.

Swartz (1997, 125) argues that a third key feature of a social field is that it both demands and imposes *specific forms of struggle* upon those in the field. Whether in a dominant or a subordinate position, agreeing to be involved in any given field is to agree to more or less play by the rules of the game established in that field (1997, 125). Another way to think about this is that those involved in any given field not only fundamentally agree that what is being struggled over is worth being struggled over, but that *how* struggles play out is equally worthy. To become invested in a field is to believe in its "stakes" and as such, "[p]layers agree, by the mere fact of playing . . . that the game is worth playing." Tacitly or explicitly, they agree (again, more or less) to play according to the rules of that game/field (Bourdieu and Wacquant 1992, 98). For example, as unhappy with a particular set of data as an Indigenous statistical analyst might be, simply fudging the numbers to produce statistics that align with their thoughts or feelings about a particular set of social relations would be extremely rare. Such practices do not fit within how they feel the game should be played within the statistical field's "rules of the engagement."[7]

Fourth and finally, what all these field characteristics mean is that social fields are more or less *autonomous* from the social world outside them. They possess their own *internal* logics, rules and mechanisms of development (Swartz 1997, 126) and as such, any given field's shape is due in large part to the longer term (and even multi-intergenerational), rule-bound struggle of the differentially located agents within it. If an Indigenous policy actor wanted to apply for a grant to increase funding to a community-based diabetes program, for example, they would be far more likely to make use of available statistical information than they would to just rely upon personal anecdotes to legitimize their arguments in the grant application (though in any given context, they could reasonably estimate the value of offering a story as an example of an underlying statistical reality). Given the relative sense of autonomy within the field, Bourdieu also suggests that all external logics (racism, heteropatriarchy, ableism, etc.) must necessarily be translated or refracted into the internal logics of a field. In a social field context, "racism" might mean one thing in the field of education, for example, but mean something else in the field of medicine and yet again something else in the field of criminal justice.

These four structural elements of social field:

a. as arenas of struggle over specific forms of power or capital;
b. as hierarchically organized;
c. as internally rule-bound and (as such);
d. as semi-autonomous;

together offer important lessons about how to understand the power of statistics in contemporary nation-states, particularly in relation to the dominant statistical descriptions of Indigenous nations and communities they (re)present. As we will explain at various points throughout this chapter, the tendency to talk about statistics as a *fait accompli* not only undersells the fundamentally political struggle involved in their production and dissemination, but also oversells their validity as a "truth telling" technology. Sociologist Bruce Curtis (2002, 34–35) argues, in fact, that when attempting to account for the power of statistics in modern society, it is less helpful to understand them as a reflection of their technical accuracy and more helpful to think in terms of the policy actions that statistics help make more (or less) visible.

Thus, in trying to imagine statistics as a social field, consider:

1. the wide variety of agents and forms of expertise occupying the field's different positions: data collection strategy creators, data analysts, data communicators and disseminators, funders, etc.;
2. the tremendously asymmetrical distribution of power within the field and across the agent positions;
3. the amount and kinds of expertise required for Indigenous statisticians, analysts and/or communicators to engage with other agents in the statistical field to produce forms of statistics that benefit Indigenous organizations, communities and peoples; and
4. the extent to which the situations that Indigenous People find ourselves in in the current configuration of the statistical field are the result of previous struggles in that field.

In the chapter's second part, we will continue to open the black box of statistics by laying out a discussion of the "statistical cycle" in a social field context to better understand how the statistical field often operates in practice.

Part II: The Statistical Cycle—The Statistical Field in Action

This chapter's first part was intended to inject complexity into discussions about statistics by focusing on issues of power and process to counter the popular understanding of statistics as purely factual "objects." In the chapter's second part, we lay out some of the major stages of what we have referred to here as a "statistical cycle," which is an example of a statistical field in practice. No "one cycle fits all" and as such, what to include in a discussion of a statistical cycle is an open empirical question. Nonetheless, the rest of this chapter lays out important components of this cycle with an eye for demonstrating the extent to which Indigenous voices, capacities, expertise and control—in a phrase, sovereignty—have been excluded from it. We also speculate about the impact this has had both on the statistics that are produced *and* the depictions of Indigenous communities and people that such statistics subsequently cement into public consciousness.

In their discussion of the "statistical method" (terminology more or less interchangeable with the "statistical cycle"), Mackay and Oldford (2000, 263) propose a statistical investigative model that includes five stages: problem, plan, data, analysis and conclusion (PPDAC). Additional stages are conceivable depending on the standpoint from which statistical issues are approached. But these five nonetheless appear to represent the backbone of most discussions or operationalizations of the statistical method/cycle. Mackay and Oldford (2000, 263–273) argue that each of these stages are linked in time, such that each stage both leads to the next but is dependent upon the completion of the previous ones. Wild et al. (2018) note, in this context, that movement back and forth between the different stages is possible and over time, these stages tend to act in a circular manner. Mackay and Oldford (2000) assert,

> [the] structure for statistical method is useful in two ways: first to provide a template for actively using empirical investigation and, second, to crucially review completed studies. The structure of all empirical studies, either implicitly or explicitly, can be represented by the five stage model.
> *(2000, 264)*

These stages would likely not surprise most students who have taken quantitative research methods classes. Stage one, the problem stage, focuses on defining the problem, clarifying the population and deciding on terminology. Stage two, the planning stage, includes decisions about the appropriate measurement system, sampling design and data management protocols. The third stage, data, involves the collection, storage, management and "wrangling" of the data (Wild et al. 2018, 11), all in the interests of ensuring data quality. Stage four then involves analysis of the data and stage five focuses on the interpretations, discussion, conclusions and dissemination of the data and their summaries (see Mackay and Oldford 2000, 264–274, for a fuller discussion of these stages). Wild and Pfannkuch (1999) expand Mackay and Oldford's statistical investigative model to include additional dimensions relating to paying attention to the kinds of thinking involved in statistical investigation; the "interrogative cycle" through which the data is generated, connected to ideas, interpreted, criticized and judged; and finally, the "dispositions" that statistical practitioners engage with to contextualize the data in ways that allow them to solve their perceived problems (see Wild and Pfannkuch 1999, 226–Figure 1 for a summary of all of these dimensions; also see Wild et al. 2018, 12).

Mackay and Oldford (2000) get us part of the way to our goal of understanding statistics as a political *process* by effectively laying out a template for understanding the process that most statistical investigations will follow. In a sense, they have opened Latour's black box referenced in the chapter's first part to provide a sense of the intricate interpretations and decisions required to proceed from start to finish in any statistical investigation. Unsurprisingly, their otherwise useful discussion is devoid of any consideration of the ways that colonial power and its associated interpretive politics not only shape statistical investigations but also represent constitutive parts of each stage of the process.

Likewise, Wild and Pfannkuch (1999) push the idea that data inputs and outputs are tied into the broader dispositions and contextualization efforts of the statistical investigators who create them. But the structural racism that is baked into the cake of all colonial projects is still completely absent from any discussions. Hence, the colonial politics that is constitutive of any relationship between Indigenous Peoples and statistics is completely absent from conventional discussions about statistical cycles. Nonetheless, it is useful to think about the useful complexity that a PPDAC approach brings to any discussion of contemporary statistics.

*****

Returning for a moment to the component parts of the statistical cycle that we began Part II of this chapter with—"problem, plan, data, analysis and conclusion," let us pause for a moment to think about what these different stages would look like, analytically, when framed in the context of a statistical field approach. And let's think specifically of the ways in which structural racism/colonialism and their impact on Indigenous Peoples are refracted into/infuse the statistical cycle. The power of understanding statistics in terms of a field is especially apparent when we think about it in terms of a complex system: the kinds of statistics that tend to get produced; the individuals and organizations that tend to be involved; the kinds of interpretative analytical decisions that tend to get made; and the limitations of the kinds of conversations that are likely to be had within the field. My point here is not that fields are deterministic or that outcomes are pre-ordained. Rather, my point is that fields powerfully shape the kinds of outcomes that *tend* to happen within them, and they tend to rely on and reproduce their own legitimacy (so for example, those in the statistical field would rarely want to get rid of the field altogether rather than improving their position within the field and, in doing so, changing what counts as legitimate statistics).

Taking each of these component parts in turn, we can get a better sense of how nation-state's colonial past and present (discussed in the previous chapter) tend to narrow the kinds of decisions that get made about what counts as legitimate statistics, who is involved in making those decisions and the kinds of broader discourses that tend to be produced through the dynamics of the statistical field.

Problem: in their discussion of how the problem stage in the "statistical method" gets framed, Wild and Pfannkuch (1999, 225) argue,

> [m]ost problems are embedded in a desire to change a "system" to improve something . . . [a] knowledge-based solution to the real problem requires better understanding of how a system works and perhaps also how it will react to changes to input streams, settings or environments.

Yet as we demonstrated in Chapter 2 (and as Maggie Walter discusses in Chapter 4), until recently the overwhelming tendency of the statistical field in most countries with Indigenous Peoples and populations has been to present the issues in narrow, deficit-based contexts. Problems are defined in a manner that encourages individual rather than structural interventions. As such, they are often over-simplistic and reductionist visions in which solutions and, likewise, the "problems" always seem to lie with "fixing" Indigenous communities rather than the colonial system that these communities are forced to contend with (see Smith 2021 for a broader discussion of this research tendency).

Plan: as Walker et al. (2017) have argued, the kinds of measures and sampling design through which statistical measures are created rarely take place in the context of strong partnerships between Indigenous organizations, communities or nations and statistical organizations. As such, narrow and unimaginative questions and answer categories are created and consistently reused, which Indigenous data users are then forced to undertake analysis with. This dynamic within the field has severely limited the kinds of stories about Indigenous communities that statistics can be used to tell and over the past century, this has firmly cemented stereotypes about Indigenous communities and people.

Data: if the data stage includes a prioritization of data collection, management and "cleaning," this has led to a long-standing dynamic through which Indigenous nations, communities and individuals often do not own the data that gets collected. The broader scientific community has not covered itself in glory with respect to the many unauthorized and certainly unknown uses to which it has put data collected from Indigenous communities. Though outside the immediate scope of our discussion here, it is nonetheless important to realize that comparable power inequities exist between these statistical and more broadly scientific contexts: both are the result of the disavowal and sometimes even outright dismissal of Indigenous Data Sovereignty. In a Canadian context, First Nations created OCAP® principles (ownership, control, access and possession) precisely to assert sovereignty over data collected by an "external" government from their citizens (see Walker et al. 2017 for a discussion about the manner in which OCAP® principles have, in a Canadian context, helped co-create governance processes for use of routinely collected health data with Indigenous Peoples).

Analysis: Indigenous failure to be involved in the formative stages of the statistical cycle means that limited options are available too at the stage of analysis. Moreover, the kinds of questions used to collect data will shape the kinds of analysis that can be undertaken once the data have been "cleaned." Generally speaking, however, analyses—particularly those undertaken by state-based statistical agencies—tend to be undertaken in ways that can be linked to previous data collection, the better to explore trends over time. Likewise, many of these categories have their origins in previous categories created without the benefit of Indigenous expertise and input; as such, they are often less culturally meaningful to Indigenous communities than might otherwise be the case. In these cases, analyses tend to reflect state policy concerns rather than the policy desires of Indigenous Peoples.

Conclusion: the sum total of a lack of Indigenous involvement in previous stages of the statistical cycle shapes publicly presented conclusions about the data in predictable ways. Data are often summarized and communicated according to conventions and policies of non-Indigenous statistical agencies, (again) according to categories that reflect state-sponsored requirements. Data is rarely summarized according to a given Indigenous nation's collective socio-demographic characteristics, for example, nor do analyses begin from a strength-based orientation that emphasize the resiliency of our communities. The sum total of the statistical cycle is manifested in the damage- or deficit-based narratives that statistical information is used to support, which in turn can lead to further Indigenous disengagement with the field itself.

* * * * *

Conclusion

The fact that official statistics today form a key plank in the evidence-based policy and decision-making field in Canada is taken for granted by anyone involved in the diverse fields that comprise it. This was, as noted earlier and with specific respect to the Métis in Chapter 7, not always the case. Without descending into a philosophical discussion about the past three centuries of welfare state growth and intervention into everyday life in the Western world, suffice it to say that today, statistics represent a powerful lens (and are often seen as a powerful form of "truth") through which we understand the world around us. In this sense, it is important to appreciate that statistics do not merely "describe a world already out there." With their fundamental ability to make certain things seem true and others not, they help to constitute the social world. Thus, far from being technical, neutral things, data and the statistics derived from them are processes. And, crucially, they need to be understood for the deeply political processes that they are, because these data politics have been used to actively harm Indigenous nations and communities.

To characterize data as (the end result of) processes is simply to say that the data never "speak for themselves." Data cannot be comprehended (let alone analysed or communicated) without understanding the complicated data or statistical "cycle" that produces them. The cycle is always "local" in a sense (in Canada, local to the geographical boundaries of the nation-state of Canada, or local to a province or a city) and always exists within a set of institutions, discourses and practices, expertise, competencies, competitions, personal investments and narratives. Together, these form the web through which information is turned into data and then into statistics. From conceptualizing the problem; to thinking through the measurement system, sampling design, data management and quality assurance analyses; to the data collection, management and "cleaning"; to the analysis itself; to the interpretations, conclusions and narrative strategies for communications—all of these require hard questions.

Important questions stem from this positioning of data, perhaps especially in an Indigenous statistics context. Whose voices are in the room when surveys are being designed and whose voices are being heard? What questions are being created and for what purposes, and what answer categories are deemed appropriate? What data will be collected and what will not? Who will be doing the collecting? Where will the data be stored? Who will have access to them and under what conditions? Who will undertake the analysis and in what ways will the data be analysed? What will the analyses be taken to mean? And, finally, what narratives and stories are being told with the data? Which *can* be told according to the data's limitations? What stories cannot be told? What, regarding the vibrant complexity of our communities and nations, is being silenced when we are not able to tell our own stories? And perhaps most importantly, do we know enough as Indigenous Peoples about what we don't know in order to tell all the stories that can be told with the data (in ways that benefit our communities in nation) while understanding the limitations of that data?

Data's "world-building" power and—given their deeply political character—their central role in building *some* worlds and diminishing or erasing *others* represent two insights key to the Indigenous Data Sovereignty field. This is not least because, until recently, Indigenous Peoples have been entirely excluded from most or all parts of the data cycle through which crucial interpretations and decisions about the work of data conceptualization, collection, analysis and communication have been made. But make no mistake: statistical fields like those described in this chapter are fundamentally social arenas filled with struggles over the appropriate analyses and meanings of the data that get collected, analysed and communicated. And this struggle—particularly as it relates to Indigenous data—has long taken place in a field that is fundamentally uneven, hierarchical, unfair and, ultimately, deeply harmful to Indigenous Peoples.

All of this is to say that the data landscape in Canada, as is the case globally, is in this sense "semi-autonomous" from the social world outside of it. In other words, those involved in all parts of this landscape operate according to particular rules, logics and mechanisms that shape—and are shaped by—internal norms and values about what appropriate conduct and behaviour should look like. This sounds complicated, but it is really just to say that an expert in a statistical field (or the fields of education, legal/criminal justice, medical, oil and natural gas, to name but a few) will simply know (and know how to do) all kinds of things relating to that field that those outside the field simply will not.

To non-nerds, this chapter may seem overly dense and even arcane. There is likely a kernel of truth to both of these potential charges. Let me conclude the chapter, then, by making three points about the methodological power of social fields to shape both the meanings and the practices of when it comes to Indigenous statistics:

1. Data do not merely describe our world; they play a fundamental role in building it. As such, being in control of their protection is key to enabling Indigenous Peoples to build the world they wish to see.
2. Data are not technical "things" but complicated political processes. As such, Indigenous expertise must (ideally) play a determining role in all parts of the field that produce data about us, whether it is we who are producing the data or data that has been produced about us.
3. Finally, data's technical accuracy can be far less important than their policy relevance (see Curtis 2001, 35). "Accuracy" is always contextual, such that technically accurate data cannot overcome questions that are misaligned with Indigenous nations' and communities' principles and values, *as defined by Indigenous participants involved in the social field of Indigenous statistics*. The wholesale exclusion of Indigenous Peoples from the production of data and statistics about us makes misalignment a near certainty.

Notes

1 I adopt the term "aperture" here from the branch of physics known as *optics*. It refers to a hole through which light can travel. A narrower aperture provides more richness of detail on a very small field of focus, while effectively "blurring out" all other background features. This represents a useful way for thinking about the ways that official statistics have focused only on selected—and usually deficit-based—elements of Indigeneity and Indigenous communities, "blurring out" the rest of the fuller complexity of what makes us, us.
2 Gal (2002, 1) defines statistical literacy as "the ability to interpret, critically evaluate, and communicate about statistical information and messages." Given our engagement with Bourdieu's work, we argue here that statistical literacy is a key outcome of developing what Bourdieu has referred to more generally as a "habitus." He defines habitus to encompass "a system of lasting, transposable dispositions which functions at every moment as a matrix of perceptions, appreciations, and actions" (Bourdieu 1977, 82–83) that we acquire over our lifetime of socialization, beginning in our childhood and continuing as we enter and become conversant in particular fields.
3 Bourdieu's methodology tends to use fairly abstract concepts such as "agent," mostly due to his concern with separating his arguments from other academic literatures. They seem slightly strange at first, but we get used to them fairly quickly.
4 A full explication of Bourdieu's social field theory would require including the manner in which the forms of "master capital" (economic, social and cultural) shape other forms of capital; the power of a broader "field of power" to shape more specific fields; and the power of misrecognition that sustains any field's legitimacy. These concepts are, however, beyond the scope of this chapter. See Bourdieu and Wacquant (1992); Swartz (1997); and Hilgers and Mangez (2015) for a more extended discussion of these concepts.

5 For present purposes, I am less interested in *how* these complex dynamics operate in relation to one another (a task that would require a level of elaboration and analysis beyond the scope of this chapter—and would likely lend itself better to a networked/assemblage approach—see Kitchin 2022, 23–25) and more focused on anchoring the point *that* they do, with elaborations on why it is important to understand this premise and its implications.
6 As noted earlier, Bourdieu discusses several forms of "master" capital that many people will be aware of and may even have used in broader discussions (usually economic and cultural capital), but for Bourdieu, all fields possess a form of capital (juridical, educational, journalistic, statistical, etc.) that agents struggle to attain within that *specific* field.
7 Bourdieu argues, "a field can function only if it finds individuals socially predisposed to behave as responsible agents, to risk their money, their time, sometimes their honor or their life, to pursue the games and to obtain the profits it supposes" (Bourdieu 1982a, 46 in Bourdieu and Wacquant 1992, 102–103—fn 55).

References

Alonso, William, and Paul Starr. "Introduction." In *The Politics of Numbers*, edited by William Alonzo and Paul Starr, 1–7. New York: Russell Sage Foundation, 1987.

Bourdieu, Pierre, and Loïc Wacquant. *An Invitation to a Reflexive Sociology*. Chicago: University of Chicago Press, 1992.

Bourdieu, Pierre. *Outline of a Theory of Practice*. Translated by Richard Nice. Cambridge: Cambridge University Press, 1977.

Chilisa, Bagele. *Indigenous Research Methodologies*. Thousand Oaks, CA: SAGE Publications, Inc., 2012.

Chilisa, Bagele. *Indigenous Research Methodologies*. 2nd ed. Thousand Oaks, CA: SAGE Publications, Inc., 2019.

Curtis, Bruce. *The Politics of Population: State Formation, Statistics, and the Census of Canada, 1840–1871*. Toronto: University of Toronto Press, 2001.

Denzin, Norman K., Yvonna S. Lincoln, and Linda Tuhiwai Smith, eds. *Handbook of Critical and Indigenous Methodologies*. Thousand Oaks, CA: SAGE Publications, Inc., 2008.

Foucault, Michel. *Power/Knowledge: Selected Interviews and Other Writings, 1972–1977*. Edited by Colin Gordon. Translated by Colin Gordon, Leo Marshall, John Mepham, and Kate Soper. New York: Pantheon Books, 1980.

Gal, Iddo. "Adults' Statistical Literacy: Meanings, Components, Responsibilities." *International Statistical Review* 70, no. 1 (2002): 1–51.

Hacking, Ian. "Making Up People." In *Reconstructing Individualism: Autonomy, Individuality, and the Self in Western Thought*, edited by Thomas C. Heller, Morton Sosna, and David E. Wellbery, 222–236. Stanford, CA: Stanford University Press, 1986.

Hilgers, Mathieu, and Eric Mangez. "Introduction." In *Bourdieu's Theory of Social Fields: Concepts and Applications*, edited by Mathieu Hilgers and Eric Mangez, 1–36. London and New York: Routledge, 2015.

Kovach, Margaret. *Indigenous Methodologies: Characteristics, Conversations, and Contexts*. Toronto: University of Toronto Press, 2010.

Kovach, Margaret. *Indigenous Methodologies: Characteristics, Conversations, and Contexts*. 2nd ed. University of Toronto Press, 2021.

Latour, Bruno. *Science in Action: How to Follow Scientists and Engineers Through Society*. Cambridge, MA: Harvard University Press, 1987.

MacKay, R. John, and R. Wayne Oldford. "Scientific Method, Statistical Method, and the Speed of Light." *Statistical Science* 15, no. 3 (2000): 254–78.
Smith, Linda Tuhiwai. *Decolonizing Methodologies: Research and Indigenous Peoples*. London: Zed Books, 1999.
Smith, Linda Tuhiwai. *Decolonizing Methodologies: Research and Indigenous Peoples*. 2nd ed. London: Zed Books, 2012.
Smith, Linda Tuhiwai. *Decolonizing Methodologies: Research and Indigenous Peoples*. 3rd ed. Zed Books, 2021.
Swartz, David. *Culture and Power: The Sociology of Pierre Bourdieu*. Chicago: University of Chicago Press, 1997.
Tomaselli, Keyan, Lauren Dyll, and Michael Francis. "'Self' and 'Other': Auto-Reflexive and Indigenous Ethnography." In *Handbook of Critical and Indigenous Methodologies*, edited by Norman K. Denzin, Yvonna S. Lincoln, and Linda Tuhiwai Smith, 347–372. Thousand Oaks, CA: SAGE Publications, Inc., 2008.
Wacquant, Loïc. "Bourdieu Comes to Town: Pertinence, Principles, Applications." *International Journal of Urban and Regional Research* 42, no. 1 (2018): 90–105.
Walker, Jennifer, Ray Lovett, Tahu Kukutai, Carmen Jones, and David Henry. "Indigenous Health Data and the Path to Healing." *Lancet* 390, no. 10107 (2017): 2022–2023.
Wild, Christopher J., and Maxine Pfannkuch. "Statistical Thinking in Empirical Inquiry." *International Statistical Review* 67, no. 3 (1999): 223–265.
Wild, Christopher J., Jessica Utts, and Nicholas J. Horton. "What Is Statistics?" In *International Handbook of Research in Statistics Education*, edited by Dani Ben-Zvi, Katie Makar, and Joan Garfield, 5–36. Cham, Switzerland: Springer International Publishing, 2018.
Wilson, Shawn. *Research Is Ceremony: Indigenous Research Methods*. Halifax: Fernwood Publishing, 2008.
Windchief, Sweeney, and Timothy San Pedro. *Applying Indigenous Research Methods: Storying with Peoples and Communities*. New York: Routledge, 2019.
Woolf, Stuart. "Statistics and the Modern State." *Comparative Studies in Society and History* 31, no. 3 (1989): 588–604.

4
STATISTICS AND THE NEO-COLONIAL ALLIANCE

"Seeing" the Indigene

Maggie Walter

CHAPTER LEARNING OBJECTIVES

Objective 1: Recognize population statistics as ancient methods, not a Western invention.

Objective 2: Understand contemporary statistics as methodologically linked to eugenics, colonization and hierarchies of humanity.

Objective 3: Perceive the power relations inherent in contemporary Indigenous statistics.

Objective 4: See how Indigenous-led and -framed statistics can provide the data to serve Indigenous, not nation-state, purposes.

As we noted in the introduction, statistics are powerful numbers. Defined in the online Encyclopedia Britannica (2024) as "the science of collecting, analysing, presenting and interpreting," statistics, especially statistics about population(s), are a key tool of the modern nation-state. Yet while the Britannica definition is accurate insofar as it says something about the "what" of statistics, the banality of its language belies the fact that statistics do much more than numerically summarize phenomena. Rather, as argued throughout this book, population statistics, that is statistics about people or Peoples, form an evidentiary base that not only reflects but also *constructs* the economic, social and cultural phenomena that is the object of the state's inquiry (Walter and Andersen 2013; Walter and Russo-Carroll 2020). As such, population statistics play a powerful part in defining a nation's concept of itself, inclusive of how Indigenous populations living within that nation-state are "seen" and understood.

Much like the workmanlike definition of statistics, the empirical mapping task of population statistics tends to be viewed as a straightforward count of things. The state instigates counts of items such as education level, age and gender distributions, patterns of birth, morbidity and mortality, and income dynamics at regular intervals, in national census and between census collections. But no data officials or datasets can collect data on all social and cultural phenomena. Choices of what to include and what to exclude are made by those with the power to do so. These determinations also change over time, reflecting changing nation-state priorities and information needs. For example, technological advances during the latter part of the 20th century saw national censuses in most CANZUS countries moving from asking about household telephone connections to asking questions on internet connections. The questions that are asked or excluded also reflect a nation's changing social and cultural norms. For example, up until the 1980s it was the norm in census questions in Western nations to categorize the male adult as the household head and the female adult as a dependent. Changing gender norms during the 1960s and 1970s led to changes in how households were defined. In the 2021 Australian census, for instance, any adult in a household could be nominated as Person 1 on the census form. Moreover, the Australian Bureau of Statistics (ABS) states clearly in its outline of the family/household reference person indicator (RPIP), "[T]his variable is not an indication that a person is 'head of the household'" (ABS 2017).

That the defining concepts of population statistics can and do change provide a demonstration that population statistics are never neutral numbers. As this chapter argues, measuring social and cultural phenomena through statistics merely changes the format of the data to numbers. This numeric format obscures, but does not change, the meanings that are linked to the phenomena they represent. Moreover, while the numeric format remains the same, the meaning/s attached to those numbers does change over time. As such statistics do not, and have never, spoken for themselves (see Barrowman 2018; Clayton 2020). Rather, in the ongoing aggregate mapping of the societal trends that nation-states deem most important, broader societal and cultural changes, as well as dominant ideologies, influence what items are included *and* how these are conceptualized. Social and cultural norms, ideologies and changing social mores also influence what items are excluded. Population statistics are therefore human artefacts, not just numerical counts. The data instigators who create these statistics leave their mark on them. In the vast majority of instances, those making such choices are not Indigenous. And it shows. The what, how and why of past and contemporary Indigenous statistics can thus be understood if we understand that population statistics, at their core, operate to

- define *and* construct the socio-cultural realities of the phenomena they measure; and
- reflect the values, assumptions and interests of their creators.

These characteristics slot into our central argument that Indigenous data can be viewed as products of colonization that did, and continue to, reflect the interest and purposes of those who collect them, and overwhelmingly, this has been the nation-state (Walter and Russo-Carroll 2020).

In this chapter we investigate statistics as a social and political force, beginning with a brief overview of the origins of statistics before describing how and why Indigenous population data are as they are. Our purpose is to demonstrate that the traditional ways in which the state has collected and collated, and continues to collect and collate, Indigenous data cannot and do not yield meaningful portraits of the embodied realities of Indigenous lives. The chapter also demonstrates that the state's failure to adequately reflect Indigenous realities is more than just a misrecognition. Rather, as we argue, the actuality of past and present Indigenous data is purposeful. The form of these data and the meanings that they reflect serve and continue to serve the interests of the colonizing state at the expense of Indigenous Peoples whose land the state occupies and from which it draws its wealth and identity.

The Origins of Statistics

Most articles or descriptions of the origins of statistics position the field's development as a European product. The Wikipedia (2023) entry for the "history of statistics" is a good example. Wikipedia, rather than a more scholarly tome, is used here as a source deliberately. As frequently the first, and sometimes only, source of information on a topic for many, including college and university students, Wikipedia is influential. Its portrayal of the field is therefore an important indicator of the dominance of the narrative of statistics as a European invention, a product of the era of European imperialism and colonial domination. Who is named and what is written about them, and what is not, is also illuminating.

The Wikipedia entry states that modern statistics evolved in the 18th century in Europe to meet the demands of industrialized states. Thus, while acknowledging that the ancient Greeks and Romans had systems of empirically recording key attributes of their populations and empires, the origin of statistics, at least in their modern form, is linked in the Wikipedia portrayal to the industrial revolution. While we query the European genesis, there is no doubt that this period was a pivotal one for the science of statistics. The severe social disruptions occurring in Western Europe in the 18th and 19th centuries led to large-scale and rapid overturning of long-established patterns of social life. These included the abandonment of feudalism; associated large-scale population movements from rural to urban areas, with the mass poverty afflicting these uprooted populations; and a rising criminalization of these new poor (Walter 2022). This social upheaval called for different and more powerful tools of statehood to manage, and control, its frequently restive populations.

The Wikipedia article attributes the term "statistic" to German Gottfied Achenwall. First used in 1749, the word is derived from the Latin terms for council of the state (*"statisticum collegium"*) and the Italian word for politician (*"statista"*) and reflects the purpose of statistics as a tool of statehood. As such, the article goes on to emphasize that early statistics, including the development of methods of statistical analysis, were primarily aimed at providing the nation-state with the population data needed for planning purposes (which we introduced in the introduction).

An early burst of statistical innovation in surveilling and understanding populations is recorded as occurring during the 17th and 18th centuries. Englishmen John Graunt and William Petty are credited with developing early census methods in 1662. John Arbuthnot is cited as the first to use tests of statistical significance to demonstrate, via his examination of London birth records in 1710, that the gender of babies was equally likely. The entry goes on to identify the 19th and early 20th centuries as the time of development of many of the statistical tests we still use today. Francis Galton, whose book *Natural Inheritance* published in 1889, is lauded as a founder of statistical theory and is said to have influenced the work of Karl Pearson, leading to many artefacts of modern statistics such as correlation coefficients, the chi-squared test and principal components analysis. Other major advances are linked to the work of Ronald Fisher, who was the first to use the statistical term variance in the 1920s, naming and promoting the method of maximum likelihood estimation among other statistical innovations (Wikipedia 2023).

Yet, just like the definition of statistics cited at the start of this chapter, the Wikipedia entry only hints at statistics as socio-cultural phenomena rather than numeric entities. It says little about the impetus for the field's development. It also says little about the inventors of these statistical methods and tools beyond lauding them as undoubtedly brilliant statisticians. And perhaps there is a reason for that. Englishman Francis Galton, for instance, as well as being a founder of statistical theory, also founded the racist pseudoscience of eugenics, which he defined as "the science which deals with all influences that improve and develop the inborn qualities of a race" (*Nature* 2022). For their part, the journal *Nature* apologized in 2022 for publishing Galton's work and that of other scientists whose work, inclusive of statistical analysis, underpinned and still provides rationales for systemic racism.

This clear link between statistics, leading statistical scholars and racism is more than the discipline harbouring a few individuals with racist beliefs. American statistician Clayton (2020) argues, convincingly, that statistical and eugenicist thinking is deeply intertwined, with many statistical theories and methods developed specifically to identify (apparent) racial differences. Galton, founder of statistical theory, also is prominent for his hierarchy of races, which posited "Negros" as two grades lower in intelligence than White Britons. German Karl Pearson, inventor of principal components analysis, is also known for his approval of the colonization in North America, noting, "in place of the red man, contributing practically nothing to the work and thought of the world, we have a great nation, mistress of many arts, and able . . . to contribute much to the common stock of civilized man" (cited in Clayton 2020). Englishman Fisher, of maximum likelihood estimation fame, for his part, was also prominent in seeing statistics as a way of shaping society according to his own value system. For example, he is noted as advocating the sterilization and incarceration of those he deemed socially unfit (Clayton 2020).

It is also not coincidental that the critical statistical developments of the 19th and 20th centuries co-occurred with rapid Anglo colonization. The American Revolution meant new lands were needed to feed hungry European factories with raw materials such as furs, minerals and timber. Sealing and whaling quickly became global industries with seal pelts required as machinery drive belts and rendered whale blubber to power them. New lands were also needed as a destination for the displaced poor as convicts and labourers. Therefore, it might be realistically claimed that statistics and colonization are also deeply entwined. As demonstrated earlier, leading European statisticians were motivated by more than numbers. Eugenics, racism and the lauding of Indigenous dispossession were driving values of their statistical endeavours; statistics were the tool for their social ambitions. Then, as now, the correlation between statistics and the colonial project have deep and harmful consequences for Indigenous Peoples (Wolfe 2006; Walter and Russo-Carroll 2020; Walter 2022).

The Neo-Colonial Alliance of Statistics and Policy

Indigenous population statistics reflect how the nation-state "sees" Indigenous populations and how it constructs the Indigenous socio-cultural position within the nation-state (Scott 1998; Walter 2018; Walter and Andersen 2013). Statistics have always served as a key tool of statecraft, and the collection of statistics about Indigenous populations is a common feature of the apparatus of colonization across the CANZUS countries. In Australia, for example, although Aboriginal Peoples were excluded from the national Census of Population and Housing by a clause in the 1901 Australian Constitution, this did not mean the Aboriginal population were not regularly counted. Rather, such data were meticulously collected but then excluded from formal Australian population counts. According to Marduntjara/Pitjantjatjara academic Gordon Briscoe (2003), the main purpose of counting was to reinforce the dominant "dying race" narrative. The careful collation of how many "Full-bloods" and "Half-Castes" and various other Euro-invented racial categorizations was to assure the Euro-Australian population of the receding Indigenous threat to their control of the Australian land mass. The seeming contradictory removal of Indigenous population from census figures was also purposeful. Removal ensured that states where larger numbers of Aboriginal people still survived, by virtue of later colonizations, were unable to use that population to claim a higher Commonwealth resource share (Chesterman and Galligan 1997). This exclusion was finally removed from the Australian Constitution by a referendum to amend offending clauses in 1967. The 1971 Australian census was the first to formally count Indigenous People.

The link between colonization and contemporary Indigenous population statistics is further evidenced by the uncanny resonances of official Indigenous data across CANZUS countries. In all countries, central statistics agencies' websites prominently display Indigenous data sections. Often positioned as a subset of overall national social trends, these population data are largely accepted as a straightforward, objective snapshot of an underlying reality; the nation-states' chief tool for ascertaining and presenting the official "who," "what," "where" and "how" of Indigenous life. Given the huge differences in geographic locales, culture and ways of being, knowing and doing among these diverse Indigenous Peoples, it might be expected that these statistics would provide equally diverse portrayals. This is not the case. Rather, all sites, and the data they present, provide a remarkably similar statistical narrative.

More to the point, all concentrate on Indigenous over-representation across the same development indicators: incarceration rates; health outcomes; educational attainment; labour market engagement; and so forth. We invite readers to do a quick Google search through the various national statistical agencies to confirm this parallel reality of Indigenous statistics in Anglo-colonized nation-states. All websites also reference, in one way or another, that a major purpose of the data collected, collated and presented is as an evidence base for Indigenous policy (Walter and Russo-Carroll 2020). Our explanation for the data similarity across the CANZUS countries is that these data reflect Anglo colonization and what the state deems important to know about the dispossessed Indigenous populations, rather than being an actual reflection of the Indigenous Peoples they portray (Walter and Russo-Carroll 2020).

Indigenous Data Reflect Relationships of Colonizing Power

This brings us to one of our central arguments, touched upon in the introduction: that far from being benign, Indigenous statistics are the foundational lens through which we are (mostly) known to our respective nation-states. They can, and often definitively do, determine the parameters of our relationships with government actors, shaping the national narrative of who Indigenous Peoples are, and as importantly, who we are not. At the centre of our claim is Quine's (1948) perception that accepting that numbers exist is not the same as accepting that numbers have a fixed reality. As Walter (2016) argues, the real query(ies) to ask of Indigenous statistics is not "are these numbers real?" but rather "what do these numbers mean and how are they understood?" The following section discusses Indigenous statistics through the lens of this question. To unpack the meaning making of Indigenous data we make use of two theoretical frames: Indigenous lifeworlds theory (Walter and Suina 2019; Walter 2022) and Scott's (1998) framework of "seeing like a state." These two theories have synergies but offer different insights into why most state-collected Indigenous statistics are as they are and why the status quo of state-generated/-collated Indigenous statistics has been, and continues to be, harmful to the Indigenous Peoples that are their subject. We may also understand these theories in the broader methodological context of the power of statistics as a social field.

The Indigenous Lifeworld

The concept of the Indigenous lifeworld provides a theoretical explanation for why Indigenous data in CANZUS nations possess jarring similarities in both the purpose and the substance of the collections. The theory (Walter and Suina 2019; Walter 2022) allows us to unpack this seemingly contradictory position of sameness of data about very different, culturally and historically, First Peoples. Indigenous lifeworlds theory builds on the core of Western lifeworlds literature which posits that the "taken-for-grantedness" of everyday lives is not verifiable truth but a subjective reflection of the social and cultural conditions of life experience. From this perspective, the meaning we make of our lived realities is always contextual and inseparable from our social, cultural and physical world and from our relational positioning within that world (Husserl 1970). The underpinning rationale of this lifeworld theory has salience for First Peoples across the CANZUS countries. But it does not necessarily have direct applicability: its resonance is critically incomplete. As per Porsanger (2004), interrogating Indigenous lived reality makes visible what is meaningful in the Indigenous social world via its axis of Indigenous world views, perspectives, values and lived experience. Such meaning making, therefore, translates to an Indigenous specific understanding of how the society in which we live our lives is organized and operationalized, its social hierarchies and social and cultural mores, and how we experience our own position in that society.

Essentially, this means that as Indigenous Peoples, we live our lives *as Indigenous Peoples*. Everyday life is negotiated and understood within the productive and vibrant complexity of distinctive life Indigenous circumstances, culture and worldviews. These vary across nation-states, across Indigenous nations and across urban and tribal land settings. But all reflect Indigenous ways of being. As such, any conceptualization of the Indigenous lifeworld must incorporate shared social and cultural life circumstances.

Our lives, however, are not lived in the societies of our uncolonized ancestors. We live our Indigenous lives as colonized, marginalized peoples: minorities on our own lands. Thus, the context of Indigenous lives also reflect the shared ongoing conflicted relationships with the nation-states that now govern (and largely possess) our traditional lands (Walter and Suina 2019; Walter 2022). The Indigenous lifeworld is, thus, encircled by dual intersubjectivities. These include:

1. intersubjectivity within Peoplehood, where everyday life reflects the ways of being and doing of those Peoples, inclusive of traditional and ongoing culture, belief systems, practices, identity and ways of understanding the world and our place within it; and
2. intersubjectivity as colonized, dispossessed marginalized peoples (denial of Peoplehood) where everyday life is framed through and directly impacted by our historical and ongoing relationship and interactions with the colonizing nation-state.

Seeing Like a State

Scott's (1998) thesis, *Seeing Like a State*, provides a complementary theoretical toolbox for understanding why Indigenous population statistics are as they are. Scott (1998) was interested in understanding statecraft, or more particularly, why state planning so often goes so badly wrong. Although Indigenous Peoples were not Scott's primary subject, his thesis speaks to the long-held Indigenous frustrations with state-imposed policies and their perpetual record of failure across all CANZUS countries (Walter and Russo-Carroll 2020). In short, Scott's book is a damning critique of state planning that disregards the values, wants and objections of those who are the subject of those policies and programs; a critique Indigenous Peoples understand all too well.

Scott's (1998) core argument is that four elements are needed, in combination, to create a policy disaster of truly epic proportions. These are the administrative ordering undertaken by the state to make a society legible to itself; an uncritical belief in the technology that supports this administrative ordering; an authoritarian state, willing and capable of using its coercive power to enact this process of administrative ordering; and a society that lacks the capacity to resist the state.

Both these theoretical frames, Indigenous lifeworlds and Scott's statecraft critique, are used in tandem in the following sections to explore our foundational question: what do Indigenous population statistics mean and to whom?

What Do Indigenous Population Statistics Mean?

To answer the question—what Indigenous statistics mean—we need to first ask how the state conceives of, makes sense of and uses Indigenous population data. Later we address the question from the perspective of Indigenous Peoples, but it is important to understand it from the dominant perspective of the state. We begin by revisiting the earlier discussion on how Indigenous statistics are created. Data do not make themselves (Walter and Andersen 2013). As Walter and Russo-Carroll (2020) argue, data are created and shaped by the assumptive determinations of their makers to collect some data and not others, to interrogate some objects over others and to investigate some variable relationships over others.

Applying an Indigenous lifeworlds analysis to our guiding question makes clear that the state predominantly sees Indigenous Peoples through the lens of Intersubjectivity 2. It is First Peoples' status as colonized dispossessed minorities, not as sovereign peoples in our own right, that the state is most interested in measuring and recording. More critically it is this status and the aligned conflictual relationship with the colonizing claims to nationness that is reflected in Indigenous population statistics. Indigenous data collected and/or collated by the state makes visible what is meaningful and important *for the state* to know about Indigenous Peoples. As Māori scholar Tahu Kukutai (2011, 47) states, within the world of data, Indigenous populations are "statistical creations based on aggregated individual-level data, rather than 'real world' concrete groups." They show the state what the state wants to see. Indigenous statistics, therefore, in both data and process are the cloned descendants of the data imperatives of colonization, with the enumeration of Indigenous inequality linked both overtly and covertly to the concept of Indigenous racial unfitness, or more latterly as deficit as a trait of Indigeneity (Walter 2016, 2018). This claim ties in with Tuhiwai Smith's (1999) earlier argument that data have long been used to rationalize Indigenous dispossession, marginalization and even our right to be Indigenous.

Of course, very real and enduring problems *do* get reflected in these statistics. Indigenous Peoples in all CANZUS countries *are* the least healthy, the poorest, the most incarcerated and so on. But that is not all we are. Understanding us *only* in such terms supports national narratives of Indigenous deficit. And this is purposeful. Constituting Indigenous Peoples as "the problem" also operates to obscure non-Indigenous responsibility in the creation and maintenance of that problem. Dispossession of our lands and the enforced poverty that stems from that dispossession, the ongoing and systemic racism that is part of Indigenous interactions with institutional systems such as health, education and welfare, the ignorance and the disregard of the mainstream population towards Indigenous Peoples and the international trauma that flows through our families and communities, to name just a few of the social cultural realities of Indigenous ways of life, are never measured. Again, this is purposeful. What is not measured is not counted and therefore cannot form part of the numeric discourse of Indigenous statistics, or the policy that often subsequently ensues.

The heritage and ubiquity of these statistics, across the CANZUS countries, allow the deficit narrative they depict to go largely unchallenged in public and political discourse. Walter (2016) theorizes that the result of this normalization is the deficit data/problematic people (DD/PP) correlation. In the DD/PP correlation, it is the problematic Indigenous population who, through their poor behaviour and their poor choices, are ultimately responsible for their own inequality. More problematically, by the nature of the data's limited, decontextualized, deficit format, any analysis of those data can only deliver one answer: that it is Indigenous People/s who are the problem. The power of the DD/PP correlation is such that it still works as a mechanism for ongoing Indigenous disenfranchising and dispossessing. This correlation, linked into Indigenous Lifeworld Intersubjectivity 2, underpins contemporary Indigenous/non-Indigenous race relations and the racial/social hierarchies dominant across CANZUS countries. And it is Indigenous populations statistics that provide the evidentiary base for these unequal race relations.

How Are Indigenous Population Statistics Understood?

This brings us to the second half of our guiding question. How are Indigenous statistics understood? The DD/PP correlation's grip on how the settler majority population, policy makers and statistical agencies "understand" Indigenous populations is exacerbated by the intense disjuncture between Indigenous and non-Indigenous lives. Regardless that Indigenous populations in all CANZUS countries are predominantly urban, living alongside the non-Aboriginal population, Indigenous lives remain out of sight and mind; spatially, politically, socially and culturally absent from dominant society view and notice. We live in different places even when living next door to each other (Atkinson et al. 2010). This invisibility extends to the nation-state's concept of itself and the business of state, except reluctantly as a seemingly unresolvable "equity issue."

Indigenous population statistics exacerbate this disconnect between Indigenous and non-Indigenous populations. Their ubiquity means that despite the lack of interpersonal interactions, the majority non-Indigenous population think that they know us, who we are. But the only Indigene most non-Indigenous populations know is the "statistical Indigene," and that knowing is framed via the pejorative stereotypes that 5D data necessarily invoke. It is here that the numerical form of statistics contributes to the normalization of the deficit data/problematic people correlation. Once social phenomena are perceived as "data," it is an easy step to regard these data points as social facts; a dispassionate representation of who Indigenous People are. The measure, in a sense, *becomes* the underlying conceptual perspective, and the perspective becomes reality. The advent of big data (discussed earlier), with their tendency to further distance lived social and cultural realities from their data-based embodiment, has only exacerbated the pejorative power of numbers to further marginalize and dispossess Indigenous individuals, communities and nations.

This claim is easily enough evidenced. We again invite the reader to Google any CANZUS linked Indigenous Peoples: Aboriginal and Torres Strait Islander; Māori; Native American; Métis; Native Hawaiian; Native Alaskan; or First Nations and the term "statistics." What comes back in a millisecond is a depressingly predictable list of woe(s). When this is done for "Aboriginal and Torres Strait Islander statistics," the first ten entries are associated with eight different entities presented from ten slightly different perspectives. But all focus in one way or another on statistical representations of the dire, and long-standing, socio-economic and health inequities between

Aboriginal and Torres Strait Islander peoples and non-Indigenous Australian people; the previously described 5D data. For example, the website human-rights.gov.au uses statistical data to demonstrate Indigenous inequality over multiple indicators; the top entries listed for the Australian Bureau of Statistics are reports of homelessness and education disparities and the top entry from the Australian Institute of Health and Welfare discusses Indigenous over-representation in deaths from preventable causes (Walter 2016).

If, however, the interest in Indigenous data is not directly related to the five "D"s, searches will be less productive. Apart from the growing, but still very small, Aboriginal and Torres Strait Islander led and owned data sites, such as the Mayi Kuwayu longitudinal study of Aboriginal and Torres Strait Islander health,[1] finding data that does not fit the 5D mould is a challenge (Brinckley and Lovett 2022; Kukutai and Walter 2015). More specifically, finding data that measures aspects of Indigenous Lifeworld Intersubjectivity 1, that reflect the unique Peoplehood of the different Indigenous Peoples of the land now incorporated into CANZUS nation-states, is almost an impossibility. But as discussed in later chapters, it is these data—data relating to who we are, how we live our lives as Indigenous Peoples, our languages, our cultures, our knowledges, our ways of being—that often sit at the centre of Indigenous quantitative methodologies. These data, and the statistics that emanate from them, are not only central to Indigenous understandings of who we are but also underpin the Indigenous work of nation rebuilding.

Moreover, to continue the Australian example, but which is also salient in other CANZUS nation-states, what the state wants to know about Aboriginal and Torres Strait Islander populations is different to what it deems top priority for the non-Indigenous population. For example, the initiators and funders of the large-scale Household Income and Labour Dynamics Australia (HILDA) project[2] did not feel it necessary to include an analysable Indigenous sample. When asked why not, the answer is always some version of the cost of obtaining a large enough Indigenous sample as being prohibitive (Walter pers comm 2010). The inference is clear. It is just not important to the state, the funders of this very expensive, longitudinal data collection, to know about Aboriginal and Torres Strait Islander households the sorts of things it deems critical to know about non-Indigenous households. For the Indigenous population, this is not what the state wants to "see."

The Indigenous Statistics Indigenous Policy (and Its Failure) Connection

Across Anglo-colonized nation-states, the predominant way the state engages with internal populations is via policy and the strategic actions and programs that flow from that policy. Statistics are the primary evidence base for Indigenous policy (Walter and Russo-Carroll 2020). Data-driven narratives and understandings of Indigenous populations as problematic translates directly in the formulation of national policy approaches framed via the lens of Indigenous deficit. In Canada and Australia, Indigenous population data are currently enmeshed in discourses associated with long-standing government policies that aim to "close the (socioeconomic/health) gap" between Aboriginal and non-Indigenous populations.

The unacknowledged power relations inherent in these discourses, central to a social field understanding of statistics, position the Indigenous population as in need of being "brought up" to the non-Indigenous standard in educational, labour market and other socio-economic indicators. The result is statistical configurations anchored in development or deficit-based understandings of Indigenous Peoples and communities. The rationale of a lack of Indigenous development has its roots in modernity and the colonial projects that comprise it as a field (see, for example, Andersen 2013; Desai and Potter 2002; Kothari 2005; Peet and Hartwick 2009). This literature documents the discursive shift between colonial and contemporary times of perceiving the "problem" of Indigenous People from one of inconvenient continued existence and biological inferiority to one of inconvenient cultural uniqueness and culturally linked behavioural deviation.

This discourse of Indigenous developmental delay is deeply embedded in national statistics agencies across the CANZUS countries. Despite the success of the Indigenous Data Sovereignty movement in alerting national statistical agencies of how deficit data pejoratively position Indigenous populations in national narratives, and indeed despite the efforts by some of these agencies to try and project a more "strengths-based" narrative, the fundamental problems engendered by the colonial origins of Indigenous data practices remain largely unchanged. Indeed, the broader Indigenous critique is that these data are just a continuation of the data of surveillance: a pulse check on the continued success of the colonizing settler state social structure. Still the sickest, check; still the most incarcerated, check; still the poorest, check. As argued by Indigenous scholars globally, such data have never delivered benefits to Indigenous lives (Walter 2018; Walter and Suina 2019; Rainie et al. 2019; Walter 2022).

Scott's (1998) thesis helps us to further engage with the corrosive impact of Indigenous population statistics on mainstream understanding of these data and the Peoples/people they represent. As noted, four ingredients are proposed as requisite to ensure policy failure. Scott centred statistics as the first element, used as a system of administrative ordering necessary for modern nation-states to make society legible. It is the transformation of social and cultural phenomena into statistically measurable items that Scott identifies as problematic. Transforming what are "exceptionally complex, illegible and local social practices" into standardized measures that can be centrally recorded and monitored (statistics) requires "transformative simplifications" (1998, 2). Scott then makes a critical point for understanding the meaning of Indigenous statistics for nation-states. This rationalizing and standardizing, he argues, does not actually represent the full reality of the society that is being depicted, but only the slice of that society that is of interest to the state. This slice of our social and cultural realities represented in state-collected and -collated Indigenous data do not, for the most part, align with Indigenous lived reality. While the reality of the measured markers of disadvantage and trauma are all too real, mostly we cannot recognize our individual and collective selves in those data. They do not reflect our Peoplehood (Intersubjectivity 1) and only represent a small, disconnected part of the denial of our Peoplehood (Intersubjectivity 2). Regardless, transformed and recorded into state-defined terms and categories, the resultant deficit-framed data are used as the primary tool by which the nation-state makes sense of its Indigenous population/s.

Scott's second element for policy failure is what he terms a high-modernist ideology, which can be translated into an uncritical confidence in scientific and technical progress. Such thinking is contemporaneously reflected across CANZUS countries in their embrace of big data technologies and open data rationales. In Australia, for example, the *Data Availability and Transparency Act 2022* renders administrative data from federal government departments and entities available to external researchers. And despite assurances from the Australian National Data Agency that they understood the risks of opening up administrative data in which First Peoples are overrepresented in pejorative categories such as incarceration, or drug and alcohol treatment inmates, this legislation failed to include any safeguards for the very large volume of Indigenous data contained within these datasets (see Commonwealth of Australia 2019).

The third element, an authoritarian state, willing and capable of using its coercive power to enact this process of administrative ordering, and the fourth, a society that lacks the capacity to resist the state, are realities familiar to Indigenous Peoples (Walter and Russo-Carroll 2020). Coercion is woven into the practices of state/Indigenous interactions (Chesterman and Galligan 1997) and imbalances of power is a hallmark of past and present relations between Indigenous Peoples and the non-Indigenous majority (Smith 1999). Scott (1998, 97) himself stated that colonial regimes are prone to experiment on Indigenous populations, noting, "[A]n ideology of 'welfare colonialism' combined with the authoritarian power inherent in colonial rule have encouraged ambitious schemes to remake native societies" (Walter and Russo-Carroll 2020).

Thus, in summary, statistics about Indigenous Peoples

- measure only what the state wants to know about Indigenous populations;
- render the complex social and cultural realities of Indigenous lives into simplistic and limited, and targeted, non-Indigenous terms;
- perpetuate the state's rationale of Indigenous "need" and developmental failure;
- obscure colonization's role in creating and recreating Indigenous inequalities;
- confirm/reconfirm the state's belief that statistics are an objective form of "evidence";
- through their numerical form, elide these data's social, cultural and racial dimensions;
- rationalize the ongoing imbalance of power between Indigenous Peoples and the state; and
- reinforce the normalcy of the deficit Indigenous stereotype.

The resulting national narrative traps Indigenous Peoples (across each CANZUS nation) within a numeric straitjacket lens of deficit (Walter and Anderson 2013).

Indigenous Statistics Are Political

The interests of the state in relation to its Indigenous populations are, and always have been, deeply political. As argued by Walter and Russo-Carroll (2020), the political nature of Indigenous data are revealed by the Indigenous data/policy nexus whereby data simultaneously emphasize and disguise Indigenous difference. Whether it is Indigenous difference or sameness that the state chooses to emphasize depends on whether the state needs to buttress the national narrative of Indigenous deficit or to disguise the role of violent dispossession and the continuing practices of colonization in ongoing Indigenous marginalization and disadvantage. Whatever the rationale, the outcome is policy prescriptions that reproduce, unreflexively, the pejorative presumptions of contemporary colonial race relations. In a seemingly unbroken circle, the values and attitudes formed and reaffirmed by these narratives shape how the state and its majority population "see" the Indigenous minority, dictating the direction of data interpretation and subsequent policy (Walter 2016).

As political artefacts, Indigenous statistics operate as a powerful societal truth claim. It is useful to position this argument within the established theories of the constitutive power of language. Philosophers such as

Wittgenstein (1974) and Foucault (1972) have long argued that language is neither a neutral nor a transparent medium. Rather, language shapes not only what we say but also more insidiously what we can think. Foucault (1972) furthered this argument in his definition of discourse as "(language) practices that systematically form the objects of which they speak; they do not identify objects, they constitute them and in the practice of doing so conceal their own invention" (cited in Bacchi 1999). It is our argument that statistics are also a language and create a form of discourse in the Foucauldian sense. For Indigenous Peoples, these statistical discourses, created by the state, for the state, do much more than identify the Peoples whom they record. Rather, they constitute us, for the state and the dominant society, systematically forming narratives of both who we are and who we cannot be. In doing so, Indigenous statistics both invent and conceal their own invention of the statistical Indigene. From this position of power, the state has and continues to imagine and construct the Indigenous Peoples living within their national borders. They allow the state, as Foucault (1972) astutely contends in relation to discourse, to surveil and discipline Indigenous populations in the very act of that creation.

Indigenous Statistics: Being More Than a Social Problem

The small slice of Indigenous life about which data have been collected since colonial times is as problematic for the data it does not collect as for the data that it does. Indigenous Peoples across the CANZUS countries are increasingly politically assertive and active agents in Indigenous nation rebuilding. But the data needed to undertake this work is largely absent from official collections (see the section on Governance of Indigenous Data in Chapter 2). For example, in Australia, while there exists a huge and growing body of data that speaks to Indigenous deficit, there are almost no data that allows these indicators to be examined within the socio-cultural systems in which these measures occur and reoccur across generations.

Does, for example, the level of cultural competence among a school's leadership and staff impact Indigenous children's levels of absenteeism or educational attainment? The answer is that we do not know. Because, while data on levels of low Indigenous educational attainment and high Indigenous levels of absenteeism have been collated for decades, there are still no data systematically collected on levels of cultural competence among teachers or principals. Yet, without data about the (largely non-Indigenous controlled) social and cultural milieu in which absenteeism and/or low educational outcomes occur, there can be no valid answer on "why" such patterns exist. More critically, the tiny body of work looking beyond deficit explanations (usually authored by Indigenous scholars) indicates that the broader socio-cultural settings matter very much. For example, Trudgett et al. (2017), using data from the Longitudinal Study of Indigenous Children[3] (one of the very few national datasets with an Indigenous governance committee), found that the likelihood of the child liking school was statistically correlated with whether the primary parent thought that the child's teacher understood the needs of Indigenous families. The opposite was also the case: when schools or teachers did not demonstrate an understanding of Indigenous families, Aboriginal and Torres Strait Islander children were less likely to like school. Yet the state does not collect these data.

Similarly, while it is known that many factors of Indigenous life disadvantage are linked (i.e., high childhood poverty are linked to high rates of Indigenous children being taken by the state into care), very little data exists on how other factors in Indigenous lives might operate to mitigate these. Do, for example, high levels of Indigenous community cohesion mitigate some impacts of intergenerational trauma? The answer is, again, that we do not know because the state does not collect data that measure Indigenous community functioning. But again the tiny scholarly literature indicates that such factors are likely to be important. For example, Walter (2017), also using data from the Longitudinal Study of Indigenous Children, found that how much time children spent with elders in their community was a statistically significant explanatory factor in how highly children's primary parents rated their own parenting ability. Yet, without data that measures community functioning such explanatory factors can never be established, let alone be considered as evidence in planning policies and programs. As per Scott (1998), the slice of Indigenous life measured by the state, and consequently its reduction and simplification, continues to exclude data which might provide alternative explanations of Indigenous disadvantage. The pattern of unremitting and long-standing Indigenous policy failure remains undisturbed; and that, perhaps, is the state's goal.

As the previous paragraphs have demonstrated, the data needed to explore broader dimensions of Indigenous lives remain scarce or non-existent. Walter (2018) has mapped this mismatch between the data that exist and those that Indigenous Peoples need across five categories—blaming, aggregate, decontextualized, deficit and restricted (BADDR)—of data failure. In Table 4.1, these BADDR data are paired with the largely absent lifeworld data that Indigenous Peoples need for community and nation rebuilding.

Conclusion

The discourse of Indigenous data deployed by the nation-state have, since colonization, foretold an unremitted tale of woe. But these data and their

TABLE 4.1 BADDR Data Versus Indigenous Data Needs

Dominant BADDR data	*Indigenous data needs*
Blaming data Too much data contrasts Indigenous/non-Indigenous data, rating the problematic Indigene against the normed non-Indigenous citizen	**Lifeworld data** We need data to inform a comprehensive, narrative of who we are as peoples, of our culture, our communities, our resilience, our aspirations
Aggregate data Too much data are aggregated at the national and/or state/province level implying Indigenous cultural and geographic homogeneity	**Disaggregated data** We need data that recognizes our cultural and geographical diversity and can provide evidence for tribal and community-level planning and service delivery
Decontextualized data Too much data are simplistic and decontextualized, focusing on individuals and families outside of their social/cultural context	**Contextualized data** We need data that are inclusive of the wider social structural context/complexities in which Indigenous disadvantage occurs
Deficit, government priority data Too much data are collected to service government priorities and are 5D, focusing on Indigenous disadvantage, disparity, dysfunction, difference, deficit	**Indigenous priority data** We need data that measure not just our problems but data that address our First Nation and community priorities and agendas and support nation rebuilding
Reductive data Too much data are reductive, treating Indigeneity as if it were a single category and a single way of being	**Diversity of data** We need data that reflect Indigenous diversity and ways of living and are informed by Indigenous knowledges and perspectives

Adapted from Walter (2018)

specific shape are purposeful. In summary, they operate as colonizer-settler artefacts that serve their masters and dis-serve their subjects. Yet, neither the state nor the dominant population that these data serve have given thought or consciousness about their restrictiveness. There seems little interest in the demonstrated fact that these state-sourced Indigenous data cannot, and do not, yield meaningful portraits of the embodied realities of Indigenous lives. For that we need different ways of understanding Indigenous populations. Seeing Indigenous populations through Indigenous understandings provides different data and a whole new world of Indigenous statistics: statistics that serve Indigenous purposes.

Notes

1 The Mayi Kuwayu is a national Aboriginal and Torres Strait Islander study of wellbeing which is both Indigenous designed and Indigenous led. The Mayi Kuwayu study looks at how Aboriginal and Torres Strait Islander wellbeing is linked to our cultures and was developed as a response to community concerns about the lack of understanding of the importance of Aboriginal and Torres Strait Islander cultures. Mayi Kuwaya is the first Australian national longitudinal study on Indigenous cultures and wellbeing and collects data via a biannual survey. The Mayi Kuwayu team is majority Aboriginal and Torres Strait Islander with strong Aboriginal and Torres Strait Islander governance and follows Indigenous Data Sovereignty Principles.
2 HILDA, the *Household, Income and Labour Dynamics in Australia (HILDA) Survey*, is a household-based panel study collecting data on economic and personal wellbeing, labour market dynamics and family life. Started in 2001, the HILDA Survey's purpose is to provide policy makers with unique insights about Australia, enabling them to make informed decisions across a range of policy areas, including health, education and social services.
3 Footprints in Time: The Longitudinal Study of Indigenous Children (LSIC) is a study of Aboriginal and Torres Strait Islander children selected from different locations across Australia and aims to improve understanding of the lives of Aboriginal and Torres Strait Islander children, their families and communities. The study started in 2008. It involves two groups of Aboriginal and/or Torres Strait Islander children who were aged 0 to 24 months and 3.5 to 5 years in 2008. In Wave 1, we interviewed over 1,680 families. Interviews occur annually. More than 1,200 parents and children were followed up in each wave by Aboriginal and Torres Strait Islander interviewers up to Wave 12. In 2020 and 2021, the response was impeded by COVID-19. www.dss.gov.au/about-the-department/longitudinal-studies/footprints-in-time-lsic-longitudinal-study-of-indigenous-children-overview

References

ABS. "2900.0—Census of Population and Housing: Understanding the Census and Census Data, Australia, 2016 ARCHIVED ISSUE Released at 11:30 AM (CANBERRA TIME) 08/11/2017." 2017. www.abs.gov.au/ausstats/abs@.nsf/Lookup/2900.0main+features100802016.

Andersen, Chris. "Urban Aboriginality as Distinctive, in Twelve Parts." In *Indigenous Identities and Urbanization in International Perspective: Cultural Resilience and Innovation in Four Settler Nations*, edited by Evelyn Peters and Chris Andersen. Vancouver: UBC Press, 2013.

Atkinson, Rowland, Emma Taylor, and Maggie Walter. "Burying Indigeneity: The Spatial Construction of Reality and Aboriginal Australia." *Social and Legal Studies* 19, no. 3 (2010): 311–330.

Bacchi, Carol. *Analysing Policy: What's the Problem Represented to Be?* Frenchs Forest: Pearson Australia, 1999.

Barrowman, Nick. "Why Data Is Never Raw: On the Seductive Myth of Information Free of Human Judgment." *The New Atlantis*, Summer/Fall 2018. www.thenewatlantis.com/publications/why-data-is-never-raw.

Brinckley, Mary, and Raymond Lovett. "Race, Racism, and Well-Being Impacts on Aboriginal and Torres Strait Islander Peoples in Australia." In *Handbook of Indigenous Sociology*, edited by Maggie Walter, Tahu Kukutai, Angela

Gonzales, and Robert Henry. New York: Oxford University Press, 2022. https://doi.org/10.1093/oxfordhb/9780197528778.013.39.

Briscoe, Gordon. *Counting, Health and Identity: A History of Aboriginal Health and Demography in Western Australia and Queensland, 1900–1940*. Canberra: Aboriginal Studies Press, 2003.

Chesterman, John, and Brian Galligan. *Citizens Without Rights: Aborigines and Australian Citizenship*. Cambridge: Cambridge University Press, 1997.

Clayton, Adam. "How Eugenics Shaped Statistics: Exposing the Damned Lies of Three Science Pioneers." *Nautilus*, October 27, 2020. https://nautil.us/how-eugenics-shaped-statistics-238014/.

Commonwealth of Australia, Department of the Prime Minister and Cabinet. *Data Sharing and Release Legislative Reforms Discussion Paper*. Canberra, 2019.

Desai, Vandana, and Robert Potter, eds. *The Companion to Development Studies*. Oxford: Oxford University Press, 2002.

Foucault, Michel. *The Archaeology of Knowledge and the Discourse on Language*. London: Routledge, 1972.

"History of Statistics." *Wikipedia*, 2023. https://en.wikipedia.org/wiki/History_of_statistics.

"How Nature Contributed to Science's Discriminatory Legacy." *Nature* 609 (September 28, 2022): 875–876. https://doi.org/10.1038/d41586-022-03035-6.

Husserl, Edmund. *The Crisis of European Sciences and Transcendental Phenomenology*. 1954 Reprint. Evanston: Northwestern University Press, 1970.

King, Thomas. *The Inconvenient Indian: A Curious Account of the Native People of North America*. Toronto: Doubleday Canada, 2012.

Kothari, Uma. *A Radical History of Development Studies: Individuals, Institutions and Ideologies*. London: Zed Books, 2005.

Kukutai, Tahu. "Building Ethnic Boundaries in New Zealand: Representations of Maori Identity in the Census." In *Indigenous Peoples and Demography: The Complex Relation between Identity and Statistics*, edited by Per Axelsson and Peter Sköld, 33–54. New York: Berghahn Books, 2011.

Kukutai, Tahu, and Maggie Walter. "Indigenising Statistics: Meeting in the Recognition Space." *Statistical Journal of the IAOS* 31, no. 2 (2015): 317–326.

Mayi Kuwayu. "Home." 2023. https://mkstudy.com.au/.

Peet, Richard, and Elaine Hartwick. *Theories of Development: Contentions, Arguments, Alternatives*. 2nd ed. New York: Guilford Press, 2009.

Porsanger, Jelena. "An Essay about Indigenous Methodology." *Nordlit* 15 (2004): 105–120. https://septentrio.uit.no/index.php/nordlit/article/download/1910/1776.

Quine, W. O. "On What There Is." *Review of Metaphysics* 2, no. 5 (1948): 21–38. Reprinted in *From a Logical Point of View*. Cambridge, MA: Harvard University Press, 1953.

Rainie, Stephanie Carroll, Tahu Kukutai, Maggie Walter, Oscar Luis Figueroa-Rodriguez, Jennifer Walker, and Per Axelsson. "Issues in Open Data: Indigenous Data Sovereignty." In *The State of Open Data: Histories and Horizons*, edited by Tim Davies, Steven Walker, Mor Rubinstein, and Fernando Perini, 300–319. Cape Town and Ottawa: African Minds and International Development Research Centre, 2019.

Scott, James C. *Seeing Like a State: How Certain Schemes to Improve the Human Condition Have Failed*. New Haven: Yale University Press, 1998.

Smith, Linda Tuhiwai. *Decolonizing Methodologies*. London: Zed Books, 1999.

"Statistics." *Encyclopedia Britannica*, 2024. www.britannica.com/science/statistics.

Trudgett, Michelle, Susan Page, Graham Bodkin-Andrews, Cathryn Franklin, and Andrew Whittaker. "Another Brick in the Wall? Parent Perceptions of School Educational Experiences of Indigenous Australian Children." In *Indigenous Children Growing Up Strong: A Longitudinal Study of Aboriginal and Torres Strait Islander Families*, edited by Maggie Walter, K. L. Martin, and Graham Bodkin-Andrews, 233–258. London: Palgrave Macmillan, 2017.

Walter, Maggie. Pers Comm, August 19, 2010.

Walter, Maggie. "Conceptualizing and Theorizing the Indigenous Lifeworld." In *Handbook of Indigenous Sociology*, edited by Maggie Walter, Tahu Kukutai, Angela Gonzales, and Robert Henry. New York: Oxford University Press, 2022.

Walter, Maggie. "Data Politics and Indigenous Representation in Australian Statistics." In *Indigenous Data Sovereignty: Towards an Agenda*, edited by Tahu Kukutai and John Taylor, 79–98. CAEPR Research Monograph, no. 34. Canberra: ANU Press, 2016.

Walter, Maggie. "Doing Indigenous Family." In *Indigenous Children Growing Up Strong: A Longitudinal Study of Aboriginal and Torres Strait Islander Families*, edited by Maggie Walter, K. L. Martin, and Graham Bodkin-Andrews, 123–152. London: Palgrave Macmillan, 2017.

Walter, Maggie. "The Voice of Indigenous Data: Beyond the Markers of Disadvantage." *Griffith Review* 60 (2018).

Walter, Maggie, and Chris Andersen. *Indigenous Statistics: A Quantitative Methodology*. New York: Routledge, 2013.

Walter, Maggie, and Stephanie Russo-Carroll. "Chapter 1: Indigenous Data Sovereignty, Governance and the Link to Indigenous Policy." In *Indigenous Data Sovereignty and Policy*, edited by Maggie Walter, Tahu Kukutai, Stephanie Russo Carroll, and Desi Rodriguez-Lonebear. London: Routledge, 2020.

Walter, Maggie, and Michelle Suina. "Indigenous Data, Indigenous Methodologies and Indigenous Data Sovereignty." *International Journal of Social Research Methodology* 22, no. 3 (2019): 233–243.

Wittgenstein, Ludwig. *Philosophical Investigations*. Oxford: Blackwell, 1974.

Wolfe, Patrick. "Settler Colonialism and the Elimination of the Native." *Journal of Genocide Research* 8, no. 4 (2006): 387–409. https://doi.org/10.1080/14623520601056240.

5
BEYOND COLONIAL CONSTRUCTS

The Promise of Indigenous Statistics

Tahu Kukutai

CHAPTER LEARNING OBJECTIVES

Objective 1: Identify how Indigenous statistical approaches reflect Indigenous lifeworlds, with a focus on culture, identity and kinship.

Objective 2: Understand the relationship between Indigenous statistics, the data lifecycle and data governance.

Objective 3: Examine a real example of Indigenous Data Governance in Aotearoa.

By this stage of the book we hope to have persuaded you that Indigenous statistics cannot be understood merely as a branch of applied mathematics involving the collection, description, analysis and inference of conclusions drawn from quantitative data about Indigenous Peoples. Tracing the genealogy of statistics clearly shows the myriad social and political forces at play. The development of statistics, as a science, was deeply intertwined with statecraft and, in the CANZUS countries, statistics about Indigenous Peoples were used to justify racism, eugenics, colonization and the erasure of our identities, cultures and lifeways. This is not to vilify statistics as inherently bad, nor to argue that statistics are anathema to Indigenous self-determination and self-representation. On the contrary. Statistics are increasingly crucial to Indigenous projects of sovereignty, nation building and cultural reclamation (Carroll et al. 2019). However, in seeking to reposition and repurpose statistics as a technology of power, we must also acknowledge its fraught legacies.

In the introductory chapter we argued that Indigenous statistics, as practised by governments and Global North academies, has at least two fundamental flaws. First, statistical portrayals of Indigenous lifeworlds are often fixated on problems and risk behaviours erroneously framed as inherent features of Indigenous individuals, families and communities. Meanwhile, colonization and colonialism—the "deep determinants" of Indigenous health and wellbeing—are rendered statistically invisible (Axelsson et al. 2016; Indigenous Health Group 2007). Second, statistics that genuinely reflect Indigenous lifeworlds (Walter and Suina 2019) in terms of our ways of being, resilience, goals and successes are few and far between. In many policy domains, they do not feature at all.

Having dedicated significant space to theorizing and empirically evidencing these twin problems, it is useful to reflect on what an alternative paradigm might entail. Reimagining statistics in our own image ought not to be an onerous task. Indeed, the ability to imagine and pursue future flourishing is the intergenerational fuel that collectively propels us forward.

The purpose of this chapter then is to describe Indigenous statistics as they could be. This requires transforming not only data collection, statistical models, research questions and interpretation to reflect Indigenous lifeworlds, but also broader considerations relating to the data lifecycle, of which statistics is a part. I begin by describing some of the Indigenous-led and collaborative research seeking to disrupt the dominant paradigms of "BADDR data" (see Chapter 4) and statistical erasure (Rodriguez-Lonebear 2021). These can be broadly described as strengths-based approaches which recognize and promote Indigenous capacities and capabilities. Earlier in the book we set out the dual nature of Indigenous lifeworlds which encompasses both our intersubjectivity as colonized, dispossessed peoples and our intersubjectivity as Indigenous Peoples with distinctive ways of being and doing. This chapter focuses on the latter but acknowledges the important scholarship of Indigenous researchers who have used statistics to expose structures of racism and inequity and their ongoing impacts on Indigenous health and wellbeing. In Aotearoa, for example, Kaupapa Māori epidemiology has been critical for holding the government to account for systemic health inequities and for subverting BADDR data narratives relating to Māori health (see, for example, Cormack and Paine 2020; Curtis 2016; Reid et al. 2019; Robson and Harris 2007).

The focus of this chapter is on Aotearoa and, more specifically, statistics on Māori identity, culture and kinship. Recognizing that good statistics require more than good analysis, it also considers the transformative potential of Indigenous Data Sovereignty and data governance, with an overview of the Māori Data Governance Model (Kukutai et al. 2023). It concludes with a brief consideration of future challenges and opportunities given the pace and scale of technological change and innovation.

Statistics That Recognize Indigenous Lifeworlds

Indigenous Peoples around the world have refused to surrender their collective identities despite the best efforts of settler colonial governments to exterminate, assimilate and acculturate them. For many Indigenous communities, maintaining and strengthening identity and culture is seen as central to their self-determination and collective wellbeing. Certainly this is the case in Aotearoa. Despite the 1840 Tiriti o Waitangi (Treaty of Waitangi) guaranteeing Māori *tino rangatiratanga* (chiefly authority) over their lands, villages and treasures (Orange 1987), the vast majority of Māori land was alienated by 1900 and Māori economic, political and demographic dominance was supplanted by the settler (primarily British origin) population known as Pākehā (Walker 1990).

From the outset, Māori resisted colonization and state-sponsored assimilation. However, rapid post-war Māori urbanization, labour market transformation, government assimilation policies and systemic racism produced complex cleavages within Māori communities (Kukutai 2013). The cultural dispossession that resulted came to be seen as a key factor driving the myriad negative Māori social and economic outcomes, including grossly disproportionate rates of incarceration (Awatere 1984; Durie 1997, 2001, 2003; Jackson 1987; Pere 1988). The birth of the modern Māori protest movement in the 1970s focused on the return of Māori land, honouring the promises of *te Tiriti o Waitangi*, and anti-racism collective action (Harris 2004). The so-called Māori renaissance (Royal 2005) was accompanied by Māori language[1] recovery programmes, notably Kohanga Reo (language nest) and Kura Kaupapa Māori, that enabled Māori children to be taught in a Māori language immersion environment. The revival of *mātauranga* Māori (Māori knowledges and ways of knowing), identity and culture were seen as crucial to Māori healing and advancement. Over the decades a significant body of scholarship theorized, conceptualized and documented the importance of cultural identity and institutions for individual, *whānau* (extended kinship groups) and community wellbeing (Durie 1994, 1998; Te Whāiti et al. 1997; Smith

1999; Walker 1990). Much of this work generated and deployed qualitative evidence.

Cultural Identity

The last decade has seen the emergence of a significant corpus of Indigenous statistical scholarship focused on what might be broadly described as socio-ecological and socio-cultural strengths-based approaches. The main assumption underpinning socio-ecological approaches is that participation in Indigenous cultural activities strengthens cultural identity and belonging. This, in turn, prevents health risks and promotes wellbeing (Bryant et al. 2021). In Aotearoa this has been described some by researchers as "culture as cure" (Houkamau and Sibley 2010).

Drawing on social identity theory (Tajfel and Turner 1986), much of the Māori-led culture as cure quantitative research has sought to demonstrate the positive association between aspects of Māori cultural identity and wellbeing outcomes. For example, Houkamau and Sibley (2010) examined the relationship between Māori cultural efficacy (confidence to competently engage in the Māori world), personal satisfaction and satisfaction with society in general. Their analysis showed that Māori cultural efficacy was positively associated with personal satisfaction but negatively associated with societal satisfaction. They surmised that while cultural efficacy positively influenced personal life satisfaction, it also appeared to increase exposure to alternative perspectives of how society should operate and "decreased satisfaction with the current Western-individualist model governing New Zealand society" (2010, 391).

Māori researchers also used data from the New Zealand Attitude and Values Survey (NZVAS)[2] to explore the relationship between Māori cultural efficacy, self-esteem and rumination (Matika et al. 2017). They found that cultural efficacy was positively linked with self-esteem but was partially mediated by a negative association between cultural efficacy and rumination. In short, Māori with higher cultural efficacy tended to experience lower levels of rumination, and a lower level rumination was, in turn, linked with increased self-esteem. The results were interpreted as providing additional support for a general culture as cure approach for Māori and the positive psychological and health benefits of active identity engagement. A subsequent study examined the relationship between identity (in-group warmth and ethnic identity centrality)[3] and three aspects of personal wellbeing (life satisfaction, self-esteem, personal wellbeing), finding that higher in-group warmth[4] towards Māori predicted increases in all three wellbeing measures (Houkamau et al. 2023). While the authors stressed the importance of ethnic identity affect for wellbeing, they acknowledged that the impacts of colonization on contemporary Māori identities and wellbeing determinants were complex, intergenerational and systemic.

NZVAS researchers also examined the relationship between Māori identity (Greaves et al. 2017) and economic attitudes using data from the nationwide Māori Identity and Financial Attitudes Study (MIFAS) (Houkamau and Sibley 2019). They found that Māori who were more strongly oriented towards a traditional Māori belief system (e.g., engaged with concepts of Māori spirituality and were socially and politically conscious) were less likely to be individualistic at work, more likely to prefer workplaces that respected Māori development and less likely to support commercializing tribal assets. The authors argued that respect for Māori values at work, workplace sociality and tribal land/asset preservation were "rational within a traditional Māori value system, even if they incur personal financial cost" (Houkamau and Sibley 2019, 132). They also highlighted the considerable heterogeneity within the Māori sample, noting, "contemporary Māori are not monolithic, and important nuances shape how different Māori engage with economic decisions."

Over the last decade Māori educational psychologists have also used statistical tools to explore the positive effects of identity on outcomes for *rangatahi* (Māori teens and young adults). Their research challenges the long litany of research stigmatizing Māori youth and the focus on individual and whānau problems. Also drawing on social identity theory, Webber et al. (2013) explored differences in ethnic identity between Māori, Samoan, Asian and European 13- and 14-year-olds. Ethnic identity was measured by level of connectedness, awareness of racism and embedded achievement—the belief that achievement at school is part of one's ethnic group identity. Their analysis showed that Māori and Samoan students had a higher sense of embedded achievement than their Pākehā and Asian peers. This was an important finding given that "Māori and Samoan students have a long history of being stereotyped as less academically able than their Pākehā peers" (Webber et al. 2013, 26). In a similar vein, a Māori-led team analysing data from the Youth 2000 panel survey found that Māori youth who had a strong cultural identity were more likely to experience good mental health outcomes, while discrimination had a serious negative impact (Williams et al. 2018).

Relational Worldviews and Kinship

The last decade has also seen the emergence of strength-based statistics exploring socio-cultural aspects of Māori lifeworlds. Socio-cultural approaches prioritize collective identities and practices viewed through connection to ancestry, family, community and land (Bryant et al. 2021,

1413). For Māori, the relational world view is refracted through *whakapapa*—the genealogical sequence that "places Māori in an environmental context with all other flora and fauna and natural resources as part of a hierarchical genetic assemblage with identifiable and established bonds" (Harmsworth and Awatere 2013). This cosmogonical sequence has some tribal variation but generally begins with *Te Kore* (the nothingness void) and progresses through space and time to the emerging light and the creation of the world, the separation of the primeval parents Ranginui (sky father) and Papatū-ā-nuku (earth mother), the birth of their children (forest and plants, the sea, animals and so forth) and, finally, the creation of humans (Harmsworth and Awatere 2013; Roberts et al. 2004). These *whakapapa* relationships are woven throughout traditional Māori knowledge systems and the intergenerational transmission of history, esoteric knowledge, customs and protocols for ethical behaviour (Mahuika 2019).

Within the realm of human *whakapapa* are the multi-layered assemblages of Māori kin groups most commonly expressed as *iwi* (tribe), *hapū* (clan or sub-tribe) and *whānau* (extended family groupings). These collective identities have been largely absent in contemporary statistical research on Māori but have been given new life through a growing body of work on tribal demography and *whānau* wellbeing. Using census and tribal register data, Māori researchers have produced demographic-focused reports—often directly commissioned by tribes—to inform tribal planning and programmes (Gifford and Mikaere 2019). Published papers have also explored the complexities and limitations of data on tribal self-identification in the population census, showing significant differences in tribal size and composition when comparing census data with tribe's own enrolment data (Walling et al. 2009). Female-dominated sex ratios[5] are one of the more unusual features of tribal census data with the vast majority of tribes in the census having far more females than males, particularly in the 25–44 age group (Kukutai and Rarere 2017). Analysis of data from Te Kupenga, the nationally representative Māori social survey, showed Māori women at those ages were more likely than their male counterparts to know detailed aspects of their *pepeha* (tribal identity), to explore *whakapapa* and to speak Māori. The explanation for female-dominated sex ratios in tribal census data thus had more to do with Māori women being the carriers of identity and culture than Māori men "missing" due to sex-selective migration and under-enumeration (Kukutai and Rarere 2017).

The growing literature on tribal demography and statistics has also been accompanied by statistical studies of *whānau*. For the most part, dominant statistical narratives about Māori families have tended to fixate on family structure and functioning (or dysfunction) and on the household as the economic unit of production, neither of which recognize or reflect Māori worldviews of *whānau* (Cram and Pitama 1998). A series of *whānau*-focused statistical projects commissioned for the annual *Families and Whānau Status Report* provide some insight into alternative approaches. One project analysed data from Te Kupenga to explore contemporary perceptions of *whānau* (Kukutai et al. 2016). Using a self-reported question "Who do you think your whānau are?" the analysis showed that the vast majority of Māori (99%) think of their *whānau* in terms of genealogical relationships, but the breadth of those relationships vary hugely. Around 40 per cent only thought of their *whānau* solely in terms of parents, partner, siblings, in-laws (brother/sister/parent) and children; 15 per cent included grandparents and grandchildren; nearly one-third included aunts, uncles, cousins, nephews, nieces and other in-laws; and 12.5 per cent included non-kin close friends and others. A number of factors were associated with seeing *whānau* in its broadest sense, namely older age, connectedness to ancestral *marae* (customary meeting places) and a high regard for being involved with Māori culture. Māori who included non-related individuals within their definition of *whānau* tended to have the strongest ties to Māori culture, language and institutions. The authors concluded that the broadening of the concept of *whānau* to include non-kin relationships "would appear to be evidence of the endurance and vitality of whānau values, rather than a diminution of it."

The same team also looked at the factors associated with self-reports of *whānau* wellbeing in Te Kupenga (Kukutai et al. 2017). Until then, most quantitative research on *whānau* wellbeing had relied on aggregating individual-level census data at the household level, even though *whānau* structures extend beyond household living arrangements. The study found that the mean level of *whānau* wellbeing reported in Te Kupenga was high. Only 6.3 per cent of respondents reported a *whānau* wellbeing score below the scale midpoint (5), and about three-quarters of respondents reported that their *whānau* were doing well (7–8) or very well (9–10). After age adjustments, the factors most strongly associated with self-assessed *whānau* wellbeing were the quality of *whānau* relationships and individual life satisfaction. The findings aligned with the large body of qualitative literature emphasizing the holistic nature of wellbeing for Māori and the interconnections between the wellbeing of individuals and their wider *whānau*.

Other Māori-led statistical studies have explored various aspects of relationality. For example, Greaves et al. (2021) used data from the Youth19 Rangatahi Smart Survey to develop a *"whanaungatanga"* scale, measuring active participation, a sense of belonging to social groups, and collective, reciprocal relationships. Three *whanaungatanga* subscales relating to *whānau*, friends and other adults were strongly predictive of wellbeing for Māori youth. Work is also underway on the development of Māori social capital concepts and indicators (Roskruge 2021). Eschewing conventional measures of civic and social participation (e.g., volunteering), the study explores Māori-centric measures such as participation in cultural gatherings, exchanges of traditional knowledge and connection to *whānau* and ancestral land. Taken together, all of the Indigenous statistics described here seek to give expression, in some way, to Māori lifeworlds as it pertains to Peoplehood and our distinctive ways of being and doing. However, good statistics requires more than good analysis—it also requires good governance and meaningful mechanisms of authority.

Good Statistics Requires More Than Good Analysis

Here we return to the question posed in the introductory chapters—What does Indigenous Data Governance mean and what does it look like in practice? In order to address this question, it is helpful to first consider some of the wider context of Indigenous Data Sovereignty and the emerging evidence base.

As noted earlier, Indigenous Data Sovereignty networks now exist in all four CANZUS countries and most networks have published their own charters, principles and/or guidelines (Maiam nayri Wingara & Australian Indigenous Governance Institute 2023; Te Mana Raraunga 2018; Rainie et al. 2017). Notwithstanding the significant differences across the CANZUS states with respect to treaty relationships, political configurations and so forth, there are common features that all Indigenous Data Sovereignty networks share. These include:

- a focus on self-determination and intergenerational wellbeing;
- recognizing data as a valued cultural resource;
- an emphasis on collective data rights; and
- prioritizing Indigenous values as the basis for good data governance.

The Indigenous scholars, practitioners and activists involved with these networks have supported Indigenous Data Sovereignty within their communities and advocated for its recognition across the public and private sectors in their respective countries. All of the networks are actively involved in research, with members building the evidence base for their advocacy as they go.

Although a new field of research (compared, for example, with statistics), Indigenous Data Sovereignty and Indigenous Data Governance scholarship is already creating impact. For example, the UN Rapporteur on the Right to Privacy has called on governments and the corporations to recognize and uphold Indigenous Data Sovereignty in his reports relating to big and open data (2018) and the use of personal health data (2019). Internationally, the CARE Principles for Indigenous Data Governance have been particularly effective in raising awareness of Indigenous data considerations (Carroll et al. 2019, 2020; Carroll et al. 2022). Informed by the frameworks and principles developed by domestic networks (Carroll et al. 2020), the CARE Principles were designed to address the tension between protecting Indigenous rights and interests in data and supporting open data, by setting minimum expectations for data sharing. The principles have been affirmed or adopted by several influential organizations including the global Research Data Alliance, UNESCO Recommendation on Open Science and IEEE Recommended Practice for the Provenance of Indigenous Peoples' Data. Research exploring implementation pathways for the principles has also been undertaken, and possible synergies have been explored with existing standards such as tribal research codes in the United States (Carroll et al. 2022).

Metadata—data that provides information about other data—is another significant area of Indigenous Data Sovereignty research, with key examples being the traditional knowledge (TK) and biocultural (BC) labels. In the absence of enabling legislation protecting Indigenous intellectual property rights, the labels provide an extralegal mechanism for Indigenous communities to exert their authority. In the case of the BC labels, it enables them to "identify and maintain provenance, origin and authority over biocultural material and data generated from Indigenous land and waters held in research, cultural institutions and data repositories" (Golan et al. 2022). Indigenous Data Sovereignty in relation to genetic and genomic data is a particularly sensitive, and rapidly growing, area (Hudson et al. 2020; Kukutai and Black 2024; Tsosie et al. 2019). During the pandemic, significant attention was also given to the collection, storage, use and reuse of Indigenous COVID-19 data (Carroll et al. 2021; Huyser et al. 2021; Rodriguez-Lonebear et al. 2020; Yellow Horse and Huyser 2021). Leveraging the CARE Principles, the Research Data Alliance (RDA) COVID-19 Working Group developed bespoke guidelines for working with COVID-19 data collected from Indigenous communities (Research Data Alliance COVID-19 Indigenous Data Working Group 2020). The guidelines went beyond guidance on data access, sharing, analysis and use to highlight the need for active investment in Indigenous community control of Indigenous data and greater government transparency about the data quality and access issues that impeded the use of COVID-19 data for effective public health responses.

A Practical Example: The Māori Data Governance Model

Having considered the wider research context, it is useful to revisit the earlier question of what Indigenous Data Governance looks like in practice.

The Māori Data Governance Model (the Model) (Kukutai et al. 2023) offers one illustrative example. Designed by Māori data experts for use across the Aotearoa public service, the Model was created under the auspices of the Tiriti-based Mana Ōrite relationship agreement[6] between the national statistics office Stats NZ and the Data Iwi Leaders Group (Data ILG 2019). The Data ILG advocates for the data rights and interests of the 80-plus tribes involved in the National Iwi (tribal) Chairs Forum. The Model development involved a lengthy process of engagement with Māori, tribal and pan-tribal organizations and communities, as well as all of the major public service agencies holding and/or using Māori data (Te Kāhui Raraunga 2021a, 2021b). The team developing the Model also received support from the First Nations Data Governance Strategy team who in 2020 published their own First Nations data governance strategy (FNIGC 2020).

Underpinned by the vision "Tuia te korowai o Hineraraunga—Data for self-determination," the Model sets clear expectations for the system-wide governance of Māori data held by public service agencies and provides direction on the actions, processes and activities needed to meet those expectations. Māori data is defined as "digital or digitisable data, information or knowledge (including mātauranga Māori) that is about, from or connected to Māori." It includes data about population, place, culture and environment. Although targeted at the public service, the Model is unapologetically focused on Māori priorities framed as "desirable outcomes," including better shared and autonomous decision-making; data to drive iwi-Māori economies; supporting *whānau* to flourish; and reaffirming and strengthening connections to identity, place and the Māori language.

Five overarching values guide the Model as an expression of *tikanga Māori*—customary protocols for proper conduct (Figure 5.1). Each of the values has its own interpretation so as to make explicit the intent. For example, the description of "decocolonise data ecosystems" states:

> Decolonisation requires the cessation of practices that exploit and extract from Indigenous land, life and knowledges. The decolonisation of data involves dismantling the structures that perpetuate the dispossession of Māori and Māori data, while shifting the locus of control over Māori data back to Māori.
>
> (Kukutai et al. 2023, 18)

Given that statistics, as a social field, is marked by power asymmetries and resistance, an important feature of the Model is that it explicitly recognizes the need for changes to system leadership, policies and legal settings.

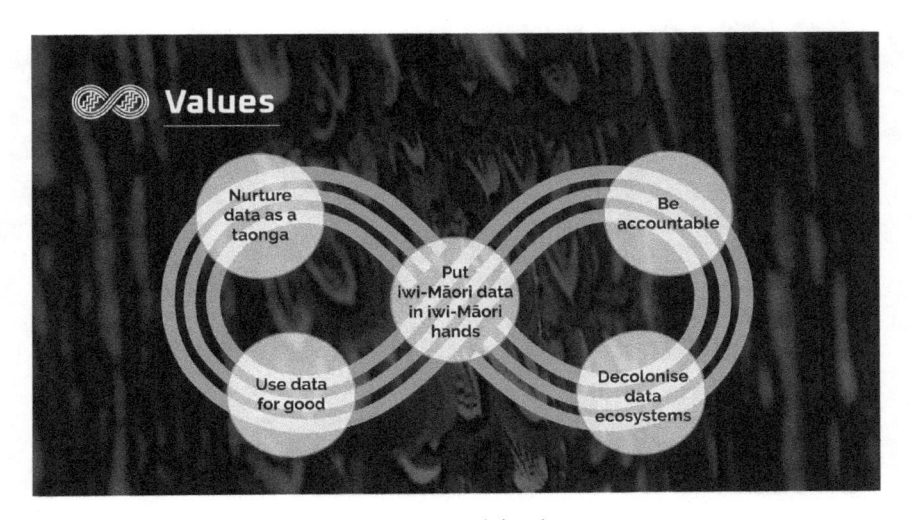

FIGURE 5.1 Māori Data Governance Model values

Reprinted with the permission of Data Iwi Leaders Group and Te Kāhui Raraunga.

This includes resourcing and implementing Māori data leadership across the government data system, government investment in a *"mana motuhake"* autonomous Māori data system that sits outside the government data system, and the development and implementation of *"sui generis"* (bespoke) Māori Data Sovereignty legislation to protect Māori data rights.

The substance of the Model comprises eight data governance *pou* or pillars which are the building blocks that represent priority areas of data governance that agencies can practically implement—from data capacities, workforce development and data infrastructure, to data access, sharing, repatriation and classification (Figure 5.2). The key features of each Māori data governance *pou* are considered below, including the action-oriented directives to agencies, and tangible exemplars of what good governance looks like.

Pou 1. Data capacities and workforce development. Here the Model calls out the power (especially resource) inequities that enable government agencies to dominate decision-making over Māori data and to develop technical capacities and capabilities that are largely inaccessible to Māori organizations and communities. Directives include the implementation of anti-racist data policies, the cessation of BADDR data (see Chapter 4 of this book) within agencies, and strategic investment in Māori data and digital expertise and leadership. The exemplar provided is "Te Mana Whakatipu," an iwi-led data collection initiative focused on building iwi data capacity and capability. The programme focuses on iwi data workforce development including short courses and micro-credentials, good data governance, digital development

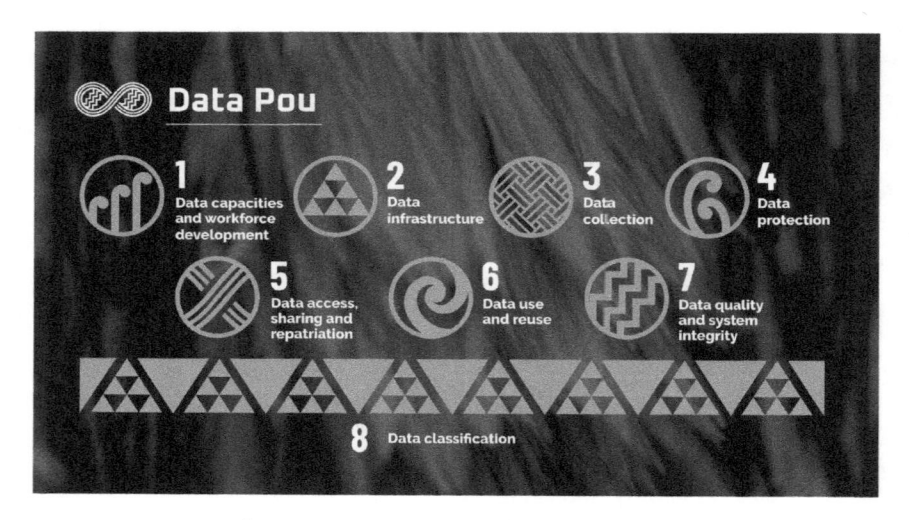

FIGURE 5.2   Māori data governance *pou* (pillars)

Reprinted with the permission of Data Iwi Leaders Group and Te Kāhui Raraunga.

and direct investment into building iwi data collection capability. Through Te Mana Whakatipu, two iwi collectives were able to pilot their own iwi data collection initiatives as part of Census 2023.

Pou 2. Data infrastructure. The Model stipulates the need for data infrastructure that works for Māori, is distributed and decentralized, and is sustainable and future focused. Infrastructure includes the hardware, software, networking services, policies and so forth that enable data consumption, storage and sharing. The Model specifies the need for data infrastructure that is flexible, scalable and interoperable and that enables the flow of information to communities where decisions need to be made. An exemplar of fit-for-purpose data infrastructure is Te Whata, a web-based data platform that has been tailored specifically "by iwi, for iwi" (see Chapter 8 of this book).

Pou 3. Data collection. The Model sets expectations for a Tiriti-led approach to data collection that involves ethical decision-making around what data should be collected, for what purposes and for whose benefit. It provides directives on how to prioritize Māori data needs, collecting data in ethical ways that strengthen relationships, collecting only what data is needed (data minimization) and returning what isn't required. An exemplar of data that prioritizes Māori information needs is the Māori social survey, Te Kupenga.

Pou 4. Data protection. The Model argues for the protection of Māori data to take a broader approach than prevailing regulatory frameworks focused on personal data protection. Instead, the application of data privacy and protection to Māori data should address collective dimensions of privacy and be guided by *tikanga* Māori and *mātauranga* Māori. The directives address issues relating to personal and collective data privacy, data de-identification, data security, data jurisdiction and the offshoring of Māori data (for more, see Kukutai et al. 2022).

Pou 5. *Data access, sharing and repatriation.* Here the timeless ritual of encounter practised by Māori known as "*pōwhiri*" is invoked as a guide for how to approach data access, sharing and repatriation. The report notes that in *pōwhiri*, "established protocols are invoked to create safe spaces and bring *mana whenua* (hosts) and *manuwhiri* (visitors) into good relations with each other" (2023, 38). Like *pōwhiri*, where information and knowledge is shared under certain conditions, contemporary processes of data access, sharing and repatriation also need to be based on relationships of reciprocity and trust and involve rules for what data can be shared, by whom and under what conditions. Particular attention is given to the process of granting data access, making Māori data open access, ensuring Māori benefit directly from Māori data, data linkage and integration, and data repatriation.

Pou 6. *Data use and reuse.* Secondary data use through data linkage is identified as an area requiring more stringent governance. This is a particular issue in Aotearoa which has one of the world's most comprehensive government data linkage programmes, notably the Integrated Data Infrastructure (IDI) stewarded by Stats NZ. The IDI is a large linked research database of de-identified microdata about people and households covering many aspects of daily life including health, education and training, benefits and social services, justice, income, work and housing.[7] The Model focuses on issues relating to consent and outlines different types of consent, emphasizing that consent should be an ongoing and negotiated process rather than a one-off exercise. Free, prior and informed (FPIC) consent is the minimum requirement, in keeping with the UNDRIP. The Model also provides directives on asking the "right" questions of data and the use of Māori data in algorithmic decision-making.

Pou 7. *Data quality and system integrity.* Data quality not only refers to data accuracy but also issues such as relevance, accessibility, timeliness and consistency. The Model notes that achieving high-quality Māori data depends on having the right systems in place and people with the appropriate knowledge and experience. System integrity requires the implementation of Māori-defined data standards and system monitoring for quality, performance and accountability. Thus, "organisations that collect, store and use Māori data need to be held accountable for providing culturally safe governance of Māori data." The directives include private sector organizations that contract to government agencies.

Pou 8. Data classification. As the Model notes, the origins of Māori data are located in *pūrakau*—ancient cosmological accounts and narratives that serve as intergenerational "knowledge codes." The exponential growth in the volume and breadth of Māori data requires innovative ways of classifying data that also recognize pre-existing structures of Māori thought. Key directives include the development of a Māori data classification framework grounded in Māori ontologies. "Having clarity over what constitutes Māori data, its level of sensitivity and its relationship to rights-holders, is integral to implementing the other Data Pou in the Model" (2023, 57). Māori metadata standards are also flagged, with the TK labels cited as an exemplar. Developed in the United States, the labels enable Indigenous communities to add local protocols for access and use to digitized cultural heritage that is held externally, such as public archives and libraries.

Finally, the Model notes, while there are many models, frameworks, roadmaps and strategies developed for use in the public service, many suffer from an implementation gap. The support of Stats NZ, as the system leader for government data, ought to provide some level of comfort around the Model implementation, but history tells us that the process will inevitably be influenced by political agendas and vagaries. Perhaps, in anticipation of that, the Model stresses the importance of investment in autonomous data systems designed by and for Māori and directly under Māori control.

Conclusion

This chapter has moved beyond theorizing Indigenous statistics as the preserve of the powerful, to give concrete expression to Indigenous agency and aspirations for a different paradigm—one that recognizes the fullness of Indigenous lifeworlds and aids our collective vision for self-determination. It has also tried to show that repurposing statistics in our own image is necessary but insufficient. The power of statistics lies not only in its collection, use and storying, but also in the power to make decisions about where data is stored and how it is classified and shared. It also requires purposeful investment in data infrastructure and human capacities and capabilities.

As we seek to navigate the very real threats of data colonialism (Couldry and Mejias 2019), surveillance capitalism (Zuboff 2019) and technologies that are invasive of individual and collective privacy (Mühlhoff 2023), Indigenous ways of thinking about statistics and data offer alternative approaches and strategies of resistance. We do not have to look far to find increasing examples of Indigenous innovators and communities reclaiming control of their data by developing their own data protection technologies (Caballar 2023). These include "privacy-first" storage systems, user permissions and apps explicitly designed to be Indigenous Data Sovereignty compliant and that prioritize community data rights and interests. In Aotearoa the independent tribal data trust Te Kāhui Raraunga has developed a distributed, decentralized sovereign data repository "Te Pā Tūwatata" that enables tribes to collect, store, protect, access and control their own data close to where they are (Waatea News 2024).

As has always been the case, the radical imaginary of Indigenous flourishing does not reside within the architecture of the colonial settler state, but within the hearts, minds and hands of Indigenous Peoples. This is as true of our data and statistics as it is of our lands, languages and identities.

Notes

1 Unlike other Indigenous Peoples in the CANZUS countries, Māori have a single language—te reo Māori—that can be readily understood across all tribes, albeit with dialectical differences. Estimates of Māori language proficiency vary, but in the 2021 General Social Survey, 23 per cent of Māori participants reported being able to hold a daily conversation in te reo Māori (Stats NZ 2022).
2 NZVAS is a 20-year longitudinal study that examines attitudes, personality and health over time for over 60,000 New Zealanders, including a Māori sample (n > 3,000).
3 Ethnic identity centrality was measured by responses to three items: "I often think about the fact that I am a member of my ethnic group," "The fact that I am a member of my ethnic group is an important part of my identity" and "Being a member of my ethnic group is an important part of how I see myself."
4 In-group warmth was measured by response to a single item asking, "Please rate the warmth of your feelings towards the following groups using the 'feeling thermometer scale' for each group. A rating of 1 indicates your feelings toward that group to be least warm (least favourable) while a rating of 10 indicates your feeling is most warm (most favourable)." The in-group warmth item used in these analyses was concerned with the Māori group.
5 A widely used measure in human demography, the sex ratio is the ratio of males to females in a population.
6 www.stats.govt.nz/about-us/what-we-do/mana-orite-relationship-agreement/
7 www.stats.govt.nz/integrated-data/integrated-data-infrastructure/data-in-the-idi/

References

Awatere, Donna. 1984. *Māori Sovereignty*. Auckland: Broadsheet Publications.
Axelsson, Per, Tahu Kukutai, and Rebecca Kippen. "The Field of Indigenous Health and the Role of Colonisation and History." *Journal of Population Research* 33 (2016): 1–7. https://doi.org/10.1007/s12546-016-9163-2.
Bryant, Joanne, Reuben Bolt, Jessica Botfield, Kacey Martin, Michael Doyle, Dean Murphy, Simon Graham, Christy Newman, Stephen Bell, Carla Treloar, Annette J. Browne, and Peter Aggleton. "Beyond Deficit: 'Strengths-based Approaches'

in Indigenous Health Research." *Sociology of Health and Illness* 43, no. 5 (2021): 1405–1421. https://doi.org/10.1111/1467-9566.13311.

Caballar, Rina. "How Indigenous Groups Are Leading the Way on Data Privacy." *Scientific American*, 2023. www.scientificamerican.com/article/how-indigenous-groups-are-leading-the-way-on-data-privacy/.

Carroll, Stephanie Russo, Randall Akee, Pryou Chung, Donna Cormack, Tahu Kukutai, Ray Lovett, Michelle Suina, and Robyn Rowe. "Indigenous Peoples' Data During COVID-19: From External to Internal." *Frontiers in Sociology* 6 (2021): 62.

Carroll, Stephanie Russo, Irbrahim Garba, Oscar Figueroa-Rodríguez, Jarita Holbrook, Ray Lovett, Simeon Materechera, Mark Parsons, Kay Raseroka, Desi Rodriguez-Lonebear, and Robyn Rowe. "The CARE Principles for Indigenous Data Governance." *Data Science Journal* 19, no. 1 (2020): 43. https://doi.org/10.5334/dsj-2020-043.

Carroll, Stephanie Russo, Ibrahim Garba, Rebecca Plevel, Desi Small-Rodriguez, Vanessa Hiratsuka, Maui Hudson, and Nanibaa' A Garrison. "Using Indigenous Standards to Implement the CARE Principles: Setting Expectations through Tribal Research Codes." *Frontiers in Genetics* 13 (2022): 823309. https://doi.org/10.3389/fgene.2022.823309.

Carroll, Stephanie Russo, Desi Rodriguez-Lonebear, and Andrew Martinez. "Indigenous Data Governance: Strategies from United States Native Nations." *Data Science Journal* 18, no. 1 (2019): 31. https://doi.org/10.5334/dsj-2019-031.

Cormack, Donna, and Sarah-Jane Paine. "Dear Epidemiology: A Letter from Two Māori Health Researchers." *The Pantograph Punch*, 2020. https://pantographpunch.com/posts/dear-epidemiology.

Couldry, Nick, and Ulises Mejias. "Data Colonialism: Rethinking Big Data's Relation to the Contemporary Subject." *Television & New Media* 20, no. 4 (2019): 336–349. https://doi.org/10.1177/1527476418796632.

Cram, Fiona and Suzanne Pitama. "Ko toku whānau, ko toku mana." In *The Family in Aoteaora New Zealand*, edited by Vivienne Adair and Robyn Dixon, 130–157. Auckland: Longman, 1998.

Curtis, Elana. "Indigenous Positioning in Health Research: The Importance of Kaupapa Māori Theory-Informed Practice." *AlterNative: An International Journal of Indigenous Peoples* 12, no. 4 (2016): 396–410. https://doi.org/10.20507/AlterNative.2016.12.4.5.

Data Iwi Leaders Group (Data ILG). *Mana Ōrite Relationship Agreement*. Rotorua: Data Iwi Leaders Group, 2019.

Durie, Arohia. "Te Aka Matua: Keeping a Maori Identity." In *Mai i Rangiatea: Māori Wellbeing and Development*, edited by Pania Te Whaiti, Marie McCarthy, and Arohia Durie, 142–162. Auckland: Auckland University Press/Bridget Williams Books, 1997.

Durie, Mason. *Mauri Ora: The Dynamics of Māori Health*. Auckland: Oxford University Press, 2001.

Durie, Mason. *Ngā Kāhui Pou: Launching Māori Futures*. Wellington: Huia, 2003.

Durie, Mason. *Te Mana, Te Kāwanatanga: The Politics of Māori Self-determination*. Auckland: Oxford University Press, 1998.

Durie, Mason. *Whaiora—Māori Health Development*. Auckland: Oxford University Press, 1994.

First Nations Information Governance Centre (FNIGC). *A First Nations Data Governance Strategy*, 2020. https://fnigc.ca/news/introducing-a-first-nations-data-governance-strategy/.

Gifford, Heather, and Kirikowhai Mikaere. "Te Kete Tū Ātea. Towards Reclaiming Rangitīkei Iwi Data Sovereignty." *Journal of Indigenous Wellbeing. Te Mauri—Pimatisiwin* 4, no. 1 (2019): 6–14.

Golan, Jacob, Katie Lee Riddle, Maui Hudson, Jane Anderson, Natalie Kusabs, and Tim Coltman. "Benefit Sharing: Why Inclusive Provenance Metadata Matter." *Frontiers in Genetics* 13 (2022). www.frontiersin.org/articles/10.3389/fgene.2022.1014044.

Greaves, Lara, Jade Le Grice, Ariel Schwencke, Sue Crengle, Sonia Lewycka, Logan Hamley, and Terryann Clark. "Measuring Whanaungatanga and Identity for Well-being in Rangatahi Māori: Creating a Scale Using the Youth19 Rangatahi Smart Survey." *MAI Journal* 10, no. 2 (2021): 93–105. https://doi.org/10.20507/MAIJournal.2021.10.2.3.

Greaves, Lara, Sam Manuela, Emerald Muriwai, Lucy Cowie, Cinnamon Lindsay, Correna Matika, Carla A. Houkamau, and Chris Sibley. "The Multidimensional Model of Māori Identity and Cultural Engagement: Measurement Equivalence Across Diverse Māori Groups." *The New Zealand Journal of Psychology* 46, no. 1 (2017): 24–35.

Harmsworth, Garth, and Shaun Awatere. "Indigenous Māori Knowledge and Perspectives of Ecosystems." In *Ecosystem Services in New Zealand—Conditions and Trends*, edited by John R. Dymond, 274–286. Wellington: Manaaki Whenua Press, 2013.

Harris, Aroha. *Hīkoi: Forty Years of Māori Protest*. Wellington: Huia Publishers, 2004.

Houkamau, Carla A., Petar Milojev, Lara Greaves, Kiri Dell, Chris Sibley, and Jean Phinney. "Indigenous Ethnic Identity, In-Group Warmth, and Psychological Wellbeing: A Longitudinal Study of Māori." *Current Psychology* 42 (2023): 3542–3558.

Houkamau, Carla A., and Chris Sibley. "Māori Cultural Efficacy and Subjective Wellbeing: A Psychological Model and Research Agenda." *Social Indicators Research* 103 (2010): 379–398. https://doi.org/10.1007/s11205-010-9705-5.

Houkamau, Carla A., and Chris Sibley. "The Role of Culture and Identity for Economic Values: A Quantitative Study of Māori Attitudes." *Journal of the Royal Society of New Zealand* 49, sup 1 (2019): 118–136.

Hudson, Maui, Nanibaa' A. Garrison, Rogena Sterling, Nadine Caron, Keolu Fox, Joseph Yracheta, Jane Anderson, Phil Wilcox, Laura Arbour, Alex Brown et al. "Rights, Interests and Expectations: Indigenous Perspectives on Unrestricted Access to Genomic Data." *Nature Reviews Genetics* 21, no. 6 (2020): Article 6. https://doi.org/10.1038/s41576-020-0228-x.

Huyser, Kimberly, Aggie Yellow Horse, Alena Kuhlemeier, and Michelle R. Huyser. "COVID-19 Pandemic and Indigenous Representation in Public Health Data." *American Journal of Public Health* 111, no. S3 (2021): S208–S214.

Indigenous Health Group. *Social Determinants and Indigenous Health: The International Experience and Its Policy Implications*. Report on Specially Prepared Documents and Discussion at the International Symposium on the Social Determinants of Indigenous Health, Adelaide, for the Commission on Social Determinants of Health, 2007.

Jackson, Moana. *The Maori and the Criminal Justice System: A New Perspective: He Whaipaanga Hou*. Wellington: Department of Justice, 1987.

Kukutai, Tahu. "The Structure of Urban Māori Identities." In *Indigenous in the City: Contemporary Identities and Cultural Innovation*, edited by Evelyn Peters and Chris Andersen, 311–333. Vancouver: UBC Press, 2013.

Kukutai, Tahu, and Amanda Black. "CARE-ing for Indigenous Non-Human Genomic Data: Rethinking Our Approach." *Science* 385, no. 6708 (2024). https://doi.org/10.1126/science.adr2493.

Kukutai, Tahu, Kyla Campbell-Kamariera, Aroha Mead, Kirikowhai Mikaere, Caleb Moses, Jesse Whitehead, and Donna Cormack. *Māori Data Governance Model*. Rotorua: Te Kāhui Raraunga, 2023.

Kukutai, Tahu, Vanessa Clark, Chris Culnane, and Vanessa Teague. *Māori Data Sovereignty and Offshoring Māori Data*. Rotorua: Te Kāhui Raraunga, 2022.

Kukutai, Tahu, and Moana Rarere. "Iwi Sex Ratios in the New Zealand Population Census: Why Are Women So Dominant?" *New Zealand Population Review* 43 (2017): 63–92.

Kukutai, Tahu, Andrew Sporle, and Matthew Roskruge. "Expressions of Whānau." In *Families and Whānau Status Report 2016*. Wellington: Social Policy Research and Evaluation Unit, 2016.

Kukutai, Tahu, Andrew Sporle, and Matthew Roskruge. *Subjective Whānau Wellbeing in Te Kupenga*. Wellington: Social Policy Research and Evaluation Unit, 2017.

Mahuika, Nepia. *Rethinking Oral History and Tradition: An Indigenous Perspective*. Oxford: Oxford University Press, 2019.

Maiam nayri Wingara Data Sovereignty Collective, the Australian Indigenous Governance Institute & Lowitja Institute. *Indigenous Data Governance Communiqué*. Maiam nayri Wingara, 2023.

Matika, Correna, Sam Manuela, Emerald Muriwai, Carla A. Houkamau, and Chris Sibley. "Cultural Efficacy Predicts Increased Self-Esteem for Māori: The Mediating Effect of Rumination." *New Zealand Journal of Psychology* 56, no. 3 (2017): 176–185.

Mühlhoff, Rainer. "Predictive Privacy: Collective Data Protection in the Context of Artificial Intelligence and Big Data." *Big Data & Society* 10, no. 1 (2023): 20539517231166886.

Orange, Claudia. *The Treaty of Waitangi*. Wellington: Bridget Williams Books, 1987.

Pere, Rangimarie. "Te Wheke: Whaia Te Maramatanga Me Te Aroha." In *Women and Education in Aotearoa*, edited by Susan Middleton, 6–19. Auckland: Allen & Unwin, 1988.

Rainie, Stephanie Carroll, Desi Rodriguez-Lonebear, and Andrew Martinez. *Policy Brief: Indigenous Data Sovereignty in the United States*. Tucson: Native Nations Institute, University of Arizona, 2017.

Reid, Papaarangi, Donna Cormack, and Sarah-Jane Paine. "Colonial Histories, Racism and Health—The Experience of Māori and Indigenous Peoples." *Public Health* 172 (2019): 119–124.

Research Data Alliance COVID-19 Indigenous Data Working Group. "Data Sharing Respecting Indigenous Data Sovereignty." In *RDA COVID-19 Working Group: Recommendations and Guidelines on Data Sharing*. Research Data Alliance, 2020.

Roberts, Mere, Bradford Haami, Richard Benton, Tere Satterfield, Melissa L. Finucane, Mark Henare, and Manuka Henare. "Whakapapa as a Māori Mental Construct: Some Implications for the Debate Over Genetic Modification of Organisms." *The Contemporary Pacific* 16, no. 1 (2004): 1–28.

Robson, Bridget, and Ricci Harris, eds. *Hauora: Māori Standards of Health IV. A Study of the Years 2000–2005*. Wellington: Te Rōpū Rangahau Hauora a Eru Pōmare, 2007.

Rodriguez-Lonebear, Desi. "The Blood Line: Racialized Boundary Making and Citizenship Among Native Nations." *Sociology of Race and Ethnicity* 7, no. 4 (2021): 527–542.

Rodriguez-Lonebear, Desi, Nicolás E. Barceló, Randall Akee, and Stephanie Russo Carroll. "Research Full Report: American Indian Reservations and COVID-19:

Correlates of Early Infection Rates in the Pandemic." *Journal of Public Health Management and Practice* 26, no. 4 (2020): 371.
Roskruge, Matthew. *Māori Social Capital and Wellbeing*. Paper presented at the New Zealand Association of Economists, Wellington, June 23, 2021.
Royal, Te Ahukaramū Charles. "Māori—Urbanisation and Renaissance." *Te Ara—The Encyclopedia of New Zealand*, 2005. https://teara.govt.nz/en/maori/page-5.
Smith, Linda Tuhiwai. *Decolonizing Methodologies: Research and Indigenous Peoples*. New York: Zed Books, 1999.
Special Rapporteur on the Right to Privacy. *Big Data and Open Data Taskforce Report* (A/73/438). New York: Office of the High Commissioner for Human Rights (UN Human Rights), 2018. www.ohchr.org/en/documents/thematic-reports/a73438-report-special-rapporteur-right-privacy.
Special Rapporteur on the Right to Privacy. *Report on the Protection and Use of Health-Related Data* (A/74/277). New York: Office of the High Commissioner for Human Rights (UN Human Rights), 2019. www.ohchr.org/en/calls-for-input/report-thee-protection-and-use-health-related-data.
Stats NZ. "Te Reo Māori Proficiency and Support Continues to Grow." 2022. www.stats.govt.nz/news/te-reo-maori-proficiency-and-support-continues-to-grow/.
Tajfel, Henri, and John Turner. "The Social Identity Theory of Intergroup Behavior." In *Psychology of Intergroup Relations*, edited by Stephen Worchel and William G. Austin, 7–24. Chicago: Nelson Hall, 1986.
Te Kāhui Raraunga. *Māori Data Governance Co-Design Review*. Rotorua: Te Kāhui Raraunga, 2021b.
Te Kāhui Raraunga. *Tawhiti Nuku: Māori Data Governance Co-Design Outcomes Report*. Rotorua: Te Kāhui Raraunga, 2021a.
Te Mana Raraunga. *Principles of Māori Data Sovereignty*, 2018. https://www.temanararaunga.maori.nz/nga-rauemi.
Te Whaiti, Pania, Marie McCarthy, and Arohia Durie. *Mai i Rangiātea: Māori Wellbeing and Development*. Auckland: Auckland University Press and Bridget Williams Books, 1997.
Tsosie, Krystal, Joseph Yracheta, and Donna Dickenson. "Overvaluing Individual Consent Ignores Risks to Tribal Participants." *Nature Reviews Genetics* 20 (2019): 497–498. https://doi.org/10.1038/s41576-019-0161-z.
Waatea News. "World-First Data Storage Infrastructure Solution Built by Iwi Māori, for Iwi Māori." June 4, 2024. https://waateanews.com/2024/06/04/world-first-data-storage-infrastructure-solution-built-by-iwi-maori-for-iwi-maori/.
Walling, Julie, Desi Small-Rodriguez, and Tahu Kukutai. "Tallying Tribes: Waikato-Tainui in the Census and Iwi Register." *Social Policy Journal of New Zealand* 36 (2009): 2–15.
Walker, Ranginui. *Ka Whawhai Tonu Mātou: Struggle Without End*. Auckland: Penguin, 1990.
Walter, Maggie, and Michelle Suina. "Indigenous Data, Indigenous Methodologies and Indigenous Data Sovereignty." *International Journal of Social Research Methodology* 22, no. 3 (2019): 233–243. https://doi.org/10.1080/13645579.2018.1531228.
Webber, Melinda, Elizabeth McKinely, and John Hattie. "The Importance of Race and Ethnicity: An Exploration of New Zealand Pāhekā, Māori, Samoan and Chinese Adolescent Identity." *New Zealand Journal of Psychology* 42, no. 2 (2013): 17–28.
Williams, Ashlea D., Terryann C. Clark, and Sonia Lewycka. "The Associations Between Cultural Identity and Mental Health Outcomes for Indigenous Māori Youth in New Zealand." *Frontiers in Public Health* 6 (2018): 319.

Yellow Horse, Aggie J., and Kimberly Huyser. "Indigenous Data Sovereignty and COVID-19 Data Issues for American Indian and Alaska Native Tribes and Populations." *Journal of Population Research* (2021): 1–5.

Zuboff, Shoshana. *The Age of Surveillance Capitalism: The Fight for a Human Future at the New Frontier of Power*. London: Profile Books, 2019.

6
STATISTICS, STIGMATIZATION AND STEREOTYPING

The Importance of Authentic Partnering and Community Engagement to Validate Indigenous Statistical Research

Chelsea Gabel

> **CHAPTER LEARNING OBJECTIVES**
>
> **Objective 1**: Draw upon specific cases of deficit-based, statistical research in healthcare to explore the incompatibility of statistical research and Indigenous Peoples in the absence of community-engaged, strength-based approaches that benefit Indigenous nations, communities and people.
>
> **Objective 2**: Argue the need for Indigenous researchers and communities to be supported in developing technical capacity to effectively counter, participate in or lead statistical research.
>
> **Objective 3**: Explore an Indigenous Data Sovereignty case study to describe why statistics and their distinctive benefits can be critically important for Indigenous health, wellbeing, governance and nation rebuilding.

Introduction

This manuscript's argument to date has been that statistics have been used primarily outside of Indigenous communities, nearly always without their knowledge, consent or involvement in any part of the research process that led to their creation. This, in turn, has reinforced stereotypes and deficit-based approaches that pathologize Indigenous life experiences in our communities and nations. Nonetheless, statistics—particularly in a research context—remain an important part of the many improvements in human health and wellbeing over the past centuries. They offer powerful tools for explaining and predicting health outcomes, they help influence decision-makers in making public health decisions and can help guide the direction of human responses to epidemics and pandemics. In particular, statistics in research are responsible for many improvements in marginalized populations, including Indigenous health and wellbeing. However, historically Indigenous Peoples have been research subjects rather than participants; they have been subjected to unethical experiments, misrepresented in academic literature, and have had their knowledge exploited (Lux 1998; Mosby 2013; Smith 2012). While the long history of Indigenous communities being subject to unethical behaviour by researchers is well documented, research data continues to be taken and used without permission, resulting in extreme breaches of trust. For example, in 2017 the Chief of Pictou Landing First Nation in Nova Scotia, Canada, willingly participated in a medical study but was subjected to additional scans without her knowledge or consent as part of a separate study on the livers of Indigenous subjects (Jones 26 February 2024). As a result of these unethical practices, some communities have organized their own research and ethics processes—the Manitoulin Anishinaabek Research Review Committee (MARRC) and the Six Nations Research Ethics Committee, for example. These community-based policies and processes can help ensure that researcher priorities align with community goals, concerns and cultural norms, particularly given the diversity of Indigenous communities in Canada (Maar et al. 2007) which university and hospital research ethics boards are not necessarily positioned to understand. Furthermore, Indigenous scholars are conducting research using their own methods and methodologies (Andersen and Gabel 2024; Walter and Andersen 2013; Kovach 2010), which present an avenue to the production of knowledge that is meaningful in Indigenous contexts, created by and for Indigenous Peoples. Hayward and colleagues further note,

> there is a need for decolonizing and Indigenizing quantitative research methods . . . to better address the public health needs of Indigenous populations who continue to face health inequities because of colonial systems, as well as inaccurate and incomplete data collection about themselves.
> *(2021, 2; Walter and Andersen 2013)*

This chapter is adapted from a previously published article entitled *Deficit-Based Indigenous Health Research and the Stereotyping of Indigenous Peoples* (see Hyett et al. 2019), which described the ways in which deficit-based discourses in Indigenous health research have historically perpetuated negative characterizations of Indigenous Peoples. As was explored in Chapter 1, deficit-based research has more often than not included statistics to quantify absence of health and wellbeing markers or presence of illness. This often creates a narrative with far-reaching effects for Indigenous communities already subjected to stigmatization, especially when researchers fail to explore the structural roots of health deficits—namely colonization, Westernization and intergenerational trauma. Doing so risks conflating complex structural health and wellbeing related challenges with individually based/inherent Indigenous characterizations.

Indigenous Research Ethics Protocols and Principles

Presently, ethical policy in Canada outlines the importance of free, prior and informed consent for both Indigenous and non-Indigenous research participants. Indigenous Peoples in Canada in particular have some additional protections through the Tri-Council Policy Statement: Chapter 9 Ethical Conduct for Research Involving Humans (TCPS2), that provides guidance on Research Involving First Nations, Inuit and Métis People of Canada (Canadian Institutes of Health Research, Natural Sciences and Engineering Research Council of Canada, and Social Sciences and Humanities Research Council of Canada 2018). All institutions that are eligible to administer and receive funding from the three federal funding research agencies in Canada—the Social Sciences and Humanities Research Council of Canada (SSHRC), the Canadian Institutes of Health Research (CIHR) and the Natural Science and Engineering Research Council of Canada (NSERC) must adhere to the TCPS2 guidelines. The TCPS2 chapter on Indigenous research was established as national policy in 2010 and was largely based on the prior 2007 guidelines, developed with wide Indigenous community consultation and published by the Canadian Institutes of Health Research (CIHR) (CIHR Guidelines for Health Research Involving Aboriginal People, Canadian Institutes of Health Research 2007). However, the previous CIHR guidelines were specific to health research with Indigenous Peoples, as opposed to Indigenous research in general. Having these separate guidelines specific to Indigenous health research strengthened the ethics process in many ways (Castellano and Reading 2010). The TCPS2 has gone through two other iterations in 2014 and 2018; however, Chapter 9 remained untouched until recently and is currently undergoing its first iteration which will include an updated literature review, coordination with other agency initiatives, advice from a technical advisory committee and consultation with Indigenous organizations with a national mandate.

While the TCPS2 Chapter 9 is designed to serve as a framework for the ethical conduct of research involving Indigenous Peoples, it is offered in a spirit of respect and is not intended to override or replace ethical guidance offered by Indigenous Peoples themselves. As described earlier in this manuscript, some First Nations researchers align themselves with other frameworks such as OCAP® principles (ownership, control, access and possession). For Inuit, the Qanuippitaa? National Inuit Health Survey was developed in 2018 by Inuit from across the country in partnership with Inuit Tapiriit Kanatami (ITK), the national Inuit organization in Canada. The survey makes certain that the data is reflective of Inuit life, requires adapting the ways in which data is collected and ensures that those collecting the data are from the region. ITK also released its National Inuit Strategy on Research (2018) which calls to have Inuit at the forefront of research agendas with actionable items to address the high number of non-Inuit researchers conducting work in the North. The strategy does not call on researchers to implement the First Nations Principles of OCAP®, but does reference that Inuit partnership in the governance of Inuit Nunangat research is necessary to broker Inuit access, ownership and control over Inuit Nunangat data and information. Most recently in 2022, the Government of Canada committed $6.4 million in directed funding to establish an Inuit Research Network. This funding invests in the four Inuit regions and their respective land claims organizations, Inuvialuit Regional Corporation, Nunavut Tunngavik Incorporated, Makivik Corporation and the Nunatsiavut Government, to guide research that strengthens Inuit health (Gabel and Henry 2024). Finally, Métis researchers and organizations are also developing their data governance principles. In 2023, *the Saskatchewan Métis Health Research and Data Governance Principles*© were created by Drs. Caroline Tait and Robert Henry in partnership with the Métis Nation Saskatchewan (MN-S). They were designed for use by MN-S and other Métis rights-holders in their research and data sharing partnerships, specifically health institutions such as the Ministry of Health Saskatchewan (MOH-S), the Saskatchewan Population Health and Evaluation Research Unit, Saskatchewan Health Quality Council and eHealth Saskatchewan. The principles can also be applied to other sectors such as education, justice, housing, social welfare, agriculture, environment and natural resources and are designed to recognize and support the diversity of Métis populations including rural, urban and remote communities and organizations with the aim of allowing for the flexibility of local, regional, provincial and national adaptation to research and data sharing agreements. These principles have been incorporated into a larger national Métis health data strategy (Gabel and Henry 2024) with the goal of being embedded into the latest TCPS2 chapter 9 iteration.

Additionally, the Ontario Federation of Indigenous Friendship Centres developed the Utility, Self-Voicing, Access and Inter-Relationality (USAI)

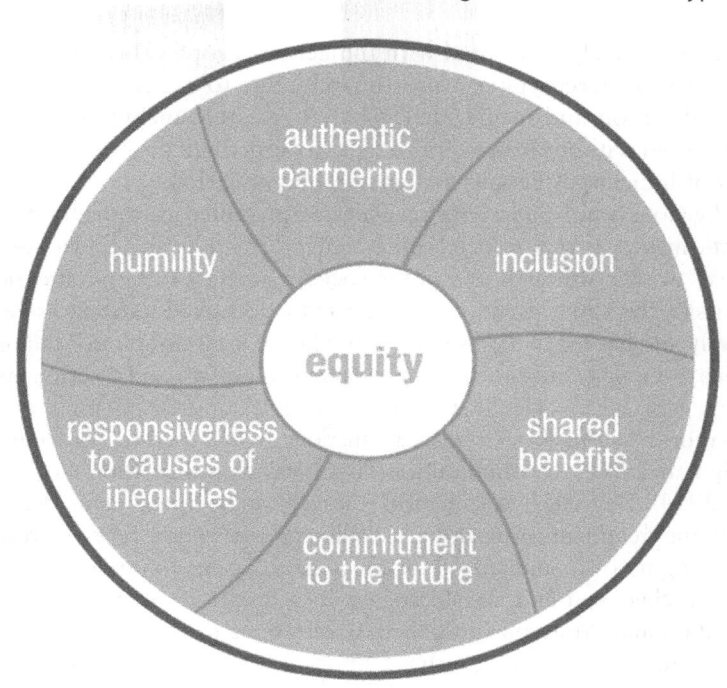

FIGURE 6.1 Canadian Coalition for Global Health Research—Principles for Global Health Research

Research Framework (USAI 2012), and the International Indigenous Data Sovereignty Interest Group (within the Research Data Alliance) developed the CARE Principles for Indigenous Data Governance (The Global Indigenous Data Alliance, GIDA-global.org, September 2019). Different frameworks may be appropriate for different projects and, in some instances, are more comprehensive than the TCPS2 guidelines (First Nations Information Governance Centre 2014). In addition, the Canadian Coalition for Global Health Research (CCGHR) Principles for Global Health Research (Figure 6.1) hold relevancy for Indigenous health research. CCGHR principles are based on a number of works including the aforementioned CIHR guidelines (Canadian Coalition for Global Health Research 2015).

From Statistics to Stereotypes: The Invention of Aboriginal Diabetes

Deficit-based, statistical research can contribute to stigmatization when problematic health and wellbeing issues are repeatedly characterized in the context of a specific population. Additionally, when any given health deficit is repetitively associated with Indigenous Peoples through research, there is risk of stereotyping. Unfortunately, due to a lack of exposure to critical education and media, deficit-based research, including the use of statistics used without proper framing, can perpetuate negative characterizations of Indigenous Peoples (Allan and Smylie 2015).

If Indigenous health and wellbeing issues are presented in academic literature with little historical and/or social contextual information, an "epidemiological paradox" arises. Although it is in the society's interest to bring attention to health risks, this same attention has repeatedly portrayed Indigenous Peoples negatively and has led to a presumed "population level pathology" that is "an insidious, pervasive and subtle form of structural racism and discrimination" (Reading et al. 2007). The First Nations Principles of OCAP® point out that information resulting from research can potentially "lead to discrimination and stigmatization" of communities (First Nations Information Governance Centre 2014). Nevertheless, statistical research can be beneficial in identifying and offering treatment for health and wellbeing challenges. To avoid transferring the stigma of a stigmatized health issue to entire communities or peoples, researchers can and should engage in a discussion of the influence of colonization and Westernization, thereby reframing the issue and reassigning the shame to such influences, rather than to Indigenous Peoples. Researchers should also consider the extent to which their research may reinforce stereotypes about Indigenous Peoples. If a given health or wellbeing issue has been extensively characterized, it may be worthwhile reframing the approach or researching topics identified as being of interest to communities, rather than potentially contributing to further stereotype reinforcement.

One example of a health challenge with associated stigma is type 2 diabetes. Research into high levels of type 2 diabetes in Indigenous communities has included substantial investigation of potential genetic explanations, sometimes referred to as the "Thrifty Gene Hypothesis." This hypothesis, which was invented by American geneticist James Neel in a 1962 study and reinforced by Robert Hegele's study of the Sandy Lake First Nation in northern Ontario in the 1990s, suggests that Indigenous People are genetically predisposed to type 2 diabetes and obesity due to their alleged hunter-gatherer genes. While both researchers retracted their findings, Canadian clinical guidelines and medical professionals continued to cite the thrifty gene hypothesis. In 2011, for example, Health Canada issued a report entitled *Diabetes in Canada*, in which it referred to genetic risk factors, specifically the thrifty gene effect, being associated with the increased rates of obesity and diabetes in the Aboriginal population (Hay 2018).

In his research that analyses the extent to which the "thrifty gene hypothesis" remains embedded within regimes of Canadian healthcare, Travis Hay argues, "metabolic myths about Indigenous Peoples remain in the registers of Canadian science and medicine long after they had been theoretically and empirically challenged, debunked and rejected. In this way, "Aboriginal diabetes" is analogous to what used to be called "Indian tuberculosis," in that settlers are blaming Indigenous biologies, not colonial policies, for poor health" (Hay 2018, 248). Statistically, Indigenous Peoples are seen to be more adversely affected by diabetes; however, as we see from Hay's analysis, without the positioning of statistics within a colonial context, genetic explanations are supported, which ignores the Indigenous experience, maintaining biological explanations.

To avoid stigmatization and deficit-based research, health issues must be contextualized. Such an example is demonstrated in a 2016 study evaluating a harvest sharing program in Northern Ontario (Gates et al. 2016). The authors highlighted a number of potentially stigmatizing deficits, including reduction in dietary quality and physical activity and an increase in obesity in First Nations communities. However, they explained that the reasons for these challenges were complex and include the transition to Western lifestyles and dietary changes that First Nations experience at a rapid rate, which at least in part contributes to their health challenges. In this way, the authors were laudably careful to contextualize their findings and to inform readers of some of the root causes of the examined deficits, thus mitigating risk of stigma. Importantly, avoidance of harm does not equate to total avoidance of research concerning stigmatized topics. For example, if a community would like to explore local prevalence of type 2 diabetes, such as in a 2009 study by Wahi and colleagues, the research can confer benefit in that they provide a community with desired community-level data and knowledge translation (Wahi et al. 2009).

Responsiveness to Community Needs

The data ecosystem framework that forms our rough methodological approach asks readers to think through the complexity of statistical data from the identification of local concerns, to the decision to undertake a statistical approach, to the collection, "cleaning," interpretation and communication of the eventual data. Indigenous presence is key to ethically undertaking each and all parts of this "chain." A significant issue that can arise in deficit-based, statistical research, in contradistinction, is a lack of responsiveness. Responsiveness is a principle that refers to the obligation of global health researchers to use research to respond to inequities affecting the participants in their research, rather than exploit inequities for research or conduct research irrelevant to the communities involved (Canadian Coalition for Global Health Research 2015). This concept of responsiveness is outlined in the CCGHR Principles and aligns with the

Inuit Tapiriit Kanatami's assertion that research must be a tool for creating social equity (National Inuit Strategy on Research 2018).

Statistics may be particularly prone to identifying inequities without explaining how such an identification acts to mitigate inequities or confer benefit. It is important to note that Indigenous Peoples may be polarized on certain topics, including whether exploration of a particular health or wellbeing deficit confers sufficient benefit or produces significant harm. In these scenarios, researchers are encouraged to engage all stakeholders to the extent possible, but to also consider the risk of increasing polarization, which may "actually impede the advancement of social justice" (Canadian Institutes of Health Research, Natural Sciences and Engineering Research Council of Canada, and Social Sciences and Humanities Research Council of Canada 2018). The CIHR guidelines recommend collaborating with community members in cases of polarization to assess conflicts of interest and to look to existing community structures and systems for resolving disputes (CIHR Guidelines for Health Research Involving Aboriginal People 2010).

Historically, lack of responsiveness has been an issue in Indigenous health research and is exemplified by, for example, nutritional experiments carried out on children who were forced into the residential school system. These experiments were carried out despite the government and researchers already recognizing malnutrition as a systemic issue in residential schools (Mosby 2013). Rather than trying to intervene to improve the nutritional status of these children, the researchers exploited the malnourished children to test various hypotheses (Mosby 2013). The research characterized by Ian Mosby demonstrates that researchers working in the residential school system not only remained unresponsive in this sense, but also exploited and perpetuated an existing inequity (starvation and malnutrition) with no benefit to those being studied. Problems relating to responsiveness are also a contemporary issue. For example, a 2011 study of the prevalence of tobacco, alcohol and drug use by Indigenous youth in Canada was characterized using existing data (Elton-Marshall et al. 2011). This information may have been useful in attracting resources or informing policy. However, such benefits were not discussed, contextualization for the issue was not provided and no disclosure of Indigenous collaboration was present. Overall, it is impossible for a reader to discern if such research was desired by or responsive to the interests of Indigenous Peoples. Deficit-based, statistical research is particularly prone to lacking responsiveness because identifying a problem, even when researchers are well intentioned, does not intrinsically result in transformative health interventions or improved social equity, since this must be done in partnership rather than as a result of concerns by only one set of stakeholders. Importantly, responsiveness can be a component of any research methodology.

Nor does an ethic of responsiveness necessarily exclude, for example, randomized controlled trials (the apogee of "scientific method") where benefit cannot be known in advance, if the involved communities agree that the trial has the potential to result in benefit.

Drawing on Community Engagement to Validate Indigenous Statistical Research

The statistical process has tended to be more prone to harming Indigenous communities when researchers fail to engage Indigenous Peoples, communities and nations as knowledge partners in the process. An important point to consider with regard to Indigenous health and wellbeing research in particular—and especially for deficit narratives—is the difficulty for Indigenous and non-Indigenous researchers to provide the full context regarding any particular deficit. Researchers must realize that they may never be an expert on the lived experience of health and wellbeing related challenges facing Indigenous Peoples, because of their lived experiences (Aveling 2012). Additionally, the potential benefit of characterizing a health deficit cannot be presumed absent Indigenous engagement (Andersen and Gabel 2024). Not recognizing Indigenous voices creates epistemic injustice by excluding members of Indigenous collectives from formulating their own research and asserting their self-determined knowledge (Carel and Kidd 2014). In their discussion of epistemic injustice in healthcare, Carel and Kidd assert that healthcare providers are epistemically privileged because they "occupy an authoritative procedural role in epistemic exchanges, for instance by acting as gatekeepers controlling which persons and groups are included, and what degree of credibility and authority they are assigned" (2014).

The same epistemic privilege applies to Western researchers. The frameworks already referenced support Indigenous engagement in all aspects of research: The First Nations Principles of OCAP®, the CCGHR principle of shared benefits and inclusion which draws upon OCAP®, the Inuit Tapiriit Kanatami's National Inuit Strategy on Research, and community-specific policies (Maar et al. 2007). The substantial resources required for meaningful engagement may have historically discouraged some researchers, as funding systems have tended to be inadequate for such approaches. The Indigenous Mentorship Networks (IMN) and the Network Environments for Indigenous Health Research (NEIHR) have both been established by CIHR and speak to the fundamental idea that Indigenous Peoples and communities are taking control of their own research and community needs (Government of Canada News Release 2019).

Another example of deficit-based research that does not disclose any sort of Indigenous engagement and participation is a 2011 study relating to effects on Inuit children of maternal "binge drinking" during pregnancy (Burden et al. 2011). With a lack of discussion around the factors related to consumption of alcohol by pregnant Inuit women, the article left readers to draw their own colonially inscribed conclusions, based on stereotypes and bias, that Inuit mothers are harmful to their children. Inuit participation could have resulted in helpful contextualization.

By contrast, an example of research that effectively demonstrated authentic partnering and privileging of Indigenous voice is a 2014 study relating to enacted stigma and HIV risk behaviours among sexual minority Indigenous youth in Canada, New Zealand and the United States (Saewyc et al. 2014). This paper included multiple Indigenous authors, Indigenous and sexual minority research team members, Indigenous advisory groups and community consultations, in all parts of the statistical process (Saewyc et al. 2011). Prior to the study, the research team additionally consulted with other Indigenous Peoples in Canada, New Zealand and Native American researchers about the "purpose, design, sampling, and measurement issues" (Saewyc et al. 2011). A Māori advisory group was consulted continuously about interpretation and dissemination, and additional advisory engagement with other Indigenous entities was sought (Saewyc et al. 2011). This work clearly prioritizes Indigenous voice and took a number of steps to engage guidance from Indigenous stakeholders.

When weighing the benefits and harms of research, one must consider restoring control to Indigenous Peoples as a benefit. Additionally, perpetuation of a deficit discourse through statistics should be considered a valid harm. An important way to restore control is to privilege Indigenous voices in Indigenous health and wellbeing statistics, including the creation, collection and communicative narratives, which will in turn reduce risk of harm from deficit-based, statistical research due to Indigenous input on framing and dissemination (Hyett et al. 2018). There may be, nonetheless, situations where disagreement about interpretation arise between researchers and the community. At minimum, if these cannot be resolved, the TCPS2 states that researchers should either provide opportunities for the community to communicate its views or accurately and fairly report the disagreement in any dissemination activities. However, researchers must be cautious to consider what harms may be associated with disseminating information that a community believes to be inaccurate, especially in relation to deficit-based topics. Some ethical principles, such as the OCAP® principle of control, suggest that Indigenous communities should always direct how knowledge is shared (Royal Commission on Aboriginal Peoples 1996).

Questioning and deconstructing deficit-based, statistical approaches to research does not mean denying the existence of health and wellbeing inequities faced by Indigenous communities. However, in 2023, it is also fair to say the majority of health and wellbeing deficits in Indigenous communities in Canada have been extensively quantified. Many health and wellbeing researchers have been advocating a switch from deficit- based narratives to a strength-based community-engaged narrative. Strength-based research can amplify existing capacities in Indigenous communities to address health issues, rather than focusing on community "shortcomings" or "deficits" (Anderson et al. 2011; Brough et al. 2004; Tsey et al. 2007). This can provide a good model through which to identify health challenges, but also to address and present them in a positive and solution-oriented way. Andersen and Gabel have further argued that Indigenous research methodologies must include *any* methods—regardless of their ontological and epistemological stances—that benefit Indigenous nations, communities and people and that the specific methods employed are less important than the ethical relationship formed with the Indigenous communities and partner organizations (2023; see also Innes 2010).

Indigenous Futures: Research Sovereignty and Evidence-Based Practices

Dion and colleagues' 2017 report entitled *Indigenous Futures: Research Sovereignty in a Changing Social Science Landscape* suggests that technological changes are bringing in a new era of social science data creation, collection, analysis and dissemination, including by governments. For example, the Canadian government collects a wide range of administrative and observational (primarily survey-based) data related to Indigenous Peoples and communities. At the federal level, Statistics Canada publishes a report summarizing key indicators related to Indigenous Peoples in Canada based on census and administrative datasets (Statistics Canada 2015). Statistics Canada also administers or maintains many surveys or special survey modules of Indigenous Peoples in Canada, including the Aboriginal Children's Survey, Aboriginal Peoples Survey and National Household Survey, among many others. Dion and colleagues' note that while survey data are useful for both Indigenous and non-Indigenous academic and government researchers, "it is unclear how extensively these data are used and to what extent Indigenous researchers or communities are using them to answer community-driven research demands" (2017, 9).

Moreover, in recent years, the Canadian government has turned their attention to the promotion and application of "evidence-based" administration, policy, programs and services. While Indigenous Peoples globally remain concerned that current Western evidence-based practice places too strong a value on Western methods and scientific rigour of research evidence over Indigenous ways of knowing (Luke et al. 2022), there remains an urgency of ensuring that Indigenous Peoples in Canada have the institutional, organizational and human resources to actively critique, participate in and lead technical research with clear policy implications, at all of its stages. Without these types of resources, Indigenous perspectives are at risk of being ignored. undervalued or stereotyped, particularly in instances of evidence-based policy making (Dion et al. 2017).

Research in sociology, economics, political science and, more recently, Indigenous Studies has become increasingly quantitative (Dion et al. 2019; Hayward et al. 2021; Walter and Andersen 2013). Thus, there is an increased urgency for Indigenous researchers and communities to understand various research methods, including qualitative and quantitative methodologies that are used by universities, government and consultants. Learning these skills could also enhance self-determination in research and nation rebuilding. Academic researchers are well positioned to lead this process in a way that emphasizes relationship building with Indigenous communities and nations, builds capacity and integrates Indigenous understandings and approaches to health and wellbeing. Dion and colleagues argue that while it is important to understand and build capacity for Indigenous participation in social science research, including non-Indigenous ways of knowing, it is not because quantitative and statistical methods provide a "better" way of knowing but, rather, an acknowledgment of the structural position of power accorded to mainstream, academic methodologies (2017, 10). They note, "If Indigenous researchers and communities are to be supported in developing sufficient technical capacity to effectively counter, participate in, or lead social science research, they need to be familiar with leading qualitative and quantitative methodologies." Institutional and organizational resources are imperative in this process-with the capacity to enforce the principles articulated by Indigenous communities (First Nations Information Governance Centre (FNIGC) n.d.) or Tri-Council Agencies (Canadian Institutes of Health Research, Natural Sciences and Engineering Research Council of Canada, and Social Sciences and Humanities Research Council of Canada 2014). Indeed, in Canadian health research, building Indigenous research capacity has been essential to ensuring that Indigenous Peoples, communities and nations were given voice and became partners or leaders in research (Anderson et al. 2011).

Indigenous Experiences With Digital Technology: An Application of Mixed-Methods Design in Community-Driven Research

Some of the important benefits of statistics, particularly concerning Indigenous Peoples, are evident by drawing upon projects that have embraced it. In this section, I briefly detail a project that embodies a mixed-methods, community-driven, strength-based approach to research and the rich benefits statistical research can deliver for researchers, communities and other partners. In March 2014, I was awarded an external grant to examine Indigenous experiences with digital technology and its impact on their health and wellbeing. The research and partnership model of the project were built upon long-standing, collaborative relationships with Indigenous communities and brought together other key stakeholders across diverse sectors (government, private sector and not-for-profit) who share a deep interest in issues of digital technology, community engagement, self-determination, public policy and health and wellbeing with the goal of better understanding how the adoption of digital technology, specifically, the use of online voting, impacts Indigenous participation, self-determination and their overall health and wellbeing (Gabel and Goodman 2019).

The project is community-based and participatory, focusing on community partners generating knowledge about themselves and their communities. This commitment shapes the project design, methodological approach and dissemination strategies. All research was carried out *with* communities, taking their guidance on research design, research questions and project outcomes. The research team worked with Whitefish River First Nation (Ontario) on their Matrimonial Real property vote in 2015, Wasauksing First Nation (Ontario) for their Land Code ratification vote in 2017 and supported enhancement of digital literacy and an opinion poll on the production and sale of cannabis in Tsuut'ina Nation (Alberta) in 2018. Relationship building spanned over six years in Whitefish River First Nation and two years in Wasauksing First Nation and included multiple community visits, meetings, presentations, submissions for community newsletters, community reports and the training of Indigenous youth and elders.

The work with Tsuut'ina Nation has spanned over six years and included multiple community visits, a presentation for chief and council and facilitation of an event to build digital skills and literacy. In each case, the research design differed based on community co-authorship of the research instruments, input and preferences for knowledge creation. In addition to interviews and focus groups, community-wide surveys were co-designed with each First Nation (Gabel et al. 2017). The team also discussed and designed community-focused outputs that would contribute to the knowledge and capacity of the community. Ethics approvals were obtained from the university research ethics board, as well as from community research ethics boards and protocols. In addition, research and data sharing agreements and memoranda of understanding were negotiated and obtained with the communities. In the previously described cases, the community-engaged approach and the statistical data gathered in each community contributed to insight into the strengths and weaknesses of internet voting and digital technology, their utility for communities of diverse geographic and demographic conditions; increased knowledge to advise member communities about technology adoption and its impact on their health and wellbeing and a recognition that digital technology can aid participation in nation rebuilding.

Conclusion

Statistical research risks contributing to the stereotyping and stigmatization of Indigenous Peoples. Strength-based and solution-oriented research provides a promising alternative to this normative approach. Ensuring that Indigenous Peoples have authority over how they are researched and how they are portrayed as a result of that research is critical to producing effective and beneficial research. Understanding the problematic history of Indigenous health and wellbeing research in Canada demands significant accountability on the part of researchers to communities. Considering how statistical research may stigmatize communities is a harm that must be addressed in any project. Likewise, researchers should consider how their work is contributing to a more equitable future for participants and how the work itself is responsive to existing inequities. Framing Indigenous health disparities in an Indigenous context must expressly encompass colonization and Westernization, so that research can contribute to how non-Indigenous Peoples view Indigenous Peoples. Finally, strength-based research provides ways for researchers to enact the significant elements in existing ethics and good practices guidance. A simple and important measure to produce good Indigenous health and wellbeing research is to privilege Indigenous voice, as Indigenous Peoples are primary stakeholders in the research with their communities. Indigenous health and wellbeing research is inextricably connected to how the wider society perceives Indigenous Peoples, and how Indigenous Peoples are perceived inherently affects their overall health and wellbeing—and this must guide the approach of statisticians, epidemiologists, ethicists and health researchers to this field of work.

References

Allan, Billie, and Janet Smylie. *First Peoples, Second Class Treatment: The Role of Racism in the Health and Well-being of Indigenous Peoples in Canada*. Toronto, ON: The Wellesley Institute, 2015.

Andersen, Chris, and Chelsea Gabel. "Deciding in Relation with Community: An Indigenous Studies Critique of the Canadian Indigenous Methodologies Field." In *Indigenous Research Design Collection*, edited by Nathan Martin and Elizabeth Sumida Huaman, Chapter 4, 59–76. Canadian Scholars Press, 2024.

Anderson, John F., Basia Pakula, Victoria Smye, Virginia Peters (Siyamex), and Leslie Schroeder. "Strengthening Aboriginal Health through a Place-Based Learning Community." *International Journal of Indigenous Health* 7, no. 1 (June 7, 2011): 42–53. https://doi.org/10.3138/ijih.v7i1.29004.

Aveling, Nado. "'Don't Talk about What You Don't Know': On (Not) Conducting Research with/in Indigenous Contexts." *Critical Studies in Education* 54, no. 2 (2012): 203–214. https://doi.org/10.1080/17508487.2012.724021.

Brough, Mark K., Chelsea Bond, and Julian Hunt. "Strong in the City: Toward a Strength Based Approach in Indigenous Health Promotion." *Health Promotion Journal of Australia* 15, no. 3 (2004): 215–220.

Burden, Michael J., Anna Westerlund, Gina Muckle, Nathan Dodge, Éric Dewailly, Charles A. Nelson, Susan W. Jacobson, and Joe L. Jacobson. "The Effects of Maternal Binge Drinking During Pregnancy on Neural Correlates of Response Inhibition and Memory in Childhood." *Alcohol Clinical and Experimental Research* 35, no. 1 (2011): 69–82.

Canadian Coalition for Global Health Research. *CCGHR Principle for Global Health Research*, 2015.

Canadian Institutes of Health Research. *Government of Canada Invests Close to $101M in Indigenous Health Research Across the Country*. Government of Canada News Release, July 16, 2019.

Canadian Institutes of Health Research, Natural Sciences and Engineering Research Council of Canada, and Social Sciences and Humanities Research Council, Tri-Council Policy Statement: Ethical Conduct for Research Involving Humans, December 2018. Accessed July 21, 2024. www.pre.ethics.gc.ca/eng/documents/tcps2-2018-en-interactive-final.pdf.

Carel, Havi, and Ian J. Kidd. "Epistemic Injustice in Healthcare: A Philosophical Analysis." *Medicine, Health Care and Philosophy* 17, no. 4 (2014): 529–40.

Castellano, Marlene Brant, and Jeffrey Reading. "Policy Writing as Dialogue: Drafting an Aboriginal Chapter for Canada's Tri-council Policy Statement: Ethical Conduct for Research Involving Humans." *The International Indigenous Policy Journal* 1, no. 2 (2010): 1–18.

Dion, Michelle, Claudia Díaz Ríos, Kelsey Leonard, and Chelsea Gabel. "Research Methodology and Community Participation: A Decade of Indigenous Social Science Research in Canada." *Canadian Review of Sociology/Revue canadienne de sociologie* (2019): 122–146. https://doi.org/10.1111/cars.12270.

Dion, Michelle, Chelsea Gabel, Claudia Milena Diaz Rios, and Kelsey Leonard. 2017. "Indigenous Futures: Research Sovereignty in a Changing Social Science Landscape." Report Prepared for the SSHRC Knowledge Synthesis Imaging Canada's Future Workshop Series. Accessed July 22, 2024. https://indigenous-futures.ca/wp-content/uploads/2017/09/20170926.

Elton-Marshall, Tara, Scott T. Leatherdale, and Robyn Burkhalter. "Tobacco, Alcohol and Illicit Drug Use Among Aboriginal Youth Living Off-Reserve: Results from the Youth Smoking Survey." *CMAJ* 183, no. 8 (May 17, 2011). https://doi.org/10.1503/cmaj.101913.

First Nations Information Governance Centre. *Ownership, Control, Access and Possession (OCAPTM): The Path to First Nations Information Governance*, 2014.

Gabel, Chelsea, Karen Bird, Nicole Goodman, and Brian Budd. "The Impact of Digital Technology on Indigenous Participation, Self-Determination and

Governance." *Canadian Journal of Native Studies* XXXVI, no. 2 (2017): 107–127. Accessed July 22, 2024. www.digitalimpactfn.com/wp-content/uploads/2018/03/CJNS-article-1-1.pdf.

Gabel, Chelsea, and Nicole Goodman. "Methodological and Academic Challenges in Canadian Political Science: The Value of a Socially-Engaged Approach for Indigenous Research." *Politics, Groups and Identities* (2019). https://doi.org/10.1080/21565503.2019.1629314.

Gabel, Chelsea, and Robert Henry. *National Métis Health Data Strategy and Principles*. A Report Prepared for the Métis National Council of Canada (MNC), 2024.

Gates, Allison, Rhona M. Hanning, Michelle Gates, and Leonard J. Tsuji. "The Food and Nutrient Intakes of First Nations Youth Living in Northern Ontario, Canada: Evaluation of a Harvest Sharing Program." *Journal of Hunger and Environmental Nutrition* 11, no. 4 (2016): 491–508.

Hay, Trevor. "Commentary: The Invention of Aboriginal Diabetes: The Role of the Thrifty Gene Hypothesis in Canadian Health Care Provision." *Ethnicity & Disease* 28, Suppl 1 (August 9, 2018): 247–252. https://doi.org/10.18865/ed.28.S1.247.

Hayward, Ashley, Larissa Wodtke, Aimee Craft, Tabitha Robin, Janet Smylie, Sarah McConkey, Alexandra Nychuk, Chloe Healey, Leona Star, and Jaime Cidro. "Addressing the Need for Indigenous and Decolonized Quantitative Research Methods in Canada." *SSM—Population Health*, no. 15 (2021): 100899. https://doi.org/10.1016/j.ssmph.2021.100899.

Hyett, Sarah, Stacey Marjerrison, and Chelsea Gabel. "Improving Indigenous Health Research Among Indigenous Peoples in Canada." *Canadian Medical Association Journal* 190, no 20 (May 22, 2018): 616–621. Accessed July 22, 2024. www.cmaj.ca/content/190/20/E616.

Innes, Robert. "Introduction: Native Studies and Native Cultural Preservation, Revitalization and Persistence." *American Indian Culture and Research Journal* 34, no. 2 (2010): 1–9.

Inuit Tapiriit Kanatami. *National Inuit Strategy on Research*. Inuit Tapiriit Kanatami, 2018. https://www.itk.ca/national-inuit-strategy-on-research/.

Jones, Lindsay. "Nova Scotia Mi'kmaq Chief Launches Lawsuit Alleging Secret Medical Research." *The Globe and Mail*, February 26, 2024. www.theglobeandmail.com/canada/article-mikmaq-lawsuit-secret-medical-research/.

Kovach, Margaret. *Indigenous Methodologies: Characteristics, Conversations, and Contexts*. Reprint ed. Toronto: University of Toronto Press, 2010.

Luke, Joanne, Ebony Verbunt, Angela Zhang, et al. "Questioning the Ethics of Evidence-Based Practice for Indigenous Health and Social Settings in Australia." *BMJ Global Health* 7 (2022). https://doi.org/10.1136/bmjgh-2022-009167.

Lux, Maureen. "Perfect Subjects: Race, Tuberculosis, and the Qu'Appelle BCG Vaccine Trial." *Canadian Bulletin of Medical History* 15, no. 2 (1998): 277–295.

Maar, Marion A., Sutherland, Mariette, and McGregor, Lorrilee. "A Regional Model for Ethical Engagement: The First Nations Research Ethics Committee on Manitoulin Island." *Aboriginal Policy Research Consortium International (APRCi)* 112 (2007). Accessed July 22, 2024. https://ir.lib.uwo.ca/aprci/112.

Mosby, Ian. "Administering Colonial Science: Nutrition Research and Human Biomedical Experimentation in Aboriginal Communities and Residential Schools, 1942–1952." *Histoire Sociale/Social History* 46, no. 91 (2013): 145–172.

Reading, Jeffrey, Andrew Kmetic, and Valerie Gideon. *First Nations Wholistic Policy & Planning Model: Discussion Paper for the World Health Organization Commission on Social Determinants of Health*. Assembly of First Nations, 2007.

Royal Commission on Aboriginal Peoples. *Volume 5: Renewal: A Twenty-Year Commitment. Report of the Royal Commission on Aboriginal Peoples. Appendix E: Ethical Guidelines for Research*. Ottawa: Canada Communication Group, 1996.

Saewyc, Elizabeth M., Terry Clark, Lesley Barney, David Brunanski, and Yuka Homma. "Enacted Stigma and HIV Risk Behaviours Among Sexual Minority Indigenous Youth in Canada, New Zealand, and the United States." *Pimatisiwin* 11, no. 3 (2014): 411–420.

Smith, Linda Tuhiwai. 2012. *Decolonizing Methodologies: Research and Indigenous Peoples*. Otago University Press.

Statistics Canada. 2015. *Aboriginal Statistics at a Glance*. 2nd ed. Ottawa, ON: Statistics Canada. Accessed July 22, 2024. www.statcan.gc.ca/pub/89-645-x/89-645-x2015001-eng.htm.

Tait, Caroline, and Robert Henry. "Saskatchewan Métis Health Research and Data Governance Principles." Métis Nation of Saskatchewan, 2023. Accessed July 22, 2024.

Tsey, Komla, Andrew Wilson, Melissa Haswell-Elkins, et al. "Empowerment-Based Research Methods: A 10-Year Approach to Enhancing Indigenous Social and Emotional Wellbeing." *Australasian Psychiatry: Bulletin of Royal Australian and New Zealand College of Psychiatrists*, 15 Suppl 1 (2007). https://doi.org/10.1080/10398560701701163.

Wahi, Gita, Alexandra Zorzi, Andrew Macnab, and Constadina Panagiotopoulos. "Prevalence of Type 2 Diabetes, Obesity and the Metabolic Syndrome among Canadian First Nations Children in a Remote Pacific Coast Community." *Paediatrics and Child Health* 14, no. 2 (2009): 79–83.

Walter, Maggie, and Chris Andersen. *Indigenous Statistics: A Quantitative Research Methodology*. 1st ed. Routledge, 2013.

7
MÉTIS POPULATION DATA IN CANADA

A Conceptual Case Study

Chris Andersen and Chelsea Gabel

CHAPTER LEARNING OBJECTIVES

Objective 1: Discuss the consequences of the Métis being largely outside of the production of statistics about them.

Objective 2: Discuss the conceptual consequences of moving Métis census conversations away from a focus on self-identification toward one on *citizenship*.

Objective 3: Examine the ramifications of the conceptual move to a focus on citizenship for understanding much of the current data on Métis peoples and what it potentially means for future data strategies for Canada, Canadian provinces and various Métis orders of government.

The first half of this book has been dedicated to a discussion of the implications of understanding data not as isolated "things." Instead, we have encouraged readers to treat statistics as processes embedded across a number of complex, power-laden *fields*. These fields involve institutions, discourses, practices and conceptual and infrastructural elements. They also involve competencies, hierarchical struggles and, ultimately, attempts to control the meaning of data themselves. In this context, we have explored the extent to which, in many cases, Indigenous leaders, rights-holders, experts and agents have largely been excluded from the complexities of the statistical field that shape data about us. This finding is particularly relevant to discussions about data pertaining to the Métis nation.

In the first half of the book we likewise noted that this exclusion both reflects and reproduces Indigenous data dependency. If Indigenous Data Sovereignty is fundamentally about the right of Indigenous nations and our communities not only to collect, analyse and communicate our own data, but also to operate in partnership with agencies and actors who collect, analyse and disseminate data *about* us, it is clear that different Indigenous nations in different countries have achieved different levels of success in these regards. For example, until recently Statistics Canada—and by necessary association, Métis policy actors—utilized a measure of the "Métis population" based on a census question that could not distinguish between respondents self-identifying as citizens of the Métis nation—with its historical leaders, events, language(s) and culture—and those self-identifying as Métis due to a racialized understanding of Métis derived from their mixed Indigenous and non-Indigenous ancestry (see Andersen 2014 for an in-depth discussion on these dynamics).

In this conceptual case study, we will explore the current data situation of the Métis nation in Canada. We will show that compared to other Indigenous nations in other nation-states (and indeed, even within Canada), Métis data sovereignty is limited to geographical regions with no current national strategy and thus is still largely reliant on existing and externally generated national census data, which in turn shape the contours and boundaries of narratives about the Métis nation, in ways that diminish it. Moreover, Métis actors continue to hold only limited power to intervene in key parts of the census process. In turns, this limits their ability to shape Métis data in ways that produce alignment with their policy objectives and aspirations.

The rest of this conceptual case study is premised on the idea, introduced in the book's first part, that robust culturally and policy-relevant data constitute a key plank of Indigenous nation rebuilding globally. The need for such data is no different for the Métis nation than it is for any other Indigenous nation. At present, however, the Métis nation has limited participation in the official statistical cycle that collects information about us. This has required making use of Métis data that are often inconsistent, contradictory and unamenable to meaningful disaggregation or contextualization in relevant policy areas. Because we cannot be certain what census respondents who self-identify as Métis are indicating (i.e., whether they are indicating a connection to the Métis nation or merely to Indigenous/non-Indigenous ancestry), we cannot trust the policy relevance of data constructed from that ambiguity. Though this is likely the case in numerous sectors of policy relevant to the Métis nation, we focus here on an issue that has most focused the attention of Canadian demographers—Métis population trends—and we summarize the demographic profiles this focus has produced.

This case study will proceed in two broad parts. First, we briefly trace Statistics Canada's presentation of census-based Métis population trends over time, noting the arc of demographic and non-demographic explanations offered for those changes. We will note the extent to which Statistics Canada's analyses are premised on the (flawed) assumption that such a single thing as a Métis population exists. We critique this assumption by offering an alternative conceptual pathway that we believe better aligns with the kinds of data production that the Métis nation needs to best support its continued building process—Métis nation control of Métis nation census data. We begin, however, with the most widely recognized communications on the "state of the Métis population"—those generated through the census and disseminated by Statistics Canada.

Part I: Métis Population Trends, in a Nutshell

The Métis are a post-contact Indigenous People whose origins lie in the buffalo hunting economy of the late 18th-/early 19th-century northern plains, where their mobile society flourished, in relations with their First Nations relatives, by the mid-19th century. Their culture evolved through a distinctive combination of identity, language, land tenure, economic niche and family kinscapes. Today, the Métis National Council defines Métis as "a person who self-identifies as Métis, is distinct from other Indigenous Peoples in Canada, is of historic Métis Nation ancestry, and is accepted by the Métis Nation" (Métis National Council 2002). Métis scholar Adam Gaudry (2018) explains identity for Métis (commonly referred to as *Red River Métis*) is "grounded in a common culture and common historical experience, and a common sense of self that emerged in the historic 'Northwest', the prairies and parkland which are now [the Canadian provinces of] Manitoba, Saskatchewan, and Alberta" (p. 166).

While the largest self-identified Métis populations are in the Canadian provinces of Alberta, Ontario and British Columbia, the largest per capita populations are in Manitoba and Saskatchewan. These provinces reflect the historical regions where the first Métis communities emerged in the late 18th century when economic and politically strategic marriages between fur traders and Indigenous women became commonplace (Macdougall 2017). The children and communities born throughout this territory during the 18th century are considered the ethnogenesis of the Métis nation, as it developed its own distinct culture, language, dress, artwork, anthem, military and flag (Hogue 2015). The Métis became skilled linguists developing their own language, Michif, which is a distinct language that combines Cree or Anishinaabe and French and is distinct from Pidgin or Creole (Bakker 1997).

It is important to note at the beginning that the Métis nation has spent much of the 20th century excluded as active agents from the Canadian statistical field and distinctions-based research overall. On the one hand, a Métis self-identification question was absent from the Canadian census for more than a century, only being added to the full long-form census in 1986 (Statistics Canada 1989). On the other hand, a national organization that advocated for Métis nationhood—the Métis National Council—was not created until 1983, the outcome of complicated Indigenous political dynamics following in the wake of the repatriation of the 1982 Constitution Act (see Royal Commission on Aboriginal Peoples, vol. 4, ch. 5). The lack of *inclusion*, coupled with a lack of Métis nation-specific data *capacity*, have together conspired to ensure a near-erasure of relevant Métis population data about—let alone by—the Métis nation.

Harper (2018, 1) argues that demographers tend to explore population trends through one or more interactive combinations of three conceptual lenses: fertility, mortality and migration. And indeed, Statistics Canada's information about "the Métis population" following the inclusion of a Métis identity question in the 1996 census noted its sharp increases between census periods, with population-level increases far beyond what traditional demographic factors might have predicted. For example, in the 1996 census, Statistics Canada reported a Métis population of 204,120 and in the 2001 census, 292,000, an increase of 43 per cent in only five years (Statistics Canada 2003, 14). In explaining this increase, it was stated,

> [n]ot all of the growth can be attributed to demographic factors. Increased awareness of Métis issues coming from court cases related to Métis rights, and constitutional discussions, as well as better enumeration of Métis communities have contributed to the increase in the population identifying as Métis.
>
> *(2003, 14)*

In this context of this apparently improving coverage, Statistics Canada suggested that "the Métis population" in 2001 was the fastest growing Indigenous population in Canada, with more than two-thirds living in an urban area, and with nearly a quarter of the total population having moved in the previous five years. Métis were younger than the non-Aboriginal population, though older than the First Nations or Inuit populations (Statistics Canada 2003, 15). In 2006, Statistics Canada reported a Métis population of 389,785, an increase of roughly one-third since 2001, and an increase of 91 per cent over the previous decade between 1996 and 2006. This continued growth was explained by reference to two factors: high fertility rates and an increasing number of respondents beginning to self-identify as Métis. Among the reasons provided for why self-identification was increasing, they note,

> Between 1996 and 2006, there were important political and legal milestones that may have encouraged individuals to identify themselves as Métis. The Métis received significant recognition in the final report of the Royal Commission on Aboriginal Peoples (1996) and in recent years, the Métis have won important court cases having an impact on their hunting rights.
> *(Statistics Canada 2006)*

Despite acknowledging the presence of non-demographic factors, Statistics Canada painted a portrait of Métis demography that included the high rates of growth over the past decade (just mentioned); the fact that nearly nine out of ten Métis lived in the western provinces and Ontario and that seven out of ten Métis lived in urban areas; that Winnipeg had the largest number of urban Métis; that the overall Métis population was still young but had aged; that Métis children were twice as likely to live with a lone parent; that crowding and need for major home repairs were more common for Métis living in rural areas; that Métis were more likely than non-Aboriginal people to move within the same census subdivision; and that older Métis were more likely to speak an Aboriginal language (Statistics Canada 2013).

In the midst of Canada's (short-lived) change from a census to a National Household Survey, Statistics Canada reported that the Métis population in Canada in 2011 was 451,795 (Statistics Canada 2013, 4). They noted that a majority of Métis lived in the western provinces and Ontario: the largest population was in Alberta, followed by Ontario, Manitoba, British Columbia and Saskatchewan. They reported further that Winnipeg, Manitoba, had the highest urban Métis population, followed by Edmonton, Alberta (Statistics Canada 2013, 12). Statistics Canada also remarked, simultaneously, "[a]bout 41,000 Métis lived in Quebec, representing 9.1% of all Métis in the country. Moreover, 5.1% of Métis lived in the Atlantic Provinces" *and* "Métis in Canada are a people with their own unique culture, traditions, way of life, collective consciousness and nationhood" (Statistics Canada 2013, 12). As a matter of logic, both of these statements could be accurate, but likely not according to the same definition of Métis.

Statistics Canada began their section on Métis demographic characteristics by relaying, "Métis hold a unique cultural and historic place among the Aboriginal peoples in Canada, with distinct traditions, culture and language (Michif)" (2017, 4).

Despite this apparent recognition of the specificity of the Métis population, they went on to report that "the Métis population" had increased by 150 per cent from 2006 and was now 587,545. They likewise reported that in 2016 Ontario had the largest Métis population of any Canadian province, representing a nearly two-thirds increase from its population a decade earlier; that Quebec's Métis population had grown by 150 per cent in the previous decade; and that the Métis populations of the Maritimes had experienced a similar increase (125%). Nearly two-thirds of the Métis population was urban (62.4%); Winnipeg possessed the largest urban Métis population; and eight city metropolitan areas (CMAs) across Canada had a Métis population of at least 10,000 or larger (Statistics Canada 2017, 4–5).

As we can see, Statistics Canada publicly positions the Métis population dynamics over the past 25 years—a population based principally on self-identification—as one of a growth that far outstripped the capacity of traditional demographic lenses like fertility, mortality and migration to account for it. However, explanations that simply attributed unexpected growth to non-demographic factors such as increased self-identification remain unpersuasive insofar as they remain ontologically "pinned" to the same orienting assumption: that such a single thing as a Métis population exists at all. Such explanations are perhaps especially unpersuasive when we consider that Statistics Canada had known for years that their "Métis question" possessed little in the way of intersubjective agreement (that is to say, they knew that different census respondents were answering that particular question in different—and often directly conflicting—ways). Yet they continued to champion self-identification as the primary dynamic of Métis population construction. As we will explain next, a number of reasons—rooted in Canada's patriarchal/colonial past and present—exist that help explain why different and conflicting responses to a single Métis question should not just be expected, but are likely inevitable. We will explain these in further detail in Part II.

Part II: Métis: What's in a Name?

As this brief overview has made clear, the Métis population in Canada is apparently growing: far more quickly than the non-Indigenous population, and until recently, even more quickly than that of First Nations and Inuit communities. However, in this section, we will demonstrate why regardless of what one might think of these numbers, they must be taken with a large grain of salt, for two reasons. First, the meanings of the term Métis have (d)evolved over time; and second, the most common marker of Métis identity, self-identification, has only very recently been contextualized in the Canadian census by reference to other necessary dynamics of Métis identity making.

Given these changing dynamics, determining the boundaries and even the contours of the meaning of Métis identity can be a fraught exercise. We will briefly lay out the changing contexts and complexities of self-identification in a Métis context, following this with an equally brief discussion of recent changes to the Canadian census that, although we believe are a step in the right direction, still reproduce a statistical field in which Métis still do not control all the possible culturally and policy-relevant meanings of the term.

The limited (and limiting) results of self-identification

By the time a Métis self-identification query was added to the 1996 census long-form questionnaire, what was ostensibly a simple question was nonetheless already long in the grip of more than a century of the Indigenous social relations it ostensibly sought to collect information about. Sound reasons exist to doubt the validity of a census question based on self-identification to produce statistical estimates respectful to the Métis nation. In this section we will briefly outline four historical dynamics: the 19th-century rise of the Métis nation on the northern plains of what is now Canada; the impact of the patriarchy of the *Indian Act*, Canada's major legislation for attempting to govern First Nation communities; an increased misrecognition based on the idea that Métis are mixed in ways that other forms of Indigeneity are not, resulting in an increased tendency to self-identify as Métis in the census; and finally, the past tendency of the federal government to frame its governance of Indigenous communities through poverty-reduction strategies (or what today we might call "closing the gap" strategies.

These historical genealogies together conspire to limit the meaning and importance of self-identification as a valid marker in the larger dynamics of Indigenous identity making. Moreover, as we discuss later, the complicated genealogy of the meanings and uses of "Métis" in Canada's history in particular mean that a single-answer category is ultimately destined to conceal as much as it reveals. We turn now to a discussion of these historical factors, beginning with the rise of the Métis nation on the northern plains of what is now often called western Canada.

a. The Rise of the Métis Nation

Appreciating why a single question or answer category the relies on self-identification is inadequate for "counting Métis" requires understanding that (at least) two competing definitions of "Métis"—one national, the other racial—were already long woven into the fabric of Canadian society by the time Statistics Canada made the decision to add the Métis self-identification answer category to the 1986 census questionnaire. As noted earlier in this chapter, Métis are a nation of Indigenous People who rose to prominence on the northern plains of what is now (roughly) western Canada at the end of the 18th/beginning of the 19th century. One of many post-contact Indigenous Peoples with post-contact origins, they were part of the Nehiyaw Pwat ("the Iron Alliance") in partnership with the Plains Ojibway, the Cree and the Assiniboine (see Innes 2013, ch. 1; Vrooman 2012, ch. 1). A primary economic force on the northern plains by the middle part of the 19th century, the Métis led two armed resistances against the Canadian state, prevailing in the first one in 1869–70 and suffering military defeat in the second, in 1885. "Métis" as defined in this context is thus associated with specific events, leaders, geographical territories, economy, land tenure, artistic styles, languages and kinship connections (see Peterson and Brown 1985; Peterson 1990; Sprague 1988; St-Onge et al. 2014 for discussions of this history).

In a contemporary context, many of the descendants of the Métis nation are represented through the efforts of the Métis National Council and its provincially based "nations" in British Columbia (the Métis nation of British Columbia); Alberta (the Métis nation of Alberta); Saskatchewan (Métis nation–Saskatchewan); Ontario (Métis nation of Ontario), and Manitoba (Manitoba Métis Federation),[1] each of whom have engaged in various nation-to-nation policy relationships with municipal, provincial and federal levels of government and, more recently, each of whom has signed "constitutional agreements" with the federal government. Nonetheless, the boundaries of these constituencies have been complicated and indeed shaped by legislative changes to the long-standing and looming presence of the Indian Act and its associated categories of Indigeneity, particularly as they relate to women and particularly as they relate(d) to the legal inability of women to pass on "Indian status" to their children.

b. Indian Act Patriarchy

"Indian" has served as the centrepiece of Statistics Canada's official data collection activities since they began in 1871. It's important to understand, however, that the term itself possessed a wider currency, also serving as a centrepiece for the Canadian government's overtly patriarchal-colonial Indian Act, omnibus legislation for which was created in 1876 but whose legislative genealogy reaches back into the 1850s (see Cannon 2019; Palmater 2011). The *Indian Act* set out a broad array of provisions for governing First Nations communities that it deemed fell under its administrative aegis. The Act codified policies aimed at achieving assimilation, enfranchisement and, ultimately, the end of the Indian. Of the many facets of its complexity, of particular interest here is its patriarchal components, which attributed legal standing to "status Indian women" by virtue of their relationship to their husband or their father (see Jamieson 1978; Kolopenuk 2012; Palmater 2011).

In this context, the Canadian state could (and did) remove the status of First Nations women in certain administrative categories for reasons specific to their sex (and for which men could not lose status), the most prominent of which was by marrying a non-status Indian partner. The 1876 Indian Act made clear any Indian woman who married "any other than an Indian or non-treaty Indian" would cease to be an "Indian" under the Act. She would not be permitted to live on her reserve or be entitled to any benefits under a treaty or other agreement (Barker 2006). Indeed, throughout the late 19th and much of the 20th centuries, thousands of women and their children lost their Indian status as a result. Due to Indian Act regulations stipulating that only status Indians could live on the reserves set aside for them under Indian Act provisions, these women and their children were forced to move away from their reserve communities. Over time, these regulations produced a growing population of "non-status Indians" for whom the government washed their hands of responsibility as they were seen to not have fiduciary responsibility, which is the basis of the Indian Act itself. Many of these individuals and their families shed their self-identification as "Indians" over time, while many others moved into Métis communities to live with relatives (see Eberts 2010; Jamieson 1978; Lawrence 2004; Palmater 2011 for a general discussion of this history). For example, in Northern Saskatchewan, some Métis communities situated adjacent to First Nations share the same family names as those in the First Nations communities of Cumberland House First Nation and Cumberland House Cree Nation. In many cases, the descendants of these families began to self-identify as Métis, for racialized reasons we will explain next.

c. Racialization and Misrecognition

Generally, censuses must and do take at their word people's identifications according to offered census categories. Tugging at this epistemological thread too firmly would quickly unravel the validity of censuses as a policy tool. And indeed, good reasons exist to trust self-identification in a contemporary context, based on the presumption that most of us "know who we are." However, scholars in various disciplines have pointed out that "identity" is not as unified as often made out to be, and in this conceptual context, numerous reasons exist for why someone might self-identify as (part of) something that does not accept them. More fundamentally, they might self-identify as something they are not (see Andersen 2014; Brubaker and Cooper 2000). In a census context the way to deal with this epistemological complexity is to create a more complex question that provides examples of is meant by the use of particular terms (see Andersen 2014, 152), but the $715M cost (for the 2021 census) of carrying out a census in Canada, coupled with the precious "real estate" of a census form, vastly complicate the addition of such complexities.

In this context and in direct contrast (and competition) with a nationalist Métis discourse, the term Métis is also understood in more baldly racialized terms to signal a fundamental "mixedness," a racialization that *also* manifests, by some, in their self-identification within the census. This racialization fuelled the growth of Canada as a colonial nation-state. The dominant discourse of racialization under which these discussions take place is premised on the idea of a pre-contact Indigenous authenticity whose purity was irrevocably transformed by the eventual presence of settlers and the march of colonialism with its various projects of dispossession and polity destruction (see Andersen 2014). In this context, the term is often used etymologically as the French term for "mixed," a translative banality often used as evidence of an essential, underlying meaning and used in baptismal recording by the Catholic Church to identify non-pure French or racialized mixedness. So-called dual origin individuals and communities—which often predated the rise of the Métis nation and which dot the geographical landscape of what is now Canada—have in turn attempted to make use of the term "Métis" to contemporarily describe themselves, their communities and their aspirations, despite the fact that none of their ancestors self-identified as Métis (see Andersen 2014; Lawrence 2004).

As such, explaining national affiliation as Métis is pretty straightforward. The bigger question, however, is why someone with no Métis ancestry would begin to self-identify as Métis (in the census or otherwise). We have argued elsewhere that the power of racialization in contemporary Canadian society has induced a misrecognition that causes such respondents to conflate of "Métis" with "mixedness" (see Andersen 2014, ch. 1), a situation that has demonstrably bolstered the ranks of the currently configured "Métis population." Whether knowingly or not, such newly self-identifying Métis rely on a form of biological essentialism rooted in the idea that mere biological proximity (i.e., ancestral connection)—rather than, say, additional connection to a contemporary Aboriginal community—constitutes a sufficient basis for making claims to identification as Aboriginal (see generally TallBear 2013).

More recently, a growing subfield of scholars have begun to analyse the growth of Métis self-identification in terms of otherwise White individuals beginning to self-identify and collectively organize based on that self-identification (see Leroux 2019; Leroux and Gaudry 2017; Gaudry 2018, etc.). We would argue that such efforts are rooted in two resonant impulses. The first is Geonpul scholar Moreton-Robinson's concept of "white possessiveness," which argues that the past five centuries of colonial projects have understood and acted upon Indigeneity as something ontologically inert and, as such, open to possession by "free" (i.e., White) subjects (see Moreton-Robinson 2015). The second is anthropologist Circe Sturm's (2011) observation that contemporary claims to Indigeneity are often rooted in "empty experiences of whiteness," such that people begin to self-identify as a means of belonging that they do not otherwise feel. This has also come to be known as race shifting. Darryl Leroux discusses race shifters and defines the "white desire to be Indigenous" as "race shifting" or as "settler self-Indigenization." All of these have powerfully impacted the manner in which "Métis" is understood and defined in contemporary Canada and, as such, the manners in which it is (and can be) measured.

In many ways, self-identifying in a census offers an ideal place to begin expressing such claims to Métisness (though the matter is slightly more complicated for reasons we explain later), since individuals can make claims without the worries or complexities of having to be claimed by anyone other than the Canadian state or, more importantly, challenged by Métis communities themselves. And while it is more than fair to say that blunt instruments like a census are neither meant nor equipped to parse through this level of identity complexity, the data they provide are nonetheless drawn upon as key empirical sources to support political claims arguably better explained by more nuanced or complex forms of evidence. Moreover, as noted earlier, a census question that fails to distinguish between multiple meanings potentially adds political weight to otherwise dubious—or more generously, misguided—collective claims that maintain colonial and dominant understandings of identity at the expense of more legitimate ones like those emanating from the Métis nation.

d. "Métis" as "In Need"

Even as individuals have begun to newly self-identify as Métis, why would various levels of Canadian government recognize them as such? Part of the answer can be explained in terms of the same colonial logics through which "Métis" is conflated with mixedness, but there is more to the story. The fact that these competing understandings of "Métis" exist is thus perhaps less important than the fact that they share an overlapping policy history with Canada's post-WWII welfare state governance. The social and political upheaval of the 1960s in Canada led to a broad questioning of what government and citizenship ought to entail (Boldt 1993; Weaver 1981). This questioning, coupled with broad public sympathy and successive governments that emphasized "active citizenship," produced a broad-based willingness to "do something" with respect to closing the gap between Indigenous communities and the rest of Canada. As such, while government actors possessed little knowledge about Native communities that would assist government agencies and ministers in producing competent policy decisions (Weaver 1981), the little research that did exist indicated that like most "Indian communities," many Métis still lived near or at the bottom of the scale for most quality of life indicators, in particular poor housing, poor diet, poor health and economic instability.

Weaver (1981) and Sawchuk (1998, 1980, 1978) argue that in Canada, the civil rights upheaval of the 1960s and the subsequent government assistance led to the reinvigoration of Native political groups, among them those organizations and locals (Métis chartered communities) that seek to represent Métis concerns. Trudeau government policy objectives in particular led the federal government in 1971 to provide grants for basic operating costs and overhead for provincial, territorial and national Native organizations (Sawchuk 1998, 72–73). Weaver (1985) argues that by the early 1970s a cottage industry had sprung up around Native program policies and monies, part of the sedimentation of a larger 1970s social justice policy paradigm "buttressed by economic prosperity in the country, an expanding bureaucratic establishment in Ottawa, a belief in enhanced policy formulation through rational-technocratic means, and a belief that social problems could be remedied by more government intervention in society" (Weaver 1985, 82).

In short, the 1970s set a policy context within which Métis communities were rendered legible to various levels of Canadian government as lagging along a number of multiple socio-demographic indicators that frame Métis experiences within a deficit perspective of being we often take as being indicative of wellbeing and as such, as being "in need" (see Chapter 2 for a broader discussion of this deficit-based discourse and its impact on government interventions into Indigenous communities). The boundaries of the term Métis were necessarily porous during that era—however Métis communities and locals knew who were a part of their community—but the needs-based interventions that characterized their relationship with other off-reserve Indigenous populations meant that political discussions over the meaning and boundaries of Métis identity remained a policy opacity. This all began to change in the lead-up to the repatriation of Canada's constitution in 1982; however, with enormous consequences for how the "Métis population" was about to be made visible (again) to the government's post-Royal Commission on Aboriginal Peoples Indigenous policy field (see Andersen 2013).

All of this is to say that by the time the events of history had caught up to Statistics Canada's 1986 formulation of a specific question in pursuit of a single Métis population, the thoroughly saturated character of Canada's colonial history—the rise of the Métis nation which predated and conflicted with Canada's expansive desires; the patriarchy of its legislation; the manner in which previous policy making was related to alleviating poverty; and the increasing misrecognized conflation of Métis with racial mixedness in everyday Canadian life—had conspired to produce a landscape of competing and indeed incommensurable understandings of "Métis" that were effectively forced to jostle for conceptual space in the question/answer categories offered in the 1986 census. It follows that any subsequent analyses that make use of any Métis data—such as that we undertook in Part I—do not and cannot analyse that conflation in any especially meaningful way: certainly not, we argue, in ways that most appropriately support nationalistic agendas and how UNDRIP is being engaged in provincial constitutional reforms of citizenship. As we will explain next, the deep racialization that saturates Métis population estimates remains, even in the face of an ostensibly positive change instituted by how Statistics Canada measures Métis in the census.

Part III: The False Promise of the (Current) Census as a Source of Métis Data

After decades of advocacy by Métis political, policy and academic actors, in the lead-up to the 2021 census, Statistics Canada enacted a significant change to how it measured the Métis population. For the previous three-and-a-half decades, Métis population identification was measured through a single self-identification question, which, with small changes over time, contained a version of something like the question in the 2016 census: "is this person an Aboriginal person, that is, First Nations (North American Indian), Métis or Inuk (Inuit)?" This question was accompanied by a short context note that the term "Indian" included both status and non-status variants, and included answer categories with four possibilities: no; yes to First Nation; yes to Métis; and yes to Inuit. Any "yes" answer included instructions to skip to an additional question for further information, though this was mainly intended for First Nation respondents. In the 2021 census, this approach was maintained, but with an additional "skip" question for those identifying as Métis: "is this person a registered member of a Métis organization or Settlement?" with response categories including the five provincially based Métis "nations" or instructions to name the Métis Settlement or other organization.

At first glance, this sea change seems to reflect exactly the kinds of logics that ground those of the provincial organizations: a movement beyond self-identification on its own as the sole marker of Métis identity and the requirement of connection to a Métis collective with pre-colonial roots and ostensibly nation-based roots, at that. And yet, the initial statistical summaries that followed in the wake of this new question demonstrate the fragility of attempting to capture nuance through census instruments. In its own publication, Statistics Canada stated, "The census counted 624,220 Métis living in Canada in 2021, up 6.3% from 2016" and "224,655 people report[ed] membership in a Métis organization or Settlement, with four-fifths (79.8%) reporting being a member of one of the five signatories of the Canada-Métis Nation Accord (2017)" (Statistics Canada 2022, 8). Doing some quick math—224,655/624,220 × .798—reveals that only a little more than a quarter (28% or about 180,000) of all those who self-identified as Métis in the census reported membership in a Métis organization that was a signatory to one of the Métis Nation Accords signed by the Canadian federal government in 2017.

Could one reading of this result be that most census respondents who identify as Métis be doing so using a logic of racialization, since a nationalist logic would have led them to self-identify with one of the provincial Métis organizations? Though this explanation would prove most convenient for our argument, in reality matter are of course more complicated, for a couple of reasons. First, though we use the term "self-identifying" to explain census methodology, in point of fact, heads of households fill out census forms and make decisions about those in their household and where they "fit" according to census categories (so, strictly speaking, censuses are not "self-identifying"). Second, the Métis provincial signatories to the Canada-Métis Accord (2017) continue to undertake membership drives to increase their documented citizenry, meaning that many Métis who are otherwise legitimately Métis have yet to undertake the process of becoming citizens of one of the five provincial Métis national bodies.

The broader issue here, however, is the extent to which the census can ever deliver on what it otherwise promises to deliver, which is to play a "vital [role] in providing consistent data over time that tell the story of Canada's ethnic, linguistic and cultural diversity." To what extent, for example, was Métis nation demographical expertise involved in all elements of the field leading up to and producing the 2021 addition (just noted)? To what extent do current census-derived estimates of the Métis population square with the citizen-demographics of the provincially based Métis nations, and what policy implications ensue from any gaps between them? What capacity exists within the provincial Métis nations or the Métis National Council to engage in all parts of the statistical field within which census estimates are produced?

In sum, what would the relationship have to look like between the Métis nation and the census at all points of the statistical cycle "compass" to produce the kinds of robust, policy-relevant data crucial to supporting continued Métis nation building—and respect Métis international engagements with UNDRIP—rather than what Métis policy actors have been forced to make due with over the past three decades and more? Moreover, to touch again on Chapter 6, in what ways could Métis data be fashioned such that it not only provided relevant data, but also could be used in concert with other research approaches that were (for example) more qualitative in character?

Note

1 It is important to note that the Manitoba Métis Federation (MMF) withdrew from the Métis National Council in 2021 due to discrepancies related to Métis citizenship. This fraction further complicates national data strategies due to jurisdictional control relating to data sovereignty, citizenship registry and definitions of Métis nationhood.

References

Andersen, Chris. *Métis: Race, Recognition, and the Struggle for Indigenous Peoplehood*. Vancouver: UBC Press, 2014.

Andersen, Chris. "Underdeveloped Identities: The Misrecognition of Aboriginality in the Canadian Census." *Economy and Society* 42, no. 4 (2013): 626–650.

Bakker, Peter. *A Language of Their Own: The Genesis of Michif, the Mixed Cree-French Language of the Canadian Métis*. New York: Oxford University Press, 1997.

Barker, Joanne. "Gender, Sovereignty, and the Discourse of Rights in Native Women's Activism: Feminism, Race, Transnationalism." *Meridians* 7, no. 1 (2006): 127–161. Accessed July 23, 2024. www.proquest.com/scholarly-journals/gender-sovereignty-discourse-rights-native-womens/docview/196938306/se-2?accountid=79256.

Boldt, Menno. *Surviving as Indians: The Challenge of Self-Government*. Toronto: University of Toronto Press, 1993.

Brubaker, Rogers, and Frederick Cooper. "Beyond Identity." *Theory and Society* 29, no. 1 (2000): 1–47.

Cannon, Martin J. *Men, Masculinity, and the Indian Act*. Vancouver: UBC Press, 2019.

Eberts, Mary. "McIvor: Justice Delayed—Again." *Indigenous Law Journal* 9, no. 1 (2010): 15–46.

Gaudry, Adam. "Communing with the Dead: The 'New Métis,' Métis Identity Appropriation, and the Displacement of Living Métis Culture." *The American Indian Quarterly* 42, no. 2 (Spring 2018): 162–190. https://www.jstor.org/stable/10.5250/amerindiquar.42.2.0162.

Government of Canada and Métis National Council. *Canada-Métis Nation Accord*. Ottawa: Government of Canada, 2017.

Guimond, Éric, Norbert Robitaille, and Sacha Senécal. "Fuzzy Definitions and Demographic Explosion of Aboriginal Populations in Canada from 1986 to 2006." In *Social Statistics and Ethnic Diversity: Cross-National Perspectives in Classifications and Identity Politics*, edited by Patrick Simon, Victor Piché, and Amélie A. Gagnon, 229–44. IMISCOE Research Series. Cham: Springer, 2015.

Harper, Sarah. *Demography: A Very Short Introduction*. Oxford: Oxford University Press, 2018.

Hogue, Michel. *Métis and the Medicine Line: Creating a Border and Dividing a People*. Chapel Hill: University of North Carolina Press, 2015.

Innes, Robert Alexander. *Elder Brother and the Law of the People: Contemporary Kinship and Cowessess First Nation*. Winnipeg: University of Manitoba Press, 2013.

Jamieson, Kathleen. *Indian Women and the Law: Citizen Minus*. Ottawa: Minister of Supply and Services Canada for Canadian Advisory Council on the Status of Women and Equal Rights for Indian Women, 1978.

Kolopenuk, Jessica. "Canada's Indians (sic): (Re)racializing Canadian Sovereign Contours through Juridical Constructions of Indianness in McIvor v. Canada." M.A. thesis, Department of Political Science, University of Alberta, 2012.

Lawrence, Bonita. *"Real" Indians and Others: Mixed-Blood Urban Native Peoples and Indigenous Nationhood*. Lincoln: University of Nebraska Press, 2004.

Leroux, Darryl. *Distorted Descent: White Claims to Indigenous Identity*. Winnipeg: University of Manitoba Press, 2019.

Leroux, Darryl, and Adam Gaudry. "White Settler Revisionism and Making Métis Everywhere: The Evocation of Métissage in Quebec and Nova Scotia." *Critical Ethnic Studies* 3, no. 1 (2017): 116–142.

Macdougall, Brenda. *Land, Family and Identity: Contextualizing Métis Health and Well-being*. Prince George, BC: National Collaborating Centre for Indigenous Health, 2017.

Métis National Council. "Citizenship." 2002. Accessed December 4, 2024. https://www.metisnation.ca/about/citizenship.

Moreton-Robinson, Aileen. *The White Possessive: Property, Power, and Indigenous Sovereignty*. Minneapolis: University of Minnesota Press, 2015.

Palmater, Pam. *Beyond Blood: Rethinking Indigenous Identity*. Saskatoon: Purich Publishing, 2011.

Peterson, Jacqueline. "Gathering at the River: The Métis Peopling of the Northern Plains." In *The Fur Trade in North Dakota*, edited by Virginia Heidenreich, 47–70. Bismarck, ND: State Historical Society of North Dakota, 1990.

Peterson, Jacqueline, and Jennifer S. H. Brown, eds. *The New Peoples: Being and Becoming Métis in North America*. Winnipeg: University of Manitoba Press, 1985.

Royal Commission on Aboriginal Peoples. "Métis Perspectives." In *Report of the Royal Commission on Aboriginal Peoples*, Vol. 4, Perspectives and Realities, Chapter 5. Ottawa: Government of Canada, 1996.

Sawchuk, Joe. "Development or Domination: Metis and Government Funding." In *The Other Natives: The-les Métis—Volume Three*, edited by Antoine Lussier and Bruce Lussier, 101–118. Winnipeg: Manitoba Métis Federation Press & Editions Bois-Brulés, 1980.

Sawchuk, Joe. "The Métis, Non-Status Indians and the New Aboriginality: Government Influence on Native Political Awareness and Identity." *Canadian Ethnic Studies* 12, no. 2 (1985): 135–146.

Sawchuk, Joe. *The Métis of Manitoba: Reformulation of an Ethnic Identity*. Toronto: Peter Martin Associates Limited, 1978.

Sawchuk, Joe. *Métis Politics in Western Canada: The Dynamics of Native Pressure Groups*. Saskatoon: Purich Publishing, 1998.
Sprague, Doug. *Canada and the Métis, 1869–1885*. Waterloo, ON: Wilfrid Laurier Press, 1988.
Statistics Canada. *Aboriginal Peoples in Canada: First Nations People, Métis and Inuit. National Household Survey, 2011*. Ottawa: Statistics Canada, 2013.
Statistics Canada. *Aboriginal Peoples in Canada in 2006: Inuit, Métis and First Nations, 2006 Census: Métis*. Ottawa: Statistics Canada, 2006. www12.statcan.gc.ca/census-recensement/2006/as-sa/97-558/p10-eng.cfm.
Statistics Canada. "Aboriginal Peoples in Canada: Key Results from the 2016 Census." *The Daily*, October 25, 2017. Released at 8:30 a.m. Eastern Time. www.statcan.gc.ca/en/daily-hier/171025/dq171025a-eng.pdf.
Statistics Canada. *Aboriginal Peoples of Canada: A Demographic Profile. 2001 Census: Analysis Series*. Ottawa: Statistics Canada, 2003.
Statistics Canada. *General Review of the 1986 Census*. Published under the authority of the Minister of Regional Industrial Expansion. © Minister of Supply and Services Canada, 1989.
Statistics Canada. "Indigenous Population Continues to Grow and Is Much Younger than the Non-Indigenous Population, Although the Pace of Growth Has Slowed." *The Daily*, September 21, 2022. Released at 8:30 a.m. Eastern Time. www.statcan.gc.ca/o1/en/plus/3920-canadas-indigenous-population.
St-Onge, Nicole, Carolyn Podruchny, and Brenda Macdougall, eds. *Contours of a People: Métis Family, Mobility, and History*. Norman: University of Oklahoma Press, 2014.
Sturm, Circe. *Becoming Indian: The Struggle over Cherokee Identity in the Twenty-first Century*. Santa Fe: School for Advanced Research Press, 2011.
United Nations (General Assembly). 2007. *Declaration on the Rights of Indigenous People*. United Nations.
Vrooman, Nicholas C. *The Whole Country Was . . . One Robe: The Little Shell Tribe's America*. Helena: Drumlummon Institute, 2012.
Weaver, Sally M. "Federal Policy-Making for Métis and Non-Status Indians in the Context of Native Policy." *Canadian Ethnic Studies* 17, no. 2 (1985): 80–102.
Weaver, Sally M. *Making Canadian Indian Policy: The Hidden Agenda, 1968–1970*. Toronto: University of Toronto Press, 1981.

8

"FIXING" THE FIGURES

Tribal Data in the Aotearoa New Zealand 2018 Census

Tahu Kukutai

CHAPTER LEARNING OBJECTIVES

Objective 1: Critically examine how statistical methods are used to produce Indigenous population data.

Objective 2: Understand the strengths and weaknesses of using Indigenous population identifiers in official statistics.

Objective 3: Reflect on how Indigenous-led approaches to creating population statistics can produce more relevant, better quality data.

Introduction

The national population census is considered the gold standard for many government data collections, with census data being deployed for a wide range of social, economic and political purposes. While the primary purpose of a census is to simultaneously count the population within a defined territory (United Nations 2008), its real impact lies in how it is used (or not) to make people count. Despite a long and fraught history of being missed and misrecognized in the census, Indigenous Peoples in the CANZUS countries generally seek inclusion in the census to be statistically visible and to generate official data to address inequities and advance their own unique rights and interests (Kukutai and Walter 2015; Madden et al. 2016).

DOI: 10.4324/9781003173342-8
This chapter has been made available under a CC-BY-NC-ND license.

But what happens when the census goes wrong and Indigenous communities face a massive data deficit? This is what happened in Aotearoa when the 2018 census missed nearly one-third of the Māori population. The consequences were particularly grim for *iwi* (tribes) given their dependence on the census for official statistics about themselves. Due to the poor quality of the 2018 iwi data, Stats NZ took the unprecedented step of announcing that it had failed to do its job and was unable to release official iwi counts. Rather than face a five-year data void, Stats NZ and the national tribal leaders forum partnered to develop new methodologies to try and produce useful interim figures for tribes.

This chapter examines the joint government-tribal efforts to "fix" Census 2018 iwi data. In doing so it illustrates a central theme of this book—that all statistics are culturally embedded and inherently political. Working through the methodology shows that the production of the adjusted iwi counts relied as much on judgements about Māori demography, contemporary tribal politics and Māori identity as it did on the application of statistical methods. It also reveals a more fundamental problem underlying the production of iwi statistics arising from the conceptual mismatch between tribal definitions of belonging rooted in *whakapapa* (genealogical connection) and individuals' self-identification in a government-controlled context. The chapter concludes with a reflection on the future of the census in Aotearoa and how devolving authority to tribes to define their own population parameters will likely produce better quality and more meaningful tribal data.

The Collection of Iwi Data in the Census

Kinship structures lie at the heart of Māori society. Iwi are one of the largest Māori kinship groupings and generally comprise several (and sometimes many) *hapū* or sub-tribes whose members descend from an eponymous ancestor. Though the signing of the 1840 *Tiriti o Waitangi* between Māori chiefs and agents of Queen Victoria represents the inception of the colonial government, the first Māori census was not conducted until 1858 (Fenton 1859). Its stated purpose was to estimate the number of Māori in each region and provide an overview of their social and material conditions. Significant space was dedicated to assessing rates of Māori fecundity, consanguineous marriage and the demographic viability of Māori as a "race" (Kukutai 2012). Counts were also attempted for a small number of tribes, with the census report listing the respective names of men, women and children. The next Māori census did not occur until 1874, followed by another in 1878, and then every five years thereafter. Conducted by colonial officials, and aggregated by tribe and region, the census provided a ready mechanism for the monitoring of tribes in terms of their size, distribution and location. However, by the turn of the century most tribal lands had been either confiscated or acquired by other (often dubious) means, and the demographic "swamping" of Māori by settlers had cemented tribal economic and political dispossession. After 1901 there was no longer a compelling need for the government to statistically surveil tribes. Māori continued to be separately enumerated throughout the 20th century but using the racial logics of "blood quantum" rather than tribal membership (for an historical overview of census categorizations of Māori, see Kukutai 2012).

Some 90 years later an iwi affiliation question was introduced in the 1991 census, ostensibly to support the devolution of some limited responsibilities and service functions to tribes. While the legislation enabling devolution was subsequently repealed, the iwi question remained, and over time tribes came to view iwi census data as an important information source, especially given lack of iwi-specific demographic and socio-economic data available in other data collections (Rarere 2012; Walling et al. 2009). The delivery of high-quality iwi data also became a key deliverable for Stats NZ as a core part of meeting its *Tiriti* obligations to Māori.

But in 2018, it went horribly wrong. On 1 June, nearly three months after starting the census, Stats NZ announced that it only had full or partial information for around 90 per cent of the national population and needed more time to "draw on other information sources and new methods to achieve the highest quality dataset" (Stats NZ 2018a). With the data collection phase winding down, the agency needed to backfill the census dataset with other government data or risk wasting $118M of taxpayer funding. Stats had always intended to use some government administrative data for the 2018 census, which was explicitly designed as a "digital-first"[1] model but not on the scale that it was now faced with.

While the initial announcement made no mention of response rates for Māori or Pacific peoples, a well-documented history of significantly lower response rates for both populations augured badly (Statistics New Zealand 2007, 2014), and this prospect did not go unnoticed by Māori. In July the Māori Data Sovereignty Network Te Mana Raraunga (TMR) issued a public statement declaring "A call for action on Māori census data." The network noted that the census was "essential for many of the functions that underpin democracy," including the determination of Māori electoral seats and boundaries, the resourcing of services and infrastructure, policy development, and action to address systemic social, economic and health inequities affecting Māori and Pacific peoples. TMR expressed concerns about the "inevitable" impacts of lower response rates on the quality of Māori and iwi data and supported an independent review of Census 2018 to identify what went wrong and hold Stats NZ to account (Te Mana Raraunga 2018).

The network had to wait a year for answers. In July 2019 an independent review panel released a damning report on Census 2018 (Jack and Graziadei 2019) and Stats NZ finally made public its *interim collection response rates* for Māori, as well as Pacific peoples and other groups. The interim[2] response rate compared the number of people counted at the end of the collection phase with the estimated number of people who should have been counted, expressed as a percentage. As Table 8.1 shows, the gap was significant. Nationally, the interim response rate was 83.3 per cent, increasing to 87.5 per cent if it included individuals who were counted on dwellings or household summary forms, but not on an individual form. For Māori the rates were 68.2 per cent and 74.3 per cent respectively, far lower than the national statistic, and nearly 20 percentage points lower than the individual response rate for 2013. For Pacific peoples, it was a shockingly low 65.1 per cent and 73.5 per cent. It was a data collection disaster.

Given the poor response rates—indeed, the lowest in recent memory—it is perhaps unsurprising that Stats NZ chose to highlight its high *interim census coverage rates* (Stats NZ 2019). Coverage rates compare the number of people counted in the census dataset with the estimated number who should have been counted, expressed as a percentage. As Table 8.2 shows, the interim coverage rates were far more favourable than the response rates, and in fact higher than the coverage rates for Census 2013.

The reason for the significant difference between the two rates—one suggesting failure, the other success—can be found in the underlying sources.

TABLE 8.1 Census 2018 Interim Collection Response Rates Compared With Census 2013

Interim collection response rates	2018 Individual census form only	2018 Any census form	2013 Individual census form only	2013 Any census form
National	83.3	87.5	92.2	93.2
Major ethnic groups				
Māori	68.2	74.3	88.5	89.7
Pacific	65.1	73.5	88.3	90.8
Asian	81.7	87.8	91.7	93.3

Source: Stats NZ (2019)

TABLE 8.2 Census 2018 Interim Coverage Rates Compared With Census 2013

Interim coverage rates	2018 (1)	2013 (2)
National	98.6	97.6 (+0.5)
Major ethnic groups		
Māori	96.0	93.9 (+1.3)
Pacific	96.1	95.2 (+1.5)
Asian	97.3	97.0 (+1.2)
	96.3	95.2 (+1.1)

Source: Stats NZ (2019)

Notes
(1) The interim results did not incorporate information from the 2018 Post Enumeration Survey thus no sampling errors are presented.
(2) The sampling error +/– indicates the extent to which the estimate from the 2013 Post Enumeration Survey might deviate from the "true" value.

TABLE 8.3 Sources of Census 2018 Data, by Major Ethnic Group

	Individual form response	Partial response	Administrative data
National	85	4	11
Major ethnic groups			
European	89	3	8
Māori	71	6	23
Pacific	68	9	24
Asian	84	6	10

Source: Stats NZ (2019)

The collection rates only included data collected as part of the census operation. This is the metric that usually serves as an indicator of how well the census enumeration is tracking. By contrast, the newly developed coverage rates included other government information sources used to augment the census dataset.

As Table 8.3 shows, of the total number of records in the final census dataset, 89 per cent were from Census 2018 forms (85 per cent from individual forms and 4 per cent from dwellings/household forms) and 11 per cent from other government data. The latter included birth registrations from the Department of Internal Affairs, tertiary enrolment data from the Ministry of Education, prisoner data from the Department of Corrections and data from the 2013 census (2018 Census

EDQP 2019). This repurposing of administrative data for census purposes was made possible by Stats NZ's sophisticated data linkage programme, developed as part of its census transformation agenda (Office of the Minister of Statistics 2015), and the government's ambition to be a "world leader in the trusted and inclusive use of shared data" (New Zealand Data Futures Forum 2014, 5). Importantly, Table 8.3 clearly shows that the composition of the census dataset varied significantly by ethnic group. For Māori and Pacific peoples nearly one-quarter of their census records were sourced from administrative data. For the majority European population and Asian peoples, it was only around one-tenth.

While Stats NZ was able to draw on other government data to produce population counts, at the national and sub-national level there were limitations to this approach. For some key variables, the information simply did not exist, or existed but was of insufficient quality to be used for official purposes. Such was the case for iwi data, which was missing for 29 per cent of the Māori descent population (Stats NZ 2021a). The External Data Quality Panel (EDQP), whose job it was to scrutinize the quality of Census 2018 data, gave iwi data a quality rating of "very poor" and Stats NZ were unable to release the data as official counts. The EDQP judged that there did not appear to be a robust or reliable way to address missing iwi data (2018 Census EDQP 2019).

Census 2018 threw many issues into sharp relief. One was the inherent vulnerability of tribes' reliance on Stats NZ for official data. When things went badly—as they did for Census 2018—there was little recourse. Nevertheless, the fallout of the failed census provided a catalyst for a greater level of Māori, and specifically tribal, involvement in the official statistics system and for Stats NZ to be more intentional about honouring its *Tiriti* partnership responsibilities. In late 2019 the groundbreaking Mana Ōrite (equal authority) relationship agreement was signed between Stats NZ and the Data Iwi Leaders Group (Data ILG) of the National Iwi Chairs Forum (NICF) (Data Iwi Leaders Group 2019). The Mana Ōrite agreement provided for a shared work programme to advance tribes' aspirations for data to make a sustainable and positive difference to tribal, *hapū* and *whānau* (extended family) outcomes. One of the joint projects pursued under the Mana Ōrite agreement was to explore mitigation options for Census 2018 iwi data. Although the EDQP had rated the data as "very poor"[3] and advised against the use of statistical imputation, both the Data ILG and Stats NZ thought it worthwhile to work through possible mitigation options in order to develop a better understanding of the problem and the wider iwi data context. This author, who was also part of the EDQP, was contracted to provide technical advice to the Data ILG and work with Stats NZ methodologists[4] on this project.

Māori Descent in the Census

In order to understand the mitigation approach used for Census 2018 iwi data, one needs to appreciate the relationship between iwi affiliation and Māori descent in the census. The census questionnaire is designed so that only those who respond "Yes" or "Don't Know" to the Māori descent question are prompted for their iwi affiliation.[5] The ethnic group question, which is intended to capture individuals' sense of cultural identity and includes Māori, is one of many ethnic group responses and is separate to the Māori descent and iwi questions. The 2018 questions on ethnic group, Māori descent and iwi are replicated below, in both online and paper format (Stats NZ 2018b) (Figures 8.1–8.3).

In the Census 2018 dataset, 21 per cent of the Māori descent population (184,000 individuals) were added through administrative data, and these individuals did not have iwi information (see Table 8.4). A further 8 per cent (68,000) of Māori descendants from Census 2018 gave a response that was classed as residual (e.g., not stated, response unidentifiable) (Stats NZ 2021a). The aim of the mitigation exercise was to reduce the share of the Māori descent population lacking iwi affiliation and to do so using methods that did not violate cultural or statistical sensibilities, or introduce bias.

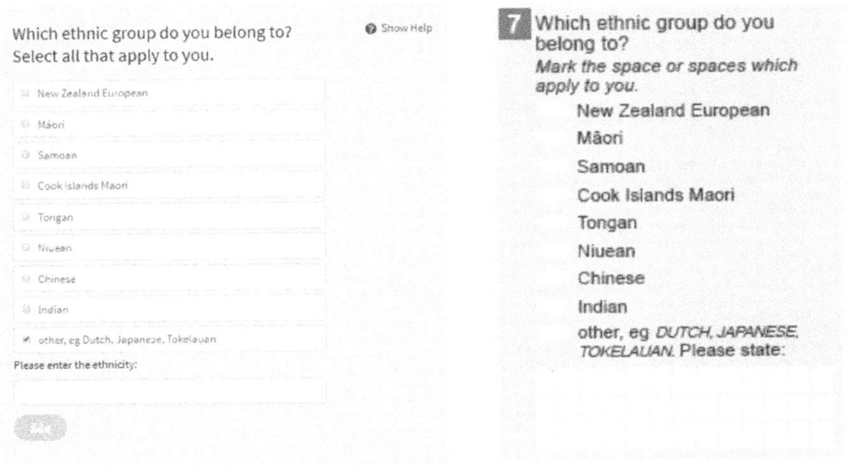

FIGURE 8.1 Ethnicity question (online and paper) in Census 2018

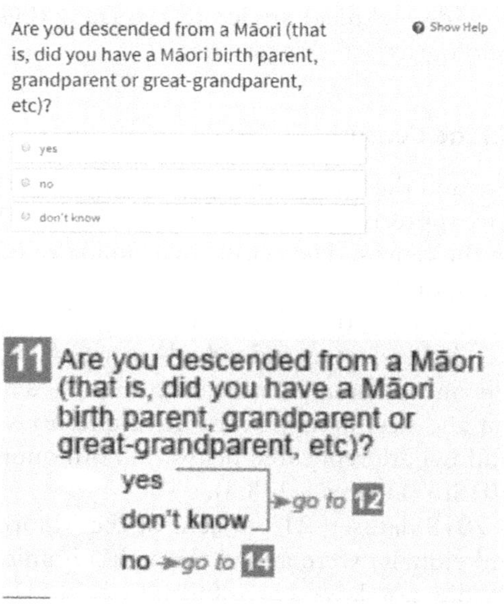

130 Indigenous Statistics

Are you descended from a Māori (that is, did you have a Māori birth parent, grandparent or great-grandparent, etc)?

- yes
- no
- don't know

11 Are you descended from a Māori (that is, did you have a Māori birth parent, grandparent or great-grandparent, etc)?

yes
don't know ⟶ go to **12**
no ⟶ go to **14**

FIGURE 8.2 Māori descent question (online and paper) in Census 2018

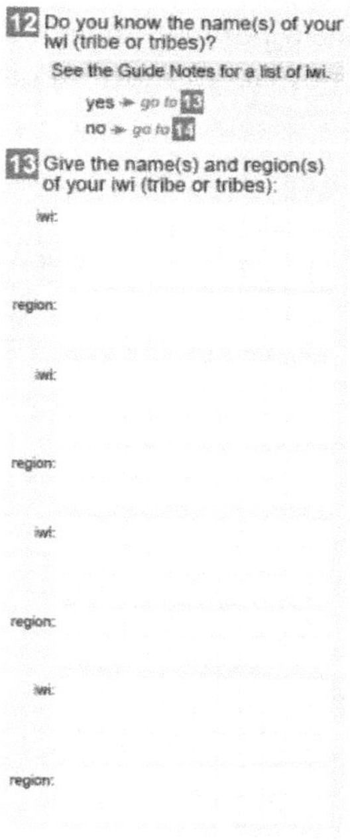

12 Do you know the name(s) of your iwi (tribe or tribes)?
See the Guide Notes for a list of iwi.
yes ⟶ go to **13**
no ⟶ go to **14**

13 Give the name(s) and region(s) of your iwi (tribe or tribes):

iwi:

region:

iwi:

region:

iwi:

region:

iwi:

region:

FIGURE 8.3 iwi affiliation question (paper and online) in Census 2018

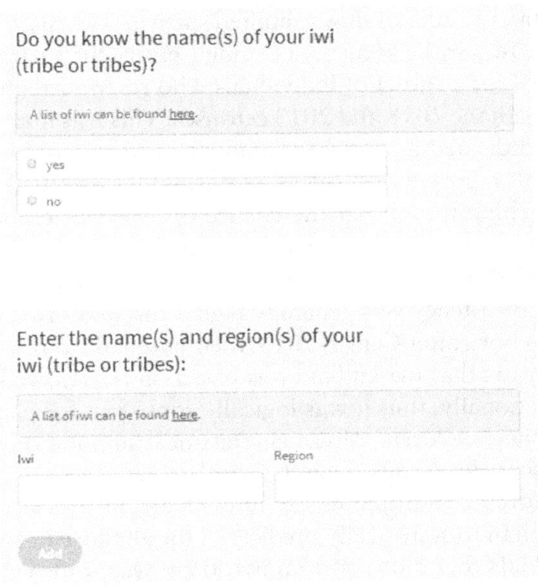

> Do you know the name(s) of your iwi
> (tribe or tribes)?
>
> A list of iwi can be found here.
>
> ○ yes
>
> ○ no
>
> Enter the name(s) and region(s) of your
> iwi (tribe or tribes):
>
> A list of iwi can be found here.
>
> Iwi   Region

FIGURE 8.3 (Continued)

TABLE 8.4 Census 2018 Māori Descent Population, by Iwi Coverage

Census 2018 Māori descent population, by iwi coverage	*Māori descent population*	
	N	%
Reported at least 1 iwi	503,000	58
Specified "Don't know"	115,000	13
Residual (not stated etc.)	68,000	8
Added from Census 2018	184,000	21
	870,999	100

"Fixing" the 2018 Iwi Census Datafile

Various mitigation methods were explored for the 130-plus unique iwi in the Stats NZ *Iwi and iwi-related groups statistical classification*, which is the list of tribes used by Stats NZ to produce iwi data (Stats NZ 2022a).[6] The first step involved locating an individual's iwi affiliation from an alternative government data source. Whereas other variables in the Census 2018 dataset could be backfilled using data from a range of sources (e.g., vital registration, education data), iwi affiliation was limited solely to Census 2013 due to data quality issues. To test the accuracy of using Census 2013 data, iwi responses were compared for a subset of individuals who responded and provided iwi affiliation in both the 2018 and 2013 censuses. This was important as earlier research had indicated a significant amount of intercensal inconsistency in how individuals reported their iwi (Kukutai and Rarere 2013, 2017). Unsurprisingly, matching found that the chance of a person reporting an iwi in 2018 that they reported in 2013 was less than 80 per cent (78 per cent). The match rate varied significantly by iwi, from a low of 56 per cent to a high of 83 per cent. Consistency was generally higher for larger iwi.

For children born after Census 2013, their parental iwi response was used. The rationale was that iwi affiliation is based on *whakapapa* that is passed on intergenerationally, thus it was logically consistent for parental iwi to be "passed" to their children. Although statistical imputation methods were used to augment the census dataset for other variables, Data ILG advised that it was more appropriate to use individuals' historical responses from Census 2013 than to statistically predict iwi for all those missing a response.

For individuals that did report an iwi, there was some evidence that the design of the iwi question in the online form had reduced the number of iwi reported. Mitigation was thus also undertaken to address this mode effect. Where individuals had an iwi response in 2018 but reported fewer affiliations than in 2013, their additional responses from 2013 were added to their 2018 response. This did not increase the number of individuals reporting at least one iwi but did increase the total number of iwi reported. Using Census 2013 iwi data for adults and children reduced the missing data from 29 per cent of the Māori descent population to 16 per cent.

The next step to mitigate the missing iwi data was to compute non-response weights. Each person with iwi data in the Census 2018 dataset was given a weight. The weights were derived from a model which "estimates the probability that a person with certain characteristics would provide iwi data, then calculating the weight as the inverse of that probability" (Stats NZ 2021a).[7] For example if 20-year-old males from Northland had a 50 per cent probability of providing iwi data in Census 2018, those without iwi data were given a weight of two. The weights served a dual purpose. One was to increase the total iwi affiliation counts by rating up the iwi responses to the total Māori descent population. The other was to reduce the potential of the estimates being biased due to the different characteristics of those providing iwi data versus those not included.

To illustrate, for Te Aupōuri iwi in Northland, of the final estimated population of 11,847, 59 per cent came from Census 2018 responses, 20.9 per cent from Census 2013, 3.4 per cent from parental iwi, and the remaining 16.7 per cent from non-response weighting adjustment (Stats NZ 2021b).

To test the robustness of the foregoing methodology (M1), the estimated counts for five iwi were compared with estimates derived from two alternative methods (M2 and M3). The second method (M2) simply adjusted the Census 2013 counts for each of the five iwi by the intercensal growth for the Māori descent population. The third method (M3) involved weighting each of the five iwi, and only adding iwi from Census 2013 if individuals had a single iwi reported in 2018 but their Census 2013 record showed more than one (i.e., increasing the number of iwi, not the number of iwi-affiliated individuals, Stats NZ 2021a).

For most iwi, the two estimates based on 2013 census data were very similar (M1 and M2). However, for 32 iwi added to the revised Iwi Classification in 2017 (Stats NZ 2017), the approach of using 2013 census data tended to be between 2 per cent and 10 per cent lower than the weighting only approach (M3). For most iwi, estimates of their population size were between 20 and 40 per cent higher than their Census 2013 counts.

The Problem for "New" Statistical Iwi

The comparative exercise showed that the first method (M1) did not work well for iwi that were only recently added to the iwi classification. This is because they were not visible in the classification at the time of the 2013 census so the level of write-in responses recorded for them in 2013 were low. Using the 2013 data to derive responses for 2018 thus resulted in a downward bias.

One option was to use the weighting only approach (M3) for all iwi added to the classification in 2017. However there was not a definitive point where the weighting only approach (M3) could be judged as more appropriate than the primary mitigation approach (M1). Moreover, the latter approach enabled a greater number of the Māori descent population to directly contribute to the iwi. Ultimately the decision was a subjective one. For iwi where the contribution from 2013 census data was less than 5 per cent and the difference between the iwi total for the two estimators (M1 and M3) was greater than 10 per cent, the weighting only approach (M3) was used. For these iwi, there was a high risk that the approach of using 2013 census data (M1) would result in the population total being significantly under-estimated.

The estimated iwi counts were finally released in June 2021, more than three years after the 2018 census began. Apart from being very late, the estimates had significant limitations. One was that they were not released as official data so could not be reliably compared with previous census years (Stats NZ 2021c). Data were only available for a limited number of variables (e.g., age or sex but not age and sex) and the quality ranged from moderate to poor depending on how the data was used. Moreover, the degree of uncertainty increased as population size decreased, meaning poorer quality data for smaller iwi.

Te Whata—A by Iwi, for Iwi Data Platform

Having developed a complex methodology to produce estimated iwi counts, the challenge remained of making the data accessible and relevant to iwi—this was especially important given the inherent limitations of the adjusted data. For Data ILG it was also crucial to deliver benefit back to the communities contributing the data as the collective data rights-holders. To increase accessibility and uptake, the estimated counts were made available through Te Whata, a bespoke "by iwi, for iwi" data platform created by Te Kāhui Raraunga. Te Whata is the Māori word for a non-carved storehouse—in this case, a virtual data storehouse. Launched in 2020, Te Whata was designed by TKR and executed by private sector data science firms, as a mechanism to put iwi data in iwi hands. More than just a repository, Te Whata touches on many aspects of the data lifecycle including data collection, classification, analysis, infrastructure and workforce development.

Most of the iwi data accessible through Te Whata—which includes census data, Ministry of Education data and estimates from the nationally representative Māori wellbeing survey Te Kupenga 2013—are available in some form on agency websites. However, Te Whata is curated with an iwi audience in mind. It is more intuitive, is visually driven (with data available as key indicators and charts rather than tables) and has inbuilt flexibility to allow iwi analysts to make comparisons with other populations of interest (e.g., the national Aotearoa population and overall Māori population). Iwi information managers who have been nominated by an Iwi Authority are able to access and tailor a customisable dashboard on behalf of their iwi, enabling them to narrate their own data and integrate it into their reporting. This customized closed access functionality proved indispensable during the COVID-19 pandemic response, enabling iwi to access Ministry of Health meshblock[8] data on Māori vaccination rates so that they could target their vaccination outreach efforts at the street level. All of the data in Te Whata are aggregated data—it does not contain de-identified microdata but has been designed to readily accommodate more complex data if needed in the future.

The Future of Iwi Data in Aotearoa

The example of Census 2018 and the "fixing" of iwi data is illustrative of the messy nature of statistics where human judgements are inevitably imperfect and where Indigenous statistics are produced within the machinery of the state. As this chapter has shown, the pros and cons of taking a particular statistical approach were weighed up at every stage, based on the available information and possible alternatives. But the question remains—did it bring Stats NZ any closer to producing data that were useful, accurate and meaningful for tribes? In this instance the answer depends less on an assessment of the statistical robustness of the methods than it does on the conceptual underpinnings of what was being measured in the first place.

For some, the census would seem to be an exercise in scientific accounting and thus an optimal forum in which to gather accurate population information. After all, its very purpose is to literally count everyone in the population. However, as we have amply demonstrated throughout this book, census-taking processes are inherently political and statistics are never produced in a value-free vacuum. Even absent operational missteps, when enumeration is tied to some form of identity—whether it be ethnicity, ancestry, iwi affiliation, religion or gender—conceptual complexity will amplify statistical messiness. The tricky question of what makes a population a population, rather than a mere category or statistical construct, is too often assumed rather than carefully scrutinized, and the assumptions that prevail tend to reflect the values and priorities of those in power.

In the case of the Aotearoa census, iwi affiliation is based on self-identification—individuals simply self-report their tribe(s). However, for Māori, *whakapapa* is the pre-eminent—and many would argue sole—criteria for belonging. It matters less who an individual thinks they are than who others recognize them as. This *whakapapa*-centric way of understanding belonging is embedded in all tribal registration processes. As a condition of enrolment most tribes require individuals to furnish at least two generations of *whakapapa* (at least grandparent) and have some form of external validation (Kukutai and Rarere 2017). This aligns with *tikanga Māori* (customary protocols) for how belonging is determined—self-identification matters far less than external collective recognition and acceptance.

With the growing call for Indigenous Data Sovereignty in Aotearoa, and the release of the Māori Data Governance Model, one might argue that there has never been a better time to shift from government collection of tribal data to tribally defined data collection and population parameters. Problems with the 2023 census may hasten this shift. Stats NZ again experienced significant challenges with its recent census, with a national interim collection response rate below 90 per cent and a Māori collection response rate of just 77 per cent (Stats NZ 2024a). Moreover, further investigations after Census 2018 revealed that the 2013 census—which up until then was seen as a very successful enumeration—had also missed 50,000 Māori, with possible constitutional implications (Stats NZ 2022b). Given declining census response rates globally, 2023 may yet turn out to be the last Aotearoa census involving significant field enumeration.

The transition to an administrative census, perhaps with some form of survey augmentation, seems unavoidable amidst pressures to cut costs (Stats NZ 2024b). If Stats NZ cannot be relied upon to provide accurate and relevant iwi data (as has shown to be the case for at least two censuses), and the census is vulnerable to system failures, credible alternatives are needed. As the Māori Data Governance Model has shown, there are ample opportunities for more distributed and decentralized approaches to data collection, sharing and storage, as well as opportunities for tribes to define their population parameters through the use of tribal registers which privilege *whakapapa*-based ways of defining membership. To do so would require a high degree of comfort on the part of tribal members for their de-identified registration data to be used for census purposes. In its report on Census 2018, the EDQP questioned both Stats NZ's claimed "social licence" to reuse other government data for census purposes and whether the average New Zealander actually had a good understanding of how their data were being used. In a post-pandemic context, where declining trust, disinformation and strained social cohesion are very real features, simply assuming a social licence for secondary data use is a shaky foundation for a future-focused data system, let alone one that purports to be world leading. The creation of tribally controlled data infrastructure would need to meet collective expectations grounded in *tikanga Māori*, as well as more mainstream concepts of accountability, transparency and trust. The foundations for this have already been laid by TMR, Data ILG, TKR and other iwi and Māori data experts. The real test will be whether the New Zealand government is ready and willing to step aside and let iwi lead. Nearly two decades ago the United Nations Permanent Forum on Indigenous Issues called for official data to "better reflect the lived experiences and information needs of indigenous communities" (2006). At a bare minimum this ought to encompass the provision for tribes to define their own population parameters.

Notes

1. Under the "digital-first" model, households received an internet access code by post before census day and were encouraged to complete the census online without the help of a census field worker. Stats NZ aimed for at least 70 per cent of respondents to complete their census forms online (Stats NZ, 2018b).
2. The rates were considered interim because official rates can only be determined by a census Post Enumeration Survey.
3. The author was a member of the EDQP that gave this rating.
4. The author warmly acknowledges the expertise provided by Stats NZ methodologist Gareth Minshall and manager Tamie Anakotta.
5. Prior to 2018, the iwi question was only asked of those who answered "Yes" to the Māori descent question. This was extended to include "Don't Know" in 2018.
6. The investigation excluded what Stats NZ calls "partially coded" iwi, which are responses that cannot be coded to a specific iwi (e.g., iwi confederation and waka (ancestral canoe) responses). A fuller description of the methodology can be found in Stats NZ (2021a, 2021b).
7. To model the probability that a person was missing iwi data, logistic regression was used with person effects of single-year age groups by sex and total personal income groupings, and area level effects for regional council and statistical area level 2.
8. Meshblocks typically comprise no more than 120 dwellings.

References

2018 Census External Data Quality Panel (2018 Census EDQP). *Initial Report of the 2018 Census External Data Quality Panel*. Wellington: Stats NZ, 2019.

Data Iwi Leaders Group (Data ILG). *Mana Ōrite Relationship Agreement*. Rotorua: Data Iwi Leaders Group, 2019.

Fenton, Francis. *Observations on the State of the Aboriginal Inhabitants of New Zealand*. Auckland: New Zealand Government, 1859.

Jack, Murray, and Connie Graziadei. *Report of the Independent Review of New Zealand's 2018 Census*. Wellington: Stats NZ, 2019.

Kukutai, Tahu. "Quantum Māori, Māori Quantum: Representations of Māori Identities in the Census, 1857/8–2006." In *Counting Stories, Moving Ethnicities: Studies from Aotearoa New Zealand*, edited by Rosalind McClean, Brad Patterson, and David Swain, 27–51. Hamilton: University of Waikato, 2012.

Kukutai, Tahu, and Moana Rarere. "Iwi Sex Ratios in the New Zealand Population Census: Why Are Women So Dominant?" *New Zealand Population Review* 43 (2017): 63–92.

Kukutai, Tahu, and Moana Rarere. "Tracking Patterns of Tribal Identification in the New Zealand Census, 1991 to 2006." *New Zealand Population Review* 39 (2013): 1–23.

Kukutai, Tahu, and Maggie Walter. "Recognition and Indigenizing Official Statistics: Aotearoa New Zealand and Australia." *Statistical Journal of the IAOS* 31, no. 2 (2015): 317–326.

Madden, Richard, Per Axelsson, Tahu Kukutai, Kalinda Griffiths, Christina Storm Mienna, Ngiare Brown, Clare Coleman, and Ian Ring. "Statistics on Indigenous Peoples: International Effort Needed." *Statistical Journal of the IAOS* 32 (2016): 37–41.

New Zealand Data Futures Forum. *Harnessing the Economic and Social Power of Data*. Wellington: New Zealand Data Futures Forum, 2014.

Office of the Minister of Statistics. *Census Transformation—A Promising Future*. Wellington: Office of the Minister of Statistics, 2015.

Rarere, Moana. *The Determinants of Tribal Population Growth in the New Zealand Census*. Unpublished master's thesis, University of Waikato, 2012.

Statistics New Zealand. *A Report on the 2006 Post-enumeration Survey*. Wellington: Statistics New Zealand, 2007.

Statistics New Zealand. *Coverage in the 2013 Census Based on the New Zealand 2013 Post-Enumeration Survey*. Wellington: Statistics New Zealand, 2014.

Stats NZ. *Stats NZ Updates Iwi Statistical Standard*. Wellington: Stats NZ, 2017. www.scoop.co.nz/stories/PO1709/S00458/stats-nz-updates-iwi-statistical-standard.htm?from-mobile=bottom-link-01.

Stats NZ. *2018 Census Update*. Wellington: Stats NZ, 2018a. www.stats.govt.nz/news/2018-census-update-2.

Stats NZ. *2018 Census: Design of Forms*. Wellington: Stats NZ, 2018b. www.stats.govt.nz/assets/Reports/2018-census-design-of-forms/2018-Census-Design-of-forms.pdf.

Stats NZ. *2018 Census: Interim Coverage Rates, Collection Response Rates, and Data Sources*. Wellington: Stats NZ, 2019. www.stats.govt.nz/reports/2018-census-interim-coverage-rates-collection-response-rates-and-data-sources.

Stats NZ. *Methodology for the 2018 Iwi Affiliation Estimated Counts*. Wellington: Stats NZ, 2021a. www.stats.govt.nz/methods/methodology-for-the-2018-iwi-affiliation-estimated-counts.

Stats NZ. *Iwi Affiliation (Estimated Counts): 2018 Data Sources and Quality by Iwi*. Wellington: Stats NZ, 2021b. www.stats.govt.nz/reports/iwi-affilation-estimated-counts-2018-data-sources-and-quality-by-iwi.

Stats NZ. *Strengths and Limitations of the 2018 Iwi Affiliation Estimated Counts*. Wellington: Stats NZ, 2021c. www.stats.govt.nz/methods/strengths-and-limitations-of-2018-iwi-affiliation-estimated-counts.

Stats NZ. *Census Iwi and Iwi-Related Groups Statistical Classification*. Wellington: Stats NZ, 2022a. https://aria.stats.govt.nz/aria/?&_ga=2.96516187.537048382.1690197223-1956376772.1669592253#ClassificationView:uri=http://stats.govt.nz/cms/ClassificationVersion/NdoVpaBrOkxg61br.

Stats NZ. *Māori Population Under-Estimation in 2013: Analysis and Findings*. Wellington: Stats NZ, 2022b. www.stats.govt.nz/reports/maori-population-under-estimation-in-2013-analysis-and-findings/#:~:text=wanting%20more%20detail.-,Summary%20of%20key%20points,ERP)%20at%2030%20June%202013.

Stats NZ. *Census Enters Next Phase Following National Collection of Census Forms*. Wellington: Stats NZ, 2023. www.stats.govt.nz/news/2023-census-enters-next-phase-following-national-collection-of-census-forms/.

Stats NZ. *Interim Coverage Rates, Collection Response Rates, and Data Sources for the 2023 Census*. Wellington: Stats NZ, 2024a. www.stats.govt.nz/reports/interim-coverage-rates-collection-response-rates-and-data-sources-for-the-2023-census/.

Stats NZ. *Modernising Our Approach to the 2028 Census. Discussion Document for Public Consultation*. Wellington: Stats NZ, 2024b. www.stats.govt.nz/consultations/modernising-our-approach-to-the-2028-census/.

Te Mana Raraunga. *Te Mana Raraunga Statement on 2018 New Zealand Census of Population and Dwellings: A Call for Action on Māori Census Data*, 2018. www.temanararaunga.maori.nz/nga-panui.

United Nations. *Principles and Recommendations for Population and Housing Censuses: Revision 2*. New York: Department of Economic and Social Affairs Statistics Division, 2008.

Walling, Julie, Desi Small-Rodriguez, and Tahu Kukutai. "Tallying Tribes: Waikato-Tainui in the Census and Iwi Register." *Social Policy Journal of New Zealand* 36 (2009): 2–15.

9
DOING INDIGENOUS STATISTICS IN AUSTRALIA

The Racial Burden of Disregard

Maggie Walter

CHAPTER LEARNING OBJECTIVES

Objective 1: Critically examine the survey initiation process and recognize that the who, what, where, when and why is central to enacting an Indigenous quantitative methodology.

Objective 2: Explore how methodologically framing the survey through the Indigenous lifeworld-centred Indigenous Peoples as knowers in exploring race relations in this city.

Objective 3: Connect how Indigenous methodology linked the initiation, design, collection, analysis and interpretation elements to ensure study coherence and serve Indigenous needs.

Introduction[1,2]

Race relations are the social, political, cultural and economic relations between different racial groupings within the same society (Park 1950). Manifesting at the individual/personal and communal levels, race relations are structurally embedded, shaping lived daily realities and life chances. Their impact, however, is uneven. All societies exhibit a racial hierarchy, with those at the top tending to be consistently privileged across social, cultural, economic and political domains as, simultaneously, those at bottom tend to be consistently disadvantaged. Race relations are thus relations of power. In the colonizer-settler nation of Australia, the primary set of race relations is that between the Euro-Australian majority and the Aboriginal Peoples of the lands the nation-state now occupies.

Aboriginal Peoples have occupied the continent of Australia for upwards of 40,000 years. British colonization from the late 18th century onwards has reduced the presence of the continent's traditional owners of many millennia to just 3 per cent of the total Australian population. The ongoing legacy of colonization means that Aboriginal people are also the most disadvantaged group in Australia. Aboriginal and Torres Strait Islander Peoples experience the highest rates of poverty, unemployment, morbidity and incarceration and the lowest rates of educational achievement and life expectancy (see AIHW 2024 for details). With three quarters of the contemporary Aboriginal population living in towns and cities (ABS 2019), these inequalities are largely enacted within the same geographic locations as socio-economic advantage is experienced by the non-Indigenous majority.

There is little dispute on the historical inequality of race relations in Australia. Frontier war, violent dispossessions, segregation, containment, the imposition of race-based laws and the forced removal of children shaped Aboriginal lives from early colonization until well into the second half of the 20th century (see Chesterman and Galligan 1997 for a detailed exploration). The continuance of unequal race relations is more contested. While the extreme level of socio-economic and health disparities is undeniable, an influential public/political discourse resists the notion that the continuation of poor Aboriginal life outcomes are race (or racism) related. The dismantling of formal discriminatory regulations throughout the 20th century underpins a dominant public and political narrative of Australia as a racially egalitarian society. The proponents of this story, however, are largely the inheritors of the benefits that have flowed to the descendants of colonialism and are directly tied to the brutal dispossession of the Peoples of the lands they now occupy and from which they draw their wealth and identity (Walter 2018). This discourse is also a cost-avoidance mechanism which allows this inheritance of colonization's spoils to be perceived in terms of deservingness and national pride. Under this logic, embedded Aboriginal inequality is understood in terms of a sad and unfair, but distant and remote, history, now replaced by a benevolent policy environment which attempts to support Aboriginal people in bettering themselves via the education and employment opportunities available to all Australians. This discourse can be clearly observed in the primary Indigenous policy framework *Closing the Gap*.[3] *Closing the Gap*, active from 2008 onwards, is built across health, education and employment targets and lists as its primary aim to "to improve the lives of Aboriginal and Torres Strait Islander Australians" (NIAA 2019). Despite ten years of the framework's acknowledged policy failure (2008–2018) (Grindlay 2017), the overarching belief that improving Aboriginal socio-economic outcomes will resolve inequality is replicated in the new "refreshed" *Closing the Gap* policy agenda.

The research presented in this chapter tests the discourse of Australia as a racially egalitarian nation. In particular it tests the link between this assumed egalitarianism and the desired model of the "good Aboriginal citizen," who betters themselves through education and employment and adopting Euro-Australian norms (Moreton-Robinson 2009), as the panacea for racially located inequality. In doing so, it takes a socio-structural lens situating the concepts of racial egalitarianism and good citizenship within the everyday lived race relation experiences of Aboriginal people. In seeking the view from the other side of the dichotomy, those who have been dispossessed from the land of more than 2,000 generations of ancestors, the research deviates from the significant, but largely descriptive, literature related to Indigenous inequality (see Productivity Commission 2016 as an example).

This research also reverses the long Indigenous history of being silenced by mainstream institutions with few opportunities to tell their own truths (Bretherton and Mellor 2006) through its use of data from a 2015 stratified sample survey of Aboriginal people. This research was commissioned by Larrakia Nation, the organization representing the traditional owners of the area from Darwin, a city of around 70,000 in the Northern Territory. Its purpose was to give voice, as knowing subjects, to Aboriginal experiences of everyday race relations. A central tenet of this giving voice was the use of specific geographic location data, rather than aggregate data, allowing the results to be contextually situated in the social milieu in which they occur. Additionally, rather than being a module or subset of data of a bigger survey, the survey instrument's topic is lived race relations. The results are framed through the theoretical lens of the race bind (Walter 2014) which identifies the self-serving contradictions inherent in Euro-Australian understandings of egalitarianism within the wider concept of relations with the country's First Nations.

The analysis and most of the literature included in this chapter refer to the Australian context. There are cautions, therefore, in presuming that the theories, concepts and empirical findings detailed here have salience for other colonized first world peoples. However, the similarity of Indigenous socio-cultural positioning in other nations built from Anglo colonization such as Canada, Aotearoa New Zealand, Hawaii and the United States suggests that the concept of the race bind and the findings around racial disregard would also be applicable in these countries.

Australian Race Relations

The Australian empirical race relations literature is a relatively small, but consistent, body of work. Primarily drawn from research on the views of the majority non-Indigenous population on Aboriginal people and culture, this literature dates from at least the late 1960s (see Beswick and Hills 1969; Western 1969; Mellor 2003; Goot and Rowse 2007; Dunn et al. 2009; Reconciliation Australia 2016). These studies indicate a persistence in racial prejudice and racialized attitudes. While these views exist across the non-Indigenous population, older, male, rural and lower educated non-Indigenous Australians are most likely to record negative racial attitudes. While there is variation across studies, mostly due to variation in question framing, the level of negative attitudes depends on the issue under question. For example, a small majority of non-Indigenous Australians tend to support generic items such as the value of Aboriginal culture to the national identity, but support drops below 50 per cent on items related to racial egalitarianism such as the impact of racism or colonization on contemporary Aboriginal inequality (Goot and Rowse 2007). For instance, Walter (2012), using data from the 2007 Australian Survey of Social Attitudes (AUSSA), found that while 53 per cent of respondents (n = 2,618) agreed with the statement: *Aboriginal people should not have to change their culture to fit into Australian society*, only 45 per cent agreed with the statement: *Aboriginal people's level of disadvantage justifies extra government assistance.*

The literature on Aboriginal perspectives is smaller but reflects a very different understanding of race relations via a focus on Aboriginal peoples' experience of racism. The 2016 Australian Reconciliation Barometer, for example, which includes an Indigenous sample of around 500, found 57 per cent of Indigenous respondents compared to 39 per cent non-Indigenous agreed with the statement that Australia is a racist country. Most of the Aboriginal perspectives literature relates to the experience of racism with studies consistently finding that a significant majority of Aboriginal respondents report such experiences as relatively common (Zubrick et al. 2005; Larson et al. 2007; Paradies and Cunningham 2009; Ferdinand et al. 2013; Cunningham and Paradies 2013) Locations of negative racially based interactions were frequently identified as shops, public spaces and educational, sport and employment settings.

The likelihood of Aboriginal people experiencing racism has also been explored. The results are mixed, again likely due to the different populations sampled and variation in the questions asked in the different studies. For example, some results suggest those aged 35–44 and those with higher income and higher education are more likely to report experiences of racism. Conversely, being a homeowner, living in a remote area (communities with Aboriginal majority population) and having relatively few Indigenous friends are associated with a lower reporting rates of experiencing racism Paradies and Cunningham (2009), Cunningham and Paradies (2013), Ferdinand et al. (2013). Aboriginal people with no permanent accommodation are particularly vulnerable to interpersonal racism (Holmes and McRae-Williams 2009; Birdsall-Jones et al. 2010).

The Race Bind: Race Relations in the Colonizing Nation-State

There is a large and voluminous theoretical sociological literature related to race and racism. This is rich literature with most based on the binary of White American/African American relations, where the central claim is that the now discredited ideas of racial biological superiority/inferiority have not been disrupted, but merely been replaced by other justifications (Kinder and Sears 1981; Bobo 1997; Sears and Henry 2005; Bonilla-Silva 2010). The theoretical concepts of this literature, of racial resentment, of the moral and cultural deficit of the racial other and the structural nature of racism have salience to contemporary Australian race relations. But of themselves they are incomplete as a conceptual framework. What they lack is a comprehension of the race relations of the colonized nation-state, where colonization, and its aftermath, are the defining feature. As argued by Glenn (2015, 54) settler colonialism is "a distinct transnational formation whose political and economic projects have shaped and continue to shape race relations in first world nations that were established through settler colonialism." Colonized first world nations are undergirded by a specific set of narratives, logics and epistemologies (Glenn 2015). These have specific effect in the shaping of race relations between a non-Indigenous majority and the colonized Indigenous group that is not directly analogous to race relations between a non-Indigenous majority and a non-Indigenous minority group (Deloria 1984; Simpson 2014). As articulated by Wolfe (1999), settler colonialism not only typically employs the organizing grammar of race but it does so within what needs to be understood as an ongoing project. Or as Wolfe terms it, invasion is a structure, not an event.

The race bind, or racial narrative paradox, incorporates the theoretical insights of Wolfe (1999, 2006) and Glenn (2015) by highlighting the inherent cognitive dissonance of colonizing settler relations that are the foundation of their own egalitarian narrative logic. Shaped by the uncomfortable legacy of the nation-state's origins, the dispossession of the Indigenous Peoples, these narratives, epistemologies, logics and grammars are the mechanism that neutralizes the paradox of the core epistemological irreconcilability of founding realities and the requisite powerful nation-building story. To achieve this discursive sleight, the race bind promulgates a set of contradictions that allow the claim of egalitarianism and the denial of racial inequality without disturbing the embedded racial hierarchy of Indigenous disadvantage and Euro-Australian privilege. Running mostly as an undercurrent, largely and deliberately invisible to the non-Indigenous majority, race-bind logics are more aggressively deployed if the status quo of race relations are challenged. My rationale in the naming of this theoretical concept as the race bind signifies the bind these logics creates for Indigenous People/s who are caught neatly between the lived consequences of highly unequal race relations and the publicly and political disavowal of the very existence of race-based inequity.

Four race-bind contradictions are identifiable in Australian discourses and practice of claims of egalitarianism. The first, *individual racially located deficit*, fits with new racism's moral and cultural differences model as per Bobo (1997) and Sears and Henry (2005). Echoing older biological inferiority beliefs, these discourses can be clearly heard in dominant explanations of Aboriginal disadvantage. An example is found in former Prime Minister Abbott's introduction to the 2014 annual *Closing the Gap* report to Parliament. The introduction states, "[F]or the gap to close we must get kids to school, adults to work and the ordinary law of the land observed. Everything flows from meeting these three objectives" (2014, 1). With these two sentences years of continued policy failure is explicitly linked to what are identified as Aboriginal peoples' morally deficit behaviours. The enabling contradiction is the individualizing but racializing logic. In this discursive device disadvantage is due to personal, but distinctly Aboriginal, failure as parents, as people and as citizens, encompassing Moreton-Robinson's (2009) "good Aboriginal citizen" model; there is an Aboriginal failure to "improve" themselves, as individuals, through educational endeavour, labour force participation and adherence to the law. In doing so, this contradiction serves its other race-bind purpose of erasing the social structural realities of Indigenous lives, inclusive of grinding intergenerational poverty, poor health, lack of basic services and ongoing socio-cultural marginalization.

The second race-bind contradiction is *national pride/national silence*, where the prideful national narrative of Australia as a bastion of egalitarianism is contradicted by the steadfast refusal to engage with the nation's genesis and the past and present impact of this on the nation's First Peoples. In this discourse any referral to past injustice is cast as irrelevant to contemporary racial relationships and an unfairness to modern-day non-Indigenous Australians who bear no responsibility. An empirical example of this contradiction is the inheritors of the benefits of colonization continuing refusal to change Australia's national day from commemorating the date British colonization formally began as the most important date in Australian history. Counter-narratives driven by long-running Aboriginal public protests at the celebration of "Invasion Day" are gaining some traction, but public and political resistance to change is fierce.

Aligned with national pride/national silence is the *racism denial/racial antipathy* contradiction. In this race-bind element an undercurrent of resentment towards Aboriginal people, who by their very presence cast a pall over the nation-state's claims to legitimacy, co-exists with what Bonilla-Silva (2010) would label "a sincerely held fiction" that Australia is not a racist country. The result is a public discourse which denies the role of race within what are clearly overt acts of racism. In a now infamous incident, Aboriginal footballer Adam Goodes pointed out to security a crowd member who was hurling racist insults. The crowd response at this and future games was a sustained booing whenever Goodes appeared on the field, effectively ending his career. Much of the extensive public commentary of the observably race-based incident absurdly insisted that the booing had nothing to do with racism but was linked to negative aspects of Goodes' own personality and that the real victim was the racially abusive football fan.

The fourth contradiction, *reconciliation but no change*, is a proclaimed commitment to make peace with Aboriginal and Torres Strait Islander people paired with an unwillingness to alter existing dynamics of race relations of power. For example, Australia was one of only four countries to vote against the United Nations Declaration of the Rights of Indigenous Peoples in 2007. More latterly the combined call from 250 Indigenous leaders for the right to be consulted on Indigenous-related legislation and policies[4] was summarily rejected. Despite being the culmination of a government-initiated consultation, then Prime Minister Turnbull's official response stated: "The Government does not believe such an addition to our national representative institutions is either desirable or capable of winning acceptance at a referendum" (Grattan 2017). This refusal was justified in terms of race being irrelevant to power structures, going on to say, "[Our] democracy is built on the foundation of all Australian citizens having equal civic rights" and therefore an Indigenous say on Indigenous related matters "is inconsistent with this fundamental principle" (Grattan 2017).

These four race-bind contradictions buttress each other with the incongruence inherent in the constructs seemingly strengthening rather than debunking claims of race egalitarianism. The incompatible juxtapositions ensure that the enduring nature of the Australian unequal racial relations are maintained, largely unchallenged. Effectively muting alternative or internally consistent narratives of Indigenous disregard, the race-bind logics support Euro-Australian privilege while stridently denying the existence of such privilege.

Method and Methodology

The research was conducted in Darwin, the capital city of the Northern Territory. At about 10 per cent of the roughly 100,000 population (ABS 2016), the Aboriginal population is comprised of permanent residents, inclusive of many Larrakia people, the traditional owners, and a smaller, but significant, visiting population. Visitors come for multiple reasons including accessing health and other services, visiting relatives, shopping, addressing legal issues, attending sporting events or sometimes just escaping the restrictions of their own "dry" communities, where no alcohol is allowed. The most visible of these, commonly referred to as "long grassers," camp in public spaces around the city.

Darwin has a long history of racial inequality. The first Europeans arrived in 1869 and enacted the Northern Territory Aboriginals *Act* (1910) as the township grew. This act and subsequent legislation and ordinances controlled nearly every aspect of Aboriginal peoples' existence. Aboriginal children were deemed wards of the state, Aboriginal people were denied the vote, restrictions were imposed on where people could work and whom they could marry and compounds, such as the notorious Khalin compound just outside the town limits of Darwin, segregated Aboriginal people from the non-Aboriginal population. It was not until the late 1970s that many of these regulations were dismantled (Chesterman and Galligan 1997). This history is a living memory for many residents and its legacy continues. Compared to non-Indigenous Darwin residents, Aboriginal people are three times as likely to be unemployed, more likely to live in overcrowded housing or be homeless and less likely to be a homeowner, and they have much lower median income and educational levels (ABS 2016).

Race relations in Darwin are also reflected in, and affected by, recent and ongoing events. In 1979 the Larrakia people launched the Kenbi land claim for their traditional country. The claim was vigorously by disputed by the Northern Territory Government but finally, in 2016 after a tortuous journey through the courts, roughly 63,000 hectares of land was placed in trust for Larrakia traditional owners. Also, in the 1970s, the Bagot Aboriginal reserve was handed back to its residents. Now home to 400 Aboriginal people there is a constant political pressure for the land to be absorbed into the surrounding high-income suburbs. Most latterly, in 2017 Darwin's Don Dale Youth Detention Center was the subject of the Royal Commission. The Commission found systematic, shocking failures, with the mostly Aboriginal detainees subjected to regular mistreatment including racial abuse, physical abuse and humiliation (Russell and Cuneen 2017).

In 2013, Larrakia Nation, the peak advocacy and support agency for traditional owners, concerned at what they perceived as a lack of Aboriginal voice in decision-making, contacted the researchers. The result was a collaborative research project, *Telling It Like It Is* (TILII), which comprised three interlinked studies: a social media phase; a qualitative phase of repeat interviews of a representative group of 40 Aboriginal people; and a survey phase, designed to evaluate more broadly the race relations insights generated from first two phases. The paper uses data from the survey phase of 470 Aboriginal residents of the Greater Darwin area.

This project consciously adopted an Indigenous methodological framework, which takes Indigenous knowledges and protocols, cultural values, ways of understanding the world and Indigenous needs and priorities as the research foundations (Walter and Andersen 2013). At the practice level this means that all aspects of the research supported Indigenous aspirations and incorporated Indigenous governance mechanisms. The research framework also emphasized the social, historical and political contexts which shape Indigenous experience, lives, positions and futures (see Tuhiwai Smith 1999; Martin 2008). Indigenous methodologies, therefore, not only reverse the traditional paradigm of the Indigene as the researched "other" but also recognize that all research is a social and cultural artefact, shaped and informed by researchers' own socio-cultural positioning.

The four project principals, three Euro-Australian and one Aboriginal (*palawa*) researcher (the author of this chapter) worked in collaboration with Larrakia Nation, its staff and the locally employed Aboriginal field staff. All were familiarized with the cultural norms and on-the-ground realities of Aboriginal people in the Greater Darwin area, and interviewer training emphasized the creation of relational rather than transactional social relationships. Gender cultural norms were respected and all non-Indigenous researchers were always accompanied by an Aboriginal team member in interactions between field staff and respondents.

The survey was conducted by a predominantly Aboriginal field team during October–November 2015, after the survey instrument was successfully piloted with 25 Aboriginal respondents. The survey instrument had six sections, with Section 1 asking about the level of interaction between respondents and White People (this term was adopted based on its usage by Aboriginal respondents in the qualitative interviews); Section 2 on White People's attitudes towards Aboriginal People; Section 3 on the respondent's own experiences of racism; Section 4 on the Aboriginal position in the legal and political system in Darwin; Section 5 on respondent's thoughts on current race relations and how they could be improved; and Section 6 on the respondent's demographic data. Surveys were undertaken face to face with the field interviewer asking the questions and noting the respondents' answers on a paper survey form. Each survey was numbered to allow the survey to be de-identified post-collection. An overview of the results of the study, including the survey, were presented at a public forum in Darwin in 2016 and an overview of survey results were sent to all respondents who indicated they would like to be kept informed of the results.

Results

A random sample of Aboriginal residents in Darwin was not possible as there is no usable sampling frame. To address representativeness, the survey sample was stratified by age, gender, housing occupancy and employment status in line with the Census 2011 Aboriginal socio-demographic profile. As shown in Table 9.1, there is a close alignment between the two. There are slightly more women in the TILII sample, slightly fewer respondents in the 18- to 24-year-old age group and slightly more in the 55 years and

TABLE 9.1 Telling It Like It Is Sample and 2011 Census of Population and Housing Comparison

Variable	Attributes	TILIT 2015 %	Census 2011 %
Gender			
	Male	44.7	48.1
	Female	55.3	51.9
Age			
	18–24	23.4	19.5
	25–34	21.3	22.5
	35–44	21.8	23.1
	45–54	19.6	17.8
	55 and over	13.9	17.1
Housing Tenure			
	Own/Mortgage	30.1	33.8
	Rent Public	43.6	41.6
	Rent Private	16.6	14.9
	Not applicable	9.3	9.7
Labour Market Status			
	Employed	46.7	45.2
	Not in Labour Force	53.3	54.8

Data Source: Census 2011 Darwin Local Government Area Community Profile (Aboriginal) and TILII Survey older age group than in the 2011 census data. Therefore, while the TILII survey makes no claim to generalization, the results are likely to be highly reflective of what would be obtained from the Aboriginal population.

To gain a broad picture of race relations in Darwin, respondents were asked to rate current Aboriginal/non-Aboriginal race relations on a five-point Likert scale where 1 equalled "very good" and 5 equalled "very bad." As shown in Table 9.2 less than one-quarter rated race relations as "good" or "very good." Based on qualitative results indicating a perception that race relations were deteriorating, respondents were also asked if they thought race relations in Darwin had improved or worsened over the last ten years. As shown in the table, the majority recorded that race relations had worsened, with only 23 per cent thinking things had gotten better.

Respondents were also asked about their own experience of racism, over three conceptual measures, again based on the responses of the qualitative interviewees. The first was *disrespect*. Survey participants were asked: *How often have you felt no respect as an Aboriginal person?* with responses on a four-point scale: "a lot," "sometimes," "hardly ever," "not at all." The second measure was *discrimination*. For this item participants responded to the question: *How often have you felt you have been treated unfairly because you are Aboriginal?* across the same four-point scale. The third measure was *alienation*. This question asked: *How often have your felt it was hard to go anywhere in Darwin because of feeling judged by White people? (for example staring at you, making you feel uncomfortable etc.)*. All measures were operationalized as how often the person experienced these in the last six months. This reference period was chosen as being long enough to provide a point of reference for frequency and short enough for respondents to recall specific incidences.

The results are displayed in Table 9.3. Just over 70 per cent of respondents reported discrimination or disrespect in the last six months "a lot" or "sometimes." A smaller majority (57%) reported "alienation" "a lot" or "sometimes" in the last six months. Only 10 per cent reported

TABLE 9.2 Perceptions of Race Relations

Race relations now (n = 471)	%	Better or worse in last 10 years (n = 469)	%
Very Good	2.8	A Lot Better	3.8
Good	22.1	A Little Better	19.2
Not Very Good	52.4	The Same	21.7
Pretty Bad	13.0	A Bit Worse	24.7
Very Bad	9.8	A Lot Worse	30.5

TABLE 9.3 Reported Experience of Interpersonal Racism

Reported level of experience (n=470)	Disrespect %	Discrimination %	Alienation %
A lot	18.3	21.1	16.5
Sometimes	52.5	49.3	40.4
Hardly ever	18.6	19.6	21.6
Not at all	10.4	10.0	21.6

no experiences of "discrimination" or "disrespect" and 22 per cent reported no experience of "alienation" in the last six months.

The impact of different socio-economic and demographic attributes was then assessed with variations found across the three measures. These are detailed in Table 9.4. As shown, gender was non-significant, with male and female respondents reporting similar levels on each measure. Experience of interpersonal racism did vary by age group, although this was only statistically significant for "disrespect" and "alienation." The pattern was similar across the three interpersonal racism types with those in the 18–24 age group reporting higher rates than those in 25–44 age groups. The level then rises for the two older age groups, except for "alienation," where those aged 55 years or more reported the lowest level.

The association between employment status and interpersonal racism was statistically significant across all three measures. Those who were unemployed, on a pension (disability or age) and full-time students reported higher levels of "disrespect," "discrimination" and "alienation" than those working full or part time. Level of education, however, was only statistically significant for "alienation" with those without post-school qualifications reporting higher levels of interpersonal racism on this measure. Housing tenure was also strongly associated with level of interpersonal racism. Homeowners reported the lowest levels of interpersonal racism, and this was especially evident on the "alienation" measure. In contrast, those living in the long grass or visiting reported very high levels of interpersonal racism across all three measures.

With the results indicating that racism is a common experience for the Aboriginal residents of Darwin, a multivariate model (ordinary least squares regression or OLS) was used to assess the influence of socio-demographic attributes. The dependent variable "racialized disregard" was derived by combining the scores of the three individual measures of *disrespect, discrimination* and *alienation* into one composite score. The mean score was inserted for six cases with a missing response on one item. No case missed more than one response on the three items. A scale test

TABLE 9.4 Level of Interpersonal Racism by Socio-Economic and Demographic Attributes

Variable	Variable attributes	Disrespect "A lot" or "Sometimes" %	Discrimination "A lot" or "Sometimes" %	Alienation "A lot" or "Sometimes" %
Gender	Male	69.8	72.1	54.6
	Female	71.9	68.9	58.6
Age Group				
	18–24	73.9*	69.1	61.2*
	25–34	67.4	71.0	52.5
	35–44	67.6	65.0	52.0
	45–54	75.3	76.4	68.8
	55+	70.8	71.2	47.0
Labour Force Status				
	Full Time (36.4%)	62.8*	61.0*	45.1**
	Part Time (10.3%)	59.2	53.0	36.7
	Unemployed (27.8%)	80.3	82.1	68.6
	On Pension (15.6%)	74.2	80.6	69.3
	At home caring for Family	69.5	60.9	65.2
	Full-Time Student	89.7	86.9	72.3
Highest Educational Level				
	No Post School Qualifications	74.4	77.9	63.8*
	Trade/Certificate/Diploma	68.6	67.0	55.5
	Bachelor Degree/Above	71.1	63.2	36.8
Housing Tenure				
	Own/Mortgage	58.8*	56.3**	37.1**
	Rent Privately	71.4	73.5	53.8
	Rent Community/Public	75.4	72.5	65.7
	Long grass/visiting	88.8	95.3	86.4

*$p<.05$ ** $p<.01$

indicated that the three measures formed a reliable item (Cronbach's alpha .722). Scores ranged from 3 to 12, representing both ends of the racial disregard spectrum, with those who scored 3 (n = 30) answering that they had experienced each of the three measures "a lot" in the last six months and those scoring 12 (n = 18) answering "not at all" to all three measures.

The set of predictor variables included the socio-economic and demographic variables examined in the bivariate analysis, with age added as a continuous variable (18–85 years). The number of people in the household, a continuous measure (1–17), was also included, based on the literature which suggests larger households are more likely to attract negative interactions with non-Indigenous authorities. Two other variables ("Who is your mob?" and "Darwin residency") were added to test whether being a traditional owner (Larrakia) or length of residence in Darwin were influential factors. These additional variable descriptions are detailed in Table 9.5.

The results from the regression model are outlined in Table 9.6. Overall the model accounted for 10.6 per cent of the variance in the level of racialized disregard experienced by participants. Once all variables were included, gender, age, level of education, length of residence and country affiliation variables yielded no statistically significant results. Unemployed respondents were statistically more likely to have a lower score (higher level of disregard) than those in full employment, but there were no statistically significant differences between those in part-time work or out of the labour market for other reasons and those in full-time employment.

The other statistically significant variables were housing tenure and household size. Compared to homeowners (outright/mortgage), those who rented publicly or privately or who had no tenure (town camps or the long grass) record statistically significantly lower "racialized disregard" scores. The difference is marked for those with no permanent housing, with coefficients substantially lower than those in owner occupier housing. Other types of tenure were also predictive of a lower racial disregard score. Household size is significant with larger households predictive of lower racial disregard scores.

Discussion

This study sought to test the dominant discourse of Australia as a racially egalitarian nation. The results largely refute this discourse. At the individual level, the majority of respondents reported experiencing interpersonal

TABLE 9.5 Additional Explanatory Variables in Regression Analysis

Variable	Description	%
Residency in Darwin		
	All life (REF)	52.1
	1–10 years	34.2
	Less than one year/visiting	13.7
Who is your mob?		
	Larrakia (REF)	15.7
	Other Northern Territory clan	71.3
	Outside of Northern Territory/Don't Know	13.0

TABLE 9.6 Burden of Racial Disregard Model Coefficients

Adj. R2 = 10.6	B	Std. Error	Sig.
Constant	8.600	.507	.000
Male	−.145	.206	−.703
Female (ref)			
Other NT	.231	.284	.417
Not from NT/Don't Know	.389	.378	.305
Larrakia (ref)			
Employed Part-Time	.240	.348	.491
Unemployed	−.613	.303	.044*
Pension/Other	−.540	.353	.127
At Home Caring	−.133	.503	.791
Full Time Student	−.799	.479	.096
Employed Full-Time (ref)			
Age in Years	−.001	.008	.937
In Darwin <=1 year or visiting	−.524	.330	.113
In Darwin 1–10 years	−.382	.232	.100
Resident in Darwin all life (ref)			
Renting Public	−.685	.275	.013*
Renting Private	−.872	.306	.005*
No Permanent Housing	−1.940	.461	.000**
Own (outright/mortgage) (ref)			
Number in household (continuous)	−.145	.041	.000**
Bachelor Degree or Higher	−.280	.419	.504
Trade/Diploma/Certificate	−.191	.221	.390
No Post School Qualifications (ref)			

Dependent Variable: Disrespect, Discrimination and Alienation Scores Combined

racism within each of the three categories in the last six months. For Aboriginal residents of Darwin, in line with the research literature, being disrespected and treated unfairly because of their race is an everyday, relatively frequent experience. Less common, but still a reality for a majority of respondents, was feeling alienated in public spaces under a perceived racialized judgemental gaze from non-Indigenous Darwin residents.

The second aspect of the racially egalitarian nation discourse is the potential of decreased inequality via the "good Aboriginal citizen" model. This aspect was tested via an examination of impact of socio-demographic factors on the likelihood of experiencing racism. In the bivariate analysis, respondent's age, employment status and housing status were all influential on the level of interpersonal racism sub-types. These results are similar to those found in previous literature. As per Cunningham and Paradies (2013), being a homeowner was associated with lower reported levels of interpersonal racism. Similarly, those with no permanent tenure inclusive of those living in the long grass are subject to high levels of negative racialized interactions (Holmes and McRae-Williams 2009; Birdsall-Jones et al. 2010; Habibis 2011). In this study age was also statistically related to reported levels of interpersonal racism. Unlike in Cunningham and Paradies (2013), the youngest age group (18–24) and older adults (45–54) reported the highest levels of "disrespect," "discrimination" and "alienation." In contrast to Ferdinand, Paradies and Kelaher (2013), the association between educational status and interpersonal racism was only statistically significant on the "alienation" measure, where those with a degree or higher reported lower levels of feeling judged pejoratively.

Once the variables were added to the full model, the influence of individual factors declined. Being unemployed, compared to those who were in full-time employment, or being an owner occupier compared to those with other housing tenures, experienced statistically significant lower levels of racial disregard. Possible explanations include a lower level of cultural capital for those unemployed, possibly due to the attendant poverty resulting in poorer dress and appearance. For homeowners, perhaps living in different areas to those renting or without permanent addresses may facilitate more regulated and familiar interactions with neighbours and local services, negating at least some of the effect of racialized disregard. Yet it is worth noting that even amongst homeowners, more than 50 per cent reported that they had felt disrespected or treated unfairly because of their race a lot or sometimes in the last six months. In the multivariate model, living in a larger household was associated with a higher experience of racialized disregard. The household size influence may be linked to the greater neighbourhood impact of large households, especially those housing visitors from outside Darwin, perhaps resulting in more negative interactions with local authorities and neighbours.

The most important result, in terms of testing the racially egalitarian nation and good Aboriginal citizen discourse, is what is not found. In the multivariate model, having a higher level of education, being older or younger, being from the local Larrakia people or from elsewhere did not, when all other factors were held equal, make any difference to the level of racial disregard experienced. Even employment status only recorded a small difference between the full-time employed and unemployed, with no significant differences between the full-time employed and those out of the labour market for other reasons. In other words, socio-demographic factors were not highly influential. Being a good Aboriginal citizen, educated and employed, does not protect an individual from racism.

The lack of association shows in the low explanatory value of the model with around 90 per cent of racialized disregard being due to factors not included in the model. This lack of statistical power strongly suggests that the socio-economic and cultural and demographic attributes of Aboriginal people do not provide an adequate empirical base to explain the level of racial disregard experienced. Rather, the explanation for the high level of racial disregard experienced by respondents largely lies outside respondents' attributes. There are no available variables to test the theory, but it is not an unreasonable conjecture, in light of the literature, to suggest that the explanation for the racial disregard experienced by the Aboriginal residents of Darwin lie in the wider (non-Indigenous) social and cultural realities in which they have no choice but to live their lives.

Theoretically, the results also illuminate the lived impact of race-bind contradictions. Research on a geographically bounded population allows the situational context of interpersonal racism to be explored alongside prevalence data, and Darwin provides a unique microcosm. With Aboriginal people a frequent visible presence in public spaces, the Aboriginal/non-Indigenous inter-racial interaction is unavoidable. In terms of the first race-bind contradiction, *individual racially located deficit*, the individualizing logic of Aboriginal disparities is contradicted by the findings that education level was not predictive of the level of racialized disregard experienced. Within employment status, only unemployment was predictive. Thus, even those fitting the description of the "good Aboriginal citizen" (Moreton-Robinson 2009) are not immune to racial disregard. These results also indicate that the opportunity to take an unracialized or undisregarded citizenship identity is not open to most Aboriginal people in Darwin.

The second race-bind contradiction, *racism denial/racial antipathy*, is demonstrated by results showing that positioning interpersonal racism as part of the past is more myth than reality. High levels of interpersonal racism were experienced by Aboriginal people in Darwin across the three measures. Therefore, despite ongoing denials of the existence of racism except as individual acts, interpersonal racism is not only a regular feature of Aboriginal/non-Aboriginal interaction but is applied regardless of socio-economic status. As per Bonilla-Silva (2010), the burden of racial disregard is systemically located: a collective experience determined by race, rather than separate acts perpetrated by individual social actors.

The results also reflect the fourth race-bind contradiction, *reconciliation/relations of power*. Refuting the dominant narrative of improved Australian race relations, more than three-quarters of respondents thought Indigenous/non-Indigenous race relations in Darwin were currently not good. More critically for the reconciliation narrative, a substantial majority, drawn from all walks of life, thought race relations in Darwin were getting worse, not better. Within the wider Darwin context, the glacial pace of land rights claim settlement suggests that any challenges to the dynamics of race relations power are being actively resisted by non-Indigenous power brokers. The relative powerlessness of Indigenous Peoples to alter these and the internalized knowledge of political and legal marginalization (Habibis et al. 2016) support this finding.

The third race-bind contradiction, *national pride/national silence*, was only indirectly addressed in this study. However, the concerns of the Larrakia Nation in the commissioning of this research, the seeming forgetting of the genesis of the city of Darwin, its traditional owners, or even the antecedents of the current socio-economic positioning of Aboriginal residents suggest that this race-bind contradiction is socially and culturally active.

Conclusion

The dominant Australian race relations narrative is of a racially egalitarian country where all are treated equally regardless of race. Reducing inequality is merely about improving socio-economic conditions for the disadvantaged, with the race of those disadvantaged people largely irrelevant. By reversing the lens, as done in this study, and asking for the views and experiences of those on the other side of race relations, Aboriginal people, a different account emerges. In this portrait, interpersonal racism is part of the everyday experience across the entire Aboriginal population, regardless of conformity to White Western cultural norms and ideals of personal responsibility and aspiration. Just being an Aboriginal person is to experience racial disregard as part of everyday life. The impact of racial disregard is magnified by the enabling contradictions of the race bind which neutralizes, at least for the non-Indigenous majority, the irreconcilability between the public and political discourse of Australian race relations and their lived reality, especially by the dispossessed Aboriginal and Torres Strait Islander population. While this study was specifically located to the Aboriginal residents of Darwin, there is nothing in the literature or in the lived experience of Aboriginal people and communities across Australia that suggests that the results could not also be applied in those locations.

Notes

1 This chapter was originally written as a journal article for a proposed special issue of the *Canadian Journal of Sociology*. It was accepted for publication, but a family tragedy at the time it was returned for reviewer revisions meant that I could not complete these within the needed time frame. While I regret not being able to uphold my commitment to the *Canadian Journal of Sociology*, I now feel that this chapter is much better placed in this volume as an example of Indigenous statistics in action.
2 I would like to acknowledge the contribution of Larrakia Nation, the organization representing the traditional owners of the area from Darwin for

commissioning this research, along with acknowledging my fellow researchers on the larger research project. I also thank with deep gratitude the team of field workers, whose local knowledge, connections and commitment to this survey were critical to its successful data collection. I also thank and acknowledge the more than 470 respondents who so generously gave of their time and perspectives on the lived reality of race relations as an Aboriginal resident of Darwin.
3 *Closing the Gap* is the primary Australian national policy framework to reduce Indigenous disadvantage. The policy was instituted in 2008 and contains six areas of policy aims with targets for improvements across six key areas: child mortality; early childhood education; school attendance; reading and numeracy; Year 12 or equivalent attainment; employment; and life expectancy. In 2020 after a decade of the *Closing the Gap* framework failing to deliver substantive gains for Aboriginal and Torres Strait Islander People across most of the target areas, it was replaced by a new Closing the Gap framework based on a National Agreement between The Coalition of the Peaks, representing First Peoples, and all levels of the Australian Government. This new Closing the Gap framework is also failing to meet its stated commitments.
4 The "Uluru Statement from the Heart" was issued from the National Constitutional Convention of 250 Indigenous leaders from across Australia at Uluru, NT, 24–26 May 2017.

References

ABS (Australian Bureau of Statistics) (2019) National Aboriginal and Torres Strait Islander Health Survey, 2018–19, ABS website, accessed 12 March 2024.

ABS (2016) Darwin. 2016 Census Aboriginal and/or Torres Strait Islander people QuickStats. *Australian Bureau of Statistics*. https://www.abs.gov.au/census/find-census-data/quickstats/2016/IQS701.

AIHW (Australian Institute of Health and Welfare) (2024) *Health and Wellbeing of First Nations people*. AIHW, Australian Government, accessed 6 December 2024.

Beswick, David G., and Michael D. Hills. "An Australian Ethnocentrism Scale." *Australian Journal of Psychology* 21, no. 3 (1969): 211–225. https://doi.org/10.1080/00049536908257791.

Birdsall-Jones, Christina, Vanessa Corunna, and Nalita Turner. 2010 "Indigenous Homelessness." *Australian Housing and Urban Research Institute Final Report No. 143*, AHURI, Melbourne.

Bobo Lawrence, D. "Race, Public Opinion, and the Social Sphere." *The Public Opinion Quarterly* 61, no. 1 (1997): 1–15.

Bonilla-Silva, Eduardo. 2010. *Racism without Racists: Colour-Blind Racism and the Persistence of Racial Inequality in the United States*. 3rd ed. MD: Rowman and Littlefield Publishers, Inc.

Bretherton, Di, and David Mellor. "Reconciliation between Aboriginal and Other Australians: The 'Stolen Generations'." *Journal of Social Issues* 62, no. 1 (2006): 81–98.

Chesterman, John, and Brian Galligan. 1997. *Citizens without Rights, Aborigines and Australian Citizenship*. Cambridge: Cambridge University Press.

Closing the Gap Prime Ministers Report 2014. Australian Government. Commonwealth of Australia, Canberra.

Cunningham, Joan, and Yin C. Paradies. "Patterns and Correlates of Self-Reported Racial Discrimination Among Australian Aboriginal and Torres Strait Islander Adults, 2008–09: Analysis of National Survey Data." *International Journal for Equity in Health* 12 (2013): 47.

Deloria, Vine, Jr. *The Nations Within: The Past and Future of American Indian Sovereignty*. New York: Pantheon Books, 1984.

Dunn, Kevin M., James Forrest, Ian Burnley, and Amy McDonald. "Constructing Racism in Australia." *Australian Journal of Social Issues* 394 (2004): 409–430.
Dunn, Kevin M., James Forrest, Rogelia Pe-pua, Maria Hynes, and Karin Maeder-Han. "Cities of Race Hatred? The Spheres of Racism and Anti-Racism in Contemporary Australian Cities." *Cosmopolitan Civil Societies: An Interdisciplinary Journal* 1, no. 1 (2009): 1–14.
Ferdinand, Angeline, S. Yin Paradies, and Margaret A. Kelaher. *Mental Health Impacts of Racial Discrimination in Victorian Aboriginal Communities: The Localities Embracing and Accepting Diversity (LEAD. Experiences of Racism Survey)*. Melbourne: The Lowitja Institute, 2013.
Glenn, Evelyn Nakano. "Settler Colonialism as Structure: A Framework for Comparative Studies of US Race and Gender Formation." *Sociology of Race and Ethnicity* 1, no. 1 (2015): 54–74.
Goot, Murray, and Tim Rowse. 2007. *Divided Nation: Indigenous Affairs and the Imagined Public*. Melbourne: Melbourne University Press.
Grattan, Michelle. "Turnbull Says No to Indigenous 'Voice to Parliament'." *The Conversation*, October 28, 2017. Accessed January 30, 2019. http://theconversation.com/turnbull-government-says-no-to-indigenous-voice-to-parliament-86421.
Grindlay, D. "Indigenous and Rural School Attendance Getting Worse Despite Investment, New Report Shows." December 6, 2017. www.abc.net.au/news/2017-12-06/indigenous-school-attendance-going-backwards/9230346.
Habibis, Daphne. "A Framework for Reimagining Indigenous Mobility and Homelessness." *Urban Policy and Research* 4, no. 4 (2011): 401–414.
Habibis, D., P. Taylor, M. Walter, and C. Elder. "Repositioning the Racial Gaze: Aboriginal Perspectives on Race, Race Relations and Governance." *Social Inclusion* (2016). https://doi.org/10.17645/si.v4i1.492.
Holmes, Catherine, and Eva McRae-Williams. 2009. *An Investigation into the Influx of Indigenous 'Visitors' to Darwin's Long Grass from Remote NT Communities—Phase 2: Being Undesirable: Law, Health and Life in Darwin's Long Grass*, National Drug Law Enforcement Research Fund, Monograph No. 33
Kinder, Donald R., and David O. Sears. "Prejudice and Politics: Symbolic Racism Versus Racial Threats to the Good Life." *Journal of Personality and Social Psychology* 40, no. 3 (1981): 414–431.
Larson, Ann I., Marissa Gillies, Peter J. Howard, and Coffin Julie. "It's Enough to Make You Sick: The Impact of Racism on the Health of Aboriginal Australians." *Australian and New Zealand Journal of Public Health* 31, no. 4 (2007): 322–329.
Martin, Karen. 2008. *Please Knock Before You Enter: Aboriginal Regulation of Outsiders and the Implications for Researchers*. Teneriffe: Post Press.
Mellor, David. "Contemporary Racism in Australia: The Experiences of Aborigines." *Personality and Social Psychology Bulletin* 29, no. 4 (2003): 474–486.
Moreton-Robinson, Aileen. "Imagining the Good Indigenous Citizen: Race War and the Pathology of Patriarchal White Sovereignty." *Cultural Studies Review* 15, no. 2 (2009): 61–79.
National Indigenous Australians Agency. *Closing the Gap*, 2019. Accessed December 19, 2019. www.niaa.gov.au/indigenous-affairs/closing-gap.
Paradies, Yin, and Joan Cunningham. "Experiences of Racism Among Urban Indigenous Australians: Findings from the DRUID Study." *Ethnic and Racial Studies* 32, no. 3 (2009): 548–573.
Park, Robert Ezra. *Race and Culture*. Edited by Everett C. Hughes et al. Glencoe, IL: Free Press, 1950.
Productivity Commission. *Overcoming Indigenous Disadvantage: Key Indicators 2016*, 2016. www.pc.gov.au/research/ongoing/overcoming-indigenous-disadvantage/2016.

Reconciliation Australia. *2016 Australian Reconciliation Barometer*, 2016. Accessed October 28, 2018. www.reconciliation.org.au/wp-content/uploads/2017/11/RA_ARB-2016_Overview-brochure_web.pdf.

Russell, Sophie, and Chris Cunneen. "Don Dale Royal Commission Reveals We Must Treat Young Better." *Sydney Morning Herald*, November 20, 2017. Accessed January 30, 2019. www.smh.com.au/comment/don-dale-royal-commission-reveals-we-must-treat-young-better-20171119-gzoqt3.html.

Sears, David, and P.J. Henry. "Over Thirty Years Later: A Contemporary Look at Symbolic Racism." *Advances in Experimental Social Psychology* 37 (2005): 95–150. https://doi.org/10.1016/S0065-2601(05)37002-X.

Simpson, A. *Mohawk Interruptus: Political Life across the Borders of Settler States*. Durham and London: Duke University Press, 2014.

Tuhiwai Smith, Linda. *Decolonizing Methodologies, Research and Indigenous Peoples*. London and New York: Zed Books, 1999.

Walter, Maggie. "Keeping Our Distance: Non-Indigenous/Aboriginal Relations." In *Australia: Identity, Fear and Governance in the 21st Century*, edited by Juliet Pietsch and Haydn Aarons, 15–32. Canberra: ANU Press, 2012.

Walter, Maggie. "The Race Bind: Denying Aboriginal Rights in Australia." In *Indivisible: Indigenous Human Rights*, edited by J. Green, 43–59. Winnipeg: Fernwood Publishing, 2014.

Walter, Maggie. "The Voice of Indigenous Data: Beyond the Markers of Disadvantage." *Griffith Review* 60 (2018).

Walter, Maggie and Chris Andersen. *Indigenous Statistics: A Quantitative Methodology*. Walnut Creek: Routledge, 2013.

Western, John. "What White Australians Think." *Race* 10 (1969): 411–434.

Wolfe, Patrick. "Settler Colonialism and the Elimination of the Native." *Journal of Genocide Research* 8, no. 4 (2006): 387–409. https://doi.org/10.1080/14623520601056240.

Wolfe, Patrick. *Settler Colonialism and the Transformation of Anthropology: The Politics and the Poetry of an Ethnographic Event*. London: Cassell, 1999.

Zubrick, Steven R., Sven R. Silburn, David Lawrence, Francis G. Mitrou, Robert, D. Dalby, Eve M. Blair, Judith Griffin, Helen Milroy, John A. De Maio, Adele Cox, and Jianghong Li. *The Western Australian Aboriginal Child Health Survey: The Social and Emotional Wellbeing of Aboriginal Children and Young People*. Perth: Curtin University of Technology and Telethon Institute for Child Health Research, 2005.

INDEX

Aboriginal 111, 115, 140, 142, 144, 146–147, 149; people, 53, 98, 109–110, 140–143, 145–147, 155–156
Aboriginal and Torres Strait Islanders 5, 8, 20–21, 58–59, 64, 66n1, 66n3, 140, 145, 157n3; populations 59, 156
ABS *see* Australian Bureau of Statistics
access 5, 16, 19, 36, 42, 44, 82, 83, 92, 134
Achenwall, Gottfried 51
AIATSIS (Australian Institute of Aboriginal and Torres Strait Islander Studies) 20–21
Alberta 1, 101, 108, 110, 113
Albuquerque Area Indian Health Board 24
alienation 149–150, 154
analysis 8, 13, 39–40, 42–44, 46n5, 69, 72–75, 77, 94, 99, 134, 139, 141; bivariate 151, 153
ancestors 115, 141
Andersen, Chris 1, 13, 99
Aotearoa / New Zealand 1, 3–4, 7, 18, 19, 22–23, 69–72, 78, 81, 83n2, 98, 124, 135, 136, 141
Arbuthnot, John 51
aspirations 65, 82, 107, 115, 128, 156
AUSSA *see* Australian Survey of Social Attitudes

Australia 1, 3–5, 7, 15, 19–20, 22–23, 60–61, 63, 66nn1–3, 140–142, 144–145, 152, 156–157
Australian Bureau of Statistics (ABS) 22, 49, 59, 140, 146
Australian Institute of Aboriginal and Torres Strait Islander Studies *see* AIATSIS
Australian Survey of Social Attitudes (AUSSA) 142
authority 4, 15, 19–20, 34, 71, 76–77, 97, 102

BADDR (categories of data failure) 64, 70, 79
big data 3, 11–13, 16–18, 58; proponents 12, 18
black box (Latour) 33, 35, 39–40
Bonilla-Silva, Eduardo 145, 155
boundaries 33, 35–36, 107, 112–113, 117, 125
Bourdieu, Pierre 32–33, 35–36, 38, 45n4, 46nn6–7
Briscoe, Gordon 53

Canadian Coalition for Global Health Research *see* CCGHR
Canadian Institutes of Health Research *see* CIHR
CANZUS (Canada, Australia, Aotearoa New Zealand and the

United States) countries 4, 7–8, 11, 16, 19, 49, 53–63, 69, 76, 83n1
capital, master 45n4, 46n6
CARE Principles for Indigenous Data Governance 20–21, 77, 93
CCGHR (Canadian Coalition for Global Health Research) Principles 93, 95, 97
census: Australian 49, 53; Canadian 109, 112; data 15, 74, 123, 133–134, 149; dataset 125–128, 132; forms 49, 115, 119; long-form 109; question 49, 107, 112, 116; questionnaire 113, 129; tribal 23
CIHR (Canadian Institutes of Health Research) 91, 93, 96–97
citizens, citizenship 15, 24, 31–32, 42, 106, 107, 117–119, 141, 144
classifications 16, 79, 133–134
Clayton, Adam 52
Closing the Gap (Australia) 5, 140–141, 144n3
colonialism 16, 34, 70, 115, 140; and Canada's history 111, 118; projects 31, 40, 52, 60, 116; regimes 61; settler 143
colonization 7, 23, 48, 50, 52–53, 57, 62, 64, 69–70, 73, 91, 94, 140, 142–144; Anglo 7–8, 54, 141; nation-state 7, 55
connectedness, connection 73, 75–76, 78, 107, 115, 119
consent 20, 81, 89, 90; FPIC (free, prior, and informed) 81, 91
cost 59, 73, 115, 117, 135
COVID-19 66n3
cultural: identity 71–72, 129; realities 58, 61–62, 155
Curtis, Bruce 38

Darwin (NT, Australia) 141, 146–150, 152–156
data: accuracy 81; administrative 61, 125, 127–128, 131; application of 18–19, 51–52, 81, 99, 124; cycles 3, 30, 44; divide 14, 16, 18; ecosystem 3, 11, 14, 17–18, 24, 30, 33; five Ds of 16; governance 19, 21, 23, 69, 71, 76, 79, 92; government 79, 82, 125, 127–128, 136; Indigenous 3–4, 10, 16–17, 19–25, 44, 50, 54, 56, 59, 61–64, 77; Indigenous dependency on 15, 18, 107; Indigenous population 50, 56, 60, 123; infrastructure 11, 22–23, 79–80, 82; iwi 124–125, 128, 131–132, 134; Māori 22, 78–82; Métis 107, 118, 120; population 14–15, 51, 53; privacy 81; revolution 3–4, 10–12, 15, 21; rights 76, 83; sovereignty 11, 18, 76, 120n1; statistical 59, 95, 102; strategies 106, 120n1, systems 24, 82; tribal 24, 124, 135; *see also* big data
Data Availability and Transparency Act (Australia) 61
deficit 2, 14, 17, 19, 57, 62–65, 94, 99; cultural 143; health 91, 97; Indigenous 13, 57, 60, 62–63; massive data 57, 60–61, 124; wellbeing 96, 99
demographic, demography 83n5, 108–111, 150–152; attributes 150–151, 155; conditions 102; Māori 71, 124–125; Métis 110–111, 119; socio- 43, 117, 148, 153–154; tribal 74
diabetes 94–95
discourses 41, 43, 60, 63–64, 106, 140–141, 144, 152; deficit-based 90, 117; dominant 115, 152; political 57, 156; public 145; public/political 140
discrimination 73, 94, 149–150, 154
dispossession 7, 57, 78, 115, 143; Indigenous 52, 57
diversity 6, 12, 21, 90, 92; geographical 65
Don Dale Youth Detention Center (Darwin) 146–147
Dyck, Noel 7
dysfunction 17, 65, 74

education 38, 44, 57, 66n2, 81, 92, 127, 140–141; level of 49, 150, 152, 155
EDQP (External Data Quality Panel) 128, 136
empiricism 39, 49, 144, 155
epistemology 16–18, 99, 114–115, 143–144
erasure 16, 44, 69, 144

Index

ethics 4, 20–21, 74, 80, 97, 101–102; processes 90–91
ethnic identity centrality 72, 83n3; *see also* identity
eugenics 48, 51–52, 69
Europe, Europeans 50–51, 73, 146
experience, lived 2, 8, 55, 97, 136, 156
External Data Quality Panel *see* EDQP

Families and Whānau Status Report 75
First Nations 19, 21, 42, 58, 65, 95, 101, 108–109, 112, 114, 118
First Nations Information Governance Centre (FNIGC) 19–20, 23, 78, 93–94, 100
First Peoples 54–55, 61, 144
Fisher, Ronald 51, 52
FNIGC *see* First Nations Information Governance Centre
Foucault, Michel 15, 32, 63
framework 2, 5, 34, 54, 77, 82, 91–93, 97, 141, 157n3

Gabel, Chelsea 99
Gal, Iddo 45n2
Galton, Francis 51–52
genealogical, genealogy 74, 112–113
geographic, geography 14; regions 107; homogeneity 65
GIDA *see* Global Indigenous Data Alliance
Global Indigenous Data Alliance (GIDA) 4, 21, 23, 93
Global North 14, 70
Goodes, Adam 145
governance 3, 14–15, 18, 20–21, 23, 89, 92, 112
government: Canadian 99, 113, 116–117; federal 112–113, 117
Graunt, John 51
Greaves, Lara 75

habitus 35, 45n2
Hacking, Ian 32
hapū (clan, sub-tribe) 74, 124, 128
Harper, Sarah 109
Hay, Travis 94
Hayward, Ashley 90, 100
health / wellbeing: challenges 94; Indigenous 70, 90; Indigenous research 70, 90–91, 93, 96; inequities 98; markers 91; Inuit 22; Māori 70; researchers 99
Hegele, Robert 94
Henry, Robert 92
hierarchy 30, 48, 52; of races 52; struggles 33, 106
HILDA *see* Household Income and Labour Dynamics Australia
Household Income and Labour Dynamics Australia (HILDA) 59, 66n2
housing 15, 53, 81, 92, 117, 146, 148, 152–153

identification, identity 7–8, 50, 55, 69, 71–74, 78, 83, 108, 112, 114, 116, 135, 140; collective 16, 71, 73–74; ethnic 6, 72–73, 83n2; self- 6, 106, 110–112, 114–116, 119, 124, 135; tribal 74
ideology 14, 49, 61
inclusion 97, 109, 123
Indian Act (Canada) 112–114
Indigene 58, 147
Indigeneity 2, 45n1, 57, 65, 112–113, 116
Indigenous: communities 15–16, 21, 24, 37, 39, 42, 45n1, 77, 89, 91, 94, 98–101, 117; control 21, 24, 31; inequality 57, 59, 141; knowledge 3, 30–31; lands 108, 113, 125, 16, 77–78; leaders and leadership 4–5, 21–23, 31–32, 106, 145, 157n4; nations 3, 11, 17, 23–24, 33, 38, 42, 45, 55, 107; researchers 2, 25, 70, 89, 100; scholars 4, 8, 19, 22–23, 30, 60, 63, 76, 90; understandings 59, 65, 100; voices 39, 97–98; ways 55, 57, 82, 99
Indigenous Data Governance 5–6, 10, 20–23, 63, 69, 76–77, 93; principles and mechanisms 4; scholarship 76; Summit 22
Indigenous Data Sovereignty 3–4, 6, 11, 16, 18–23, 34, 42, 60, 76, 83, 107; and big data technologies 11; and data governance 71; and Indigenous Data Governance scholarship 76
Indigenous Mentorship Networks (IMN) 97

inequality 35, 57, 62, 140–141
inequity 70, 79, 95–96; health 58, 90, 125
infrastructure 14, 18, 20, 36, 80, 125, 134
in-group 72, 83n4
inputs 31–33, 42, 101
International Indigenous Data Sovereignty Interest Group 20, 93
interpretation 40, 43–44, 70, 78, 95, 98
intersubjectivity 7–8, 55–56, 61, 70; *see also* Peoplehood
Inuit 22, 92, 118; health 92
Inuit Tapiriit Kanatami (ITK) 92; National Inuit Strategy on Research 97
investment 30, 33, 77, 82
iwi 74, 80, 124, 131–134, 136; affiliation 128–129, 131–132, 135; census data 125, 132; data collection initiatives 80, 128; parental 132

justice 38, 44, 81, 92; social 7, 96

K'awaika YOU Count! 24
kinship 69, 71, 73, 108, 113; groups 71; structures 124; *see also* whānau
Kitchin, Rob 12, 14
knowledge 2, 4, 13–16, 19, 31, 34–36, 74, 78, 81, 89–90, 98, 101–102; ceremonial 31; self-determined 97; systems 2; traditional 76–77; translation 95; *see also* TK
Kohanga Reo (language program) 71
Kukutai, Tahu 18–19, 57, 78

labour market 53, 60, 71, 152, 154
Larrakia: Nation 141, 147, 156; people 146, 152, 154
Latour, Bruno 33, 35, 40; *see also* black box
Lauriault, Tracey P. 12, 14
legislation 61, 77, 118, 125, 145–146
Leroux, Darryl 116
life expectancy 32, 140, 157n3
lifeworlds 2, 6–7, 19, 21, 24, 54–55, 69–70, 82; analysis 56; intersubjectivity 57, 59; Maori 73, 76
logics 35, 37–38, 44, 110, 118, 140, 143–144, 155; colonial 17, 116; narrative 143; nationalist 119; racial 119, 125, 144

Maiam nayri Wingara Indigenous Data Sovereignty Collective 20, 22
mana motuhake (power and authority) 19, 79
Mana Ōrite (agreement) 78, 128
Manitoba Métis Federation (MMF) 113, 120n1
Māori 8, 56, 58, 71–75, 78, 80–83, 83n1, 98, 124–126, 128–129, 135; culture 75; data experts 22, 78, 136; data sovereignty 18, 20; descent population 128, 131–133; identity 71, 73, 124; language 71, 78; youth, 73, 75
Māori Data Governance Model 22, 71, 77–79, 135
Māori Data Sovereignty Network 19, 125
Māori Identity and Financial Attitudes Study (MIFAS) 73
Martínez Cobo, Jose R. 6
mātauranga (ways of knowing) 71, 81
maximum likelihood estimation 51, 52
Mayi Kuwayi National Study of Aboriginal and Torres Strait Islander 22, 59, 66n1
McCarthy, Matthew T. 12, 16
methodologies 2, 8, 33, 35, 90, 124, 132; academic 100; complex 133; new 124; quantitative 1–2, 25, 59, 100, 139; storytelling 31
methods, statistical 39, 41, 47, 51, 100, 123–124
Métis 1, 8, 43, 58, 106–119; communities 108–109, 114, 116–117; identity 112, 117, 119; nation 107–109, 112–113, 115–116, 118, 120; nationhood 109, 120n1; as term 111, 115, 117
Métis National Council 108–109, 113, 119–120
Métis nation of Ontario 22, 113
Michif 109, 111
minorities, Indigenous people as 7, 17, 55–56
misrecognition 45n4, 50, 114–115
mixedness 115, 116; racial 115, 118
model: multivariate 150, 154; regression 152; sets 78
Moreton-Robinson, Aileen 144
Mosby, Ian 96

narratives 2, 21, 33, 43–44, 60, 63, 82, 107, 143; based 98–99, 146; national 57, 60
National Household Survey (Canada) 99, 110
National Inuit Health Survey 22, 92
National Inuit Strategy on Research 92, 96
National Iwi Chairs Forum (NICF) 128
nation rebuilding 19, 59, 64, 89, 100, 102
nation-states 4, 8, 15, 17, 19, 37, 43, 48–53, 55, 61, 64; modern 48, 60
Native American and Indigenous Studies Association (NAISA) 1
Hawaiians, Native 8, 58
Neel, James 94
Network Environments for Indigenous Health Research (NEIHR) 97
networks 4, 13–14, 20, 36, 76, 125–126; national 19, 21
New Zealand *see* Aotearoa / New Zealand
New Zealand Attitude and Values Survey (NZVAS) 72–73, 83n2
non-Indigenous populations 58–60, 111, 142
norms, cultural 49, 90, 147, 156
Northern Territory Aboriginals Act (Australia) 146

obesity 94–95
OCAP (ownership, control, access and possession) 19, 42, 92, 94, 97–98
outcomes 5, 41, 62, 73, 109, 128
outputs 31–33, 40
owners, traditional 140–141, 146–147, 152, 156
ownership: and application 18–19; and control 16, 92; of statistics and data 16, 18–19, 42, 92

patriarchy 112, 114, 118
Pearson, Karl 51–52
Peoplehood 7, 55, 61, 76
Petty, William 51
phenomena, cultural 48–49, 60
policies 42, 56–57, 59–60, 62, 78, 80, 97, 99, 107, 118, 145
policy makers 58, 66n2
population: Aboriginal 53, 94, 140, 146, 149, 156; Indigenous 49, 52–54, 57–62, 90; Indigenous statistics 52, 55–56, 58, 60; Maori 124, 134; Métis 107–111, 115, 117–118; non-Aboriginal / non-Indigenous 58–60, 109, 111, 142, 146; parameters 124, 135–136
positioning, socio-cultural 2, 141, 147
Post Enumeration Survey (2018) (New Zealand) 126, 136n2
pou (pillars) 22, 79–82
power, coercive 56, 61
privilege 136, 146; epistemic 97
protocols 74, 81, 102, 147; customary 78, 135

race 52, 124, 140–141, 143–145, 153–156; grammar of 143; relations 58, 139–140, 142–145, 147, 149, 155, 156; inequalities 144, 146
racialization 114–115, 118–119
racism 38, 52, 69–70, 73, 140, 142–143, 145, 147, 149–150, 153–155; experience of 142, 147, 149; interpersonal 143, 150, 153–156; structural 40, 94; systemic 52, 57, 71
RDA *see* Research Data Alliance
reconciliation 145, 155
relationships: contemporary racial 144; nation-to-nation policy 113; ongoing 7, 55; social 16, 18, 37, 112, 147; variable 17, 56
repatriation 22, 79, 81, 109, 117
research, researchers: deficit-based 91, 94–95, 97; framework 93, 147; Maori 72, 74; non-Indigenous 97, 147; questions 70, 101; statistical 89, 93–96, 98, 101–102; strength-based 99, 102
Research Data Alliance (RDA) 20, 77, 93
rights 4–5, 19–20, 123, 145; hunting 110; inalienable 18; intellectual property 77
rights-holders 82, 92, 106, 134
Rodriguez-Lonebear, Desi 16
Royal Commission on Aboriginal Peoples 98, 109–110

sampling 98, 148; design 40, 41, 43; errors 126
Saskatchewan 1, 92, 108, 110, 113

Index **165**

Saskatchewan Métis Health Research and Data Governance Principles 92
scholarship 1, 3, 11, 71; statistical 52, 72
science 33, 48, 51–52, 69
Scott, James C. 56
self-determination 3, 18–20, 71, 76, 78, 82, 100–101
settlers 71, 95, 115, 125
social field 30, 35, 37–38, 54, 78; approach 33–34; context 38–39; theory 45n4; understanding of statistics 60
socialization 35, 45n2
society 6, 12, 17, 23, 34–35, 52, 55–56, 60–61, 72, 102, 108, 139; dominant 58, 63; egalitarian 140; native 61; pre-colonial 6; pre-settler 6
sovereignty 7, 34, 39, 42, 69
spaces, public 142, 146, 153, 155
state: authoritarian 56, 61; Canadian 113–114, 116
statistical: agencies 36, 42, 53, 58, 60; approaches 69, 95, 98; cycle 24, 34, 37, 39–43, 120; erasure 70; information 31, 37, 43, 45n2; theory 51–52
statistics: application of 18–19, 51–52, 81, 99, 124; contemporary 40, 48; history of 50; state-collected Indigenous 54, 61; modern 50–51; official 3, 32, 43, 45n1, 123–124; population 8, 10, 17, 48–50, 123; wellbeing 98
Statistics Canada 99, 107–111, 113, 118–119
Statistics New Zealand (Stats NZ) 81–82, 124–128, 131–136
status 56, 114, 118
stereotypes 42, 58, 89–90, 94, 98, 102
stewardship 4, 20
stigma, stigmatization 7, 17, 91, 93–95, 98, 102
stories 24, 33, 37–38, 42, 44, 116, 119, 140
Sturm, Circe 116
subjectivity 34
survey 24, 44, 66nn1–2, 73, 92, 99, 101, 139, 141, 147–148
Swartz, David 35

systems 16, 31, 36, 40–41, 43, 73, 81, 82, 83, 97; belief 7–8, 55; institutional 57; leadership 78, 82; legal 6

Tait, Caroline 92
TCPS2 (Tri-Council Policy Statement: Chapter 9 Ethical Conduct for Research Involving Humans) 91–92, 98; guidelines 91, 93
technologies 3, 11, 13–15, 17, 33, 56, 70, 82–83
Te Kāhui Raraunga (TKR) 134, 136
Te Kore 74
Te Kupenga (survey) 74–75, 80, 134
Telling It Like It Is *see* TILII
Te Mana Raraunga (TMR) 19, 20, 125
Te Mana Whakatipu (data collective initiative) 79–80
Te Pā Tūwatata (data repository) 83
Te Tiriti o Waitangi (treaty) 22, 71, 124–125, 128
Te Whata (data platform) 80, 134
thrifty gene effect 94
tikanga Māori (protocols) 78, 81, 135–136
TILII (survey) 147–149
tino rangatiratanga (chiefly authority) 19, 71
TK (traditional knowledge) 76–77, 82
trauma 61; intergenerational 64, 91
treaty 22, 71, 114
tribes 18, 74, 83, 83n1, 124–125, 128, 131, 134–136
trust 81, 90, 107, 136, 146
truth 13, 33, 43–44, 54, 141
Tuhiwai Smith, Linda 57

UNDRIP (United Nations Declaration on the Rights of Indigenous Peoples) 19, 81, 118, 120
United Nations Declaration on the Rights of Indigenous Peoples *see* UNDRIP
United Nations Permanent Forum on Indigenous Issues (UNPFII) 6, 19, 136
United States 4, 7, 18–19, 23, 77, 82, 98, 141
United States Indigenous Data Sovereignty Network (USIDSN) 20

UNPFII *see* United Nations Permanent Forum on Indigenous Issues
USIDSN *see* United States Indigenous Data Sovereignty Network

values 11–12, 18, 21, 34, 38, 44, 45n3, 50, 52, 55–56, 62, 135, 142
variables, data 49, 131–133, 152, 154–155
violence 16, 31

Wacquant, Loïc 33–37
Wahi, Gita 95
Walter, Maggie 1, 13, 16, 17, 23, 41, 54, 56, 57, 62, 64, 90, 142
wellbeing 15, 20, 22, 66n1–2, 70, 72–75, 89–91, 94, 97, 100–102, 117; Aboriginal and Torres Strait Islander 22, 66n1; intergenerational 76; issues 93–94; measures 72
Westernization 91, 94, 102
whakapapa (relationships) 20, 74, 124, 132, 135–136
whānau (kinship groups) 71, 74–76, 78, 128; problems 73; values 75
whanaungatanga (obligations) 20, 75
Wittgenstein, Ludwig 63
Wolfe, Patrick 143
women 148; and Indian status 113–114; Indigenous 108, 113; pregnant Inuit 98; Māori 74
world, social 32, 35, 37, 43–44, 55
worldviews 55, 75

Youth19 Rangatahi Smart Survey 75